My Samsung
Galaxy Note® 4

Craig James Johnston
Guy Hart-Davis

que®

800 East 96th Street,
Indianapolis, Indiana 46240 USA

My Samsung Galaxy Note® 4

Copyright © 2015 by Pearson Education, Inc.

ISBN-13: 978-0-7897-5450-9
ISBN-10: 0-7897-5450-9

Library of Congress Control Number: 2014957651

Printed in the United States of America

First Printing: April 2015

Trademarks

All terms mentioned in this book that are known to be trademarks or service marks have been appropriately capitalized. Que Publishing cannot attest to the accuracy of this information. Use of a term in this book should not be regarded as affecting the validity of any trademark or service mark.

All Galaxy Note 4 images are provided by Samsung Electronics America.

Warning and Disclaimer

Every effort has been made to make this book as complete and as accurate as possible, but no warranty or fitness is implied. The information provided is on an "as is" basis. The author and the publisher shall have neither liability nor responsibility to any person or entity with respect to any loss or damages arising from the information contained in this book.

Special Sales

For information about buying this title in bulk quantities, or for special sales opportunities (which may include electronic versions; custom cover designs; and content particular to your business, training goals, marketing focus, or branding interests), please contact our corporate sales department at corpsales@pearsoned.com or (800) 382-3419.

For government sales inquiries, please contact governmentsales@pearsoned.com.

For questions about sales outside the U.S., please contact international@pearsoned.com.

Editor-in-Chief
Greg Wiegand

Acquisitions Editor
Michelle Newcomb

Development Editor
Charlotte Kughen,
The Wordsmithery LLC

Managing Editor
Kristy Hart

Senior Project Editor
Betsy Gratner

Copy Editor
Bart Reed

Indexer
Erika Millen

Proofreader
Debbie Williams

Technical Editor
Christian Kenyeres

Editorial Assistant
Cindy Teeters

Compositor
Tricia Bronkella

Contents at a Glance

Table of Contents

About the Authors

Craig James Johnston has been involved with technology since his high school days at Glenwood High in Durban, South Africa, when his school was given some Apple][Europluses. From that moment, technology captivated him, and he has owned, supported, evangelized, and written about it.

Craig has been involved in designing and supporting large-scale enterprise networks with integrated email and directory services since 1989. He has held many different IT-related positions in his career, ranging from sales support engineer to mobile architect for a 40,000-smartphone infrastructure at a large bank.

In addition to designing and supporting mobile computing environments, Craig cohosts the CrackBerry.com podcast as well as guest hosting on other podcasts, including iPhone and iPad Live podcasts. You can see Craig's previously published work in his books *Professional BlackBerry*, *My iMovie*, and many books in the *My* series covering devices by BlackBerry, Palm, HTC, Motorola, Samsung, and Google.

Craig also enjoys high-horsepower, high-speed vehicles and tries very hard to keep to the speed limit while driving them.

Originally from Durban, South Africa, Craig has lived in the United Kingdom, the San Francisco Bay Area, and New Jersey, where he now lives with his wife, Karen, and a couple of cats.

Craig would love to hear from you. Feel free to contact Craig about your experiences with *My Samsung Galaxy Note 4* at http://www.CraigsBooks.info.

All comments, suggestions, and feedback are welcome, including positive and negative.

Guy Hart-Davis is the author of approximately 100 computer books, including *Android Tips and Tricks*.

Dedication

"I love deadlines. I like the whooshing sound they make as they fly by."
—Douglas Adams

Acknowledgments

We would like to express our deepest gratitude to the following people on the *My Samsung Galaxy Note 4* team, who all worked extremely hard on this book:

- Michelle Newcomb, our acquisitions editor, who worked with us to give this project an edge

- Christian Kenyeres, our technical editor, who double-checked our writing to ensure the technical accuracy of this book

- Charlotte Kughen, who developed the manuscript skillfully

- Bart Reed, who edited the manuscript with a light touch

- Betsy Gratner, who kept the book project on schedule

- Tricia Bronkella, who combined the text and art into colorful pages

We Want to Hear from You!

As the reader of this book, *you* are our most important critic and commentator. We value your opinion and want to know what we're doing right, what we could do better, what areas you'd like to see us publish in, and any other words of wisdom you're willing to pass our way.

We welcome your comments. You can email or write to let us know what you did or didn't like about this book—as well as what we can do to make our books better.

Please note that we cannot help you with technical problems related to the topic of this book.

When you write, please be sure to include this book's title and author as well as your name and email address. We will carefully review your comments and share them with the authors and editors who worked on the book.

Email: feedback@quepublishing.com

Mail: Que Publishing
ATTN: Reader Feedback
800 East 96th Street
Indianapolis, IN 46240 USA

Reader Services

Visit our website and register this book at quepublishing.com/register for convenient access to any updates, downloads, or errata that might be available for this book.

In this chapter, you become familiar with the external features of the Galaxy Note 4 and the basics of getting started with the Android operating system. Topics include the following:

→ Getting to know your Galaxy Note 4's external features

→ Getting to know your Galaxy Note 4's S Pen (stylus)

→ Learning the fundamentals of Android 4.4 (KitKat) and TouchWiz

→ Setting up your Galaxy Note 4 for the first time

→ Installing desktop synchronization software

Getting to Know Your Galaxy Note 4

Let's start by getting to know more about your Galaxy Note 4 by examining the external features, device features, and how the Android 4.4 operating system works.

In addition to Android 4.4 (KitKat), this chapter covers the Samsung TouchWiz interface, which is overlaid on top of Android to adjust the way things look and function.

Your Galaxy Note 4's External Features

Becoming familiar with the external features of your Galaxy Note 4 is a good place to start because you will be using them often. This section covers some of the technical specifications of your Galaxy Note 4, including the touchscreen, camera, and S Pen. There are many versions of the Samsung Galaxy Note 4, but no matter which one you own or which wireless carrier you use to connect it, the exterior, functionality, and look and feel of the interface are exactly the same.

Front

Earpiece

Proximity/gesture sensor

Indicator light

Front camera

Light sensor

Touchscreen

Home button/ fingerprint reader

Recent Apps button

Back button

- **Proximity/gesture sensor**—Detects when you place your Galaxy Note 4 against your head to talk, which causes it to turn off the screen so that your ear doesn't inadvertently activate any onscreen items. This sensor also allows you to use gestures (in conjunction with the accelerometer). Gestures are covered later in the chapter.

- **Light sensor**—Adjusts the brightness of your Galaxy Note 4's screen based on the brightness of the ambient light.

- **Earpiece**—The part you hold against your ear while on a call.

- **Indicator light**—Indicates new events (such as missed calls, new Facebook messages, and new emails).

- **Front camera**—A 3.7-megapixel front-facing camera that you use for video chat, taking self-portraits, and even unlocking your Galaxy Note 4 using your face.

- **Touchscreen**—The Galaxy Note 4 has a 5.7" 1440×2560 pixel Quad HD Super AMOLED (Super Active-Matrix Organic Light-Emitting Diode) screen that incorporates capacitive touch.

- **Back button**—Tap to go back one screen when using an application or menu. This is a touch-sensitive button.

- **Recent Apps button**—Tap to see a list of apps you recently used. You can then touch to jump to them or swipe them off the screen to close them. Touch and hold to see additional options for the current screen. The Recent Apps button replaces the Menu button on previous Galaxy Notes.

- **Home button/fingerprint reader**—Press to go to the Home screen. The application that you are using continues to run in the background. Press twice to launch S Voice. Press and hold to launch Google Now. A fingerprint reader is built in to the Home button; you can read more about it in Chapter 2, "Customizing Your Galaxy Note 4." This is a physical button.

Back

- **Volume up/down buttons**—Enable you to control the audio volume on calls and while playing audio and video.

- **Power button**—Allows you to wake up your Galaxy Note 4 by pressing once. Press and hold for one second to reveal a menu of choices. The choices enable you to put your Galaxy Note 4 into Silent mode or Airplane mode, or to power it off completely.

- **Rear camera**—A 16-megapixel camera with autofocus and Optical Image Stabilization (OIS) that takes clear pictures close up or far away.

- **LED (light-emitting diode) camera flash**—Helps to illuminate the surroundings when you're taking pictures in low light.

- **Back cover removal point**—Allows you to remove the back cover. Insert your fingernail and pull to remove the back cover. After you have removed the back cover, you can install or swap SIM cards as well as insert or swap the Micro SD memory card.

Top

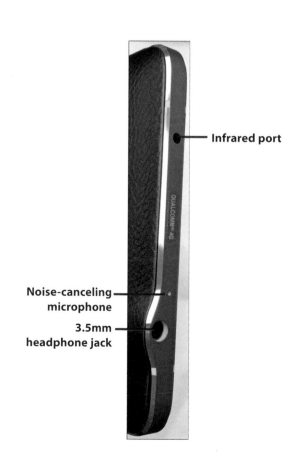

Infrared port

Noise-canceling microphone

3.5mm headphone jack

- **Infrared port**—Allows you to control your television from your Note 4 using an infrared signal.

- **3.5mm headphone jack**—Plug in your Galaxy Note 4 or third-party headset to enjoy music and talk on the phone.

- **Noise-canceling microphone**—Use in conjunction with the regular microphone to reduce background noise during phone calls. This microphone is also used when you record videos.

Bottom

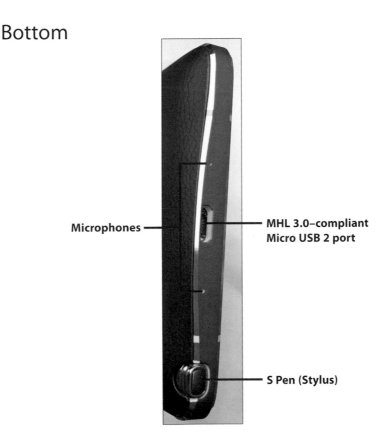

Microphones

MHL 3.0–compliant
Micro USB 2 port

S Pen (Stylus)

- **MHL 3.0–compliant Micro USB 2 port**—You can use the Micro USB 2 port to synchronize your Galaxy Note 4 to your desktop computer and charge it, but because it is Mobile High-definition Link (MHL) compliant, you can use it to play movies on your TV via high-definition multimedia interface (HDMI) using a special cable or dock. Read more about MHL 3.0 at http://en.wikipedia.org/wiki/Mobile_High-Definition_Link#MHL_3.0_features.

- **Microphones**—You use the microphones when you are on a call and holding your Galaxy Note 4 to your ear.

- **S Pen (Stylus)**—Pull the S Pen out of its holder to draw on the screen and interact with apps. Read more about the S Pen in the next section.

S Pen

Your Samsung Galaxy Note 4 comes with a stylus, which Samsung calls the S Pen. The S Pen is stored in the Galaxy Note 4 on the right side, and you pull it out from the lower right. This section covers some of the S Pen's features and functions.

Getting to Know the S Pen

Let's take a look at the S Pen itself and learn about its features.

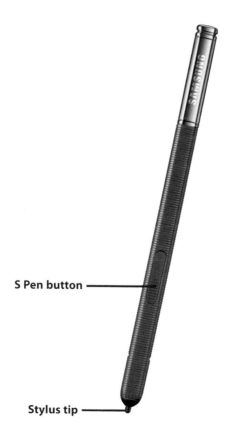

S Pen button

Stylus tip

- **Stylus tip**—The S Pen stylus tip is what makes contact with the screen as you write and draw. The stylus tip is pressure sensitive, so it knows how hard or soft you are pressing. This is particularly useful for drawing because pressure translates into line thickness.

- **S Pen button**—The S Pen button adds extra functionality to the S Pen. When you press the button as you drag the pen on the screen, you can perform functions, such as moving between screens, taking screenshots, and even cutting out parts of any screen.

Air Command

When you remove your S Pen, Air Command is the first thing that pops up. Air Command gives you quick access to useful S Pen functionality. You can also access Air Command any time by hovering your S Pen over the screen and pressing the S Pen button. It is important to note that Air Command on the Note 4 no longer includes the S Finder and Pen Window functions that used to be included on the Note 3.

- **Action Memo**—Write in a special note area and tell your Note 4 to take action on what you write. For example, write a phone number and tell Action Memo to dial that number.

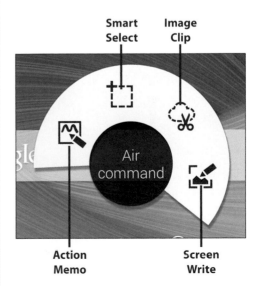

Smart Select   Image Clip

Action Memo   Screen Write

- **Smart Select**—This feature used to be called Scrap Booker. Capture a part of the screen by drawing around the area you want to capture. You can then share the captured image, save the captured area of the screen to the Scrapbook app, or, if the captured image includes text, you can take an action such as call a phone number, open a link, or send an email.

- **Screen Write**—Capture the entire screen and then write on the image of the captured screen. Your image is saved in the Screenshots album. This album can be viewed using the Photos app or the Gallery app.

Write something first...   **...then touch here...**

...and lastly choose an action

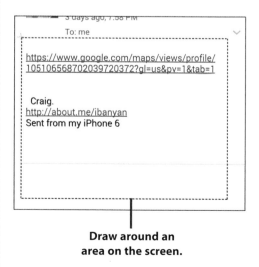

Draw around an area on the screen.

- **Image Clip**—Capture part of the screen by drawing around the area you want to capture. Your image can then be shared, or saved in the Scrapbook app.

Tap to save.

Tap to share.

Adjust the selection area to be round or square.

Draw on the captured screenshot.

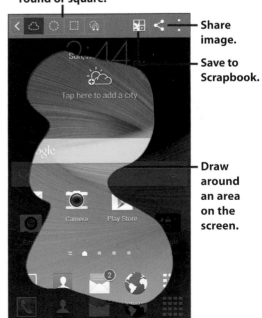

Share image.

Save to Scrapbook.

Draw around an area on the screen.

Air View

Air View is a feature that shows you a preview of information about an object and enables you to interact with it when you hover the S Pen or your finger near the screen over an object that is Air View enabled. Make sure that Air View is turned on in Settings before you try to use it. Refer to Chapter 2 to see how to turn on Air View and customize how it works. This section shows you some examples of using Air View.

Hover over an album in the Gallery app.

Hover over a menu icon.

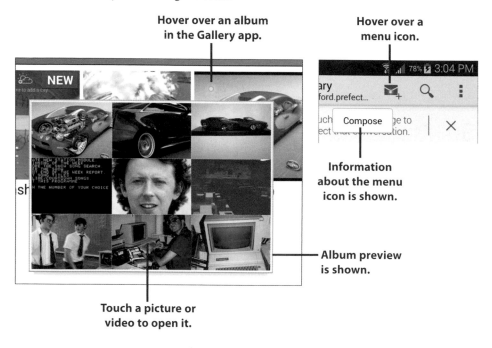

Information about the menu icon is shown.

Album preview is shown.

Touch a picture or video to open it.

Air View Is Not Always Available

Apps must be specifically written to support Air View. For example, Samsung has rewritten the Gallery app to support Air View; however, the Photos app, which Google is moving to, does not support Air View.

Scrolling Using the S Pen

You can scroll up and down by hovering your S Pen at the top or bottom of an area of the screen that scrolls, such as a message list. For this gesture, you must not press the S Pen button—just hover at the top or bottom of the scroll area. You see an arrow indicating that the scrolling gesture has been recognized.

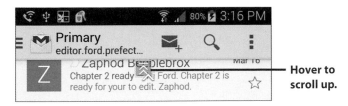

Hover to scroll up.

Gestures and Motions

Gestures and motions allow you to quickly use certain functions or features by making hand gestures or moving the Note 4 in a specific way.

- **Direct Call**—While you are looking at a missed call, reading an SMS (text message) from someone, or viewing someone's contact information, if you lift your Note 4 to your ear and hold it there, the phone number being viewed will be dialed.

- **Smart Alert**—If you have missed calls or messages, when you pick up your Note 4 from a flat surface, it vibrates.

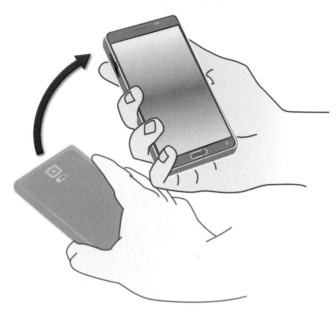

- **Mute**—To mute incoming calls and alarms, either place your hand over the screen or turn your Note 4 over.

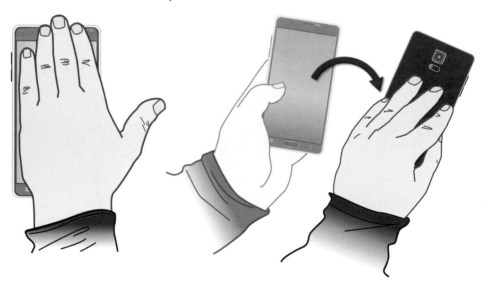

- **Palm Swipe to Capture**—You can capture a screenshot by holding your palm perpendicular to the screen, touching it on the screen and swiping it from left to right or right to left. The captured screenshot goes to the Screenshots album, which you can view using the Gallery or Photos app.

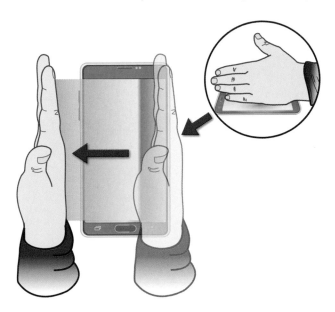

First-Time Setup

Before setting up your new Samsung Galaxy Note 4, you should have a Google account because your Galaxy Note 4 running Android is tightly integrated with Google. When you have a Google account, you can store your content in the Google cloud, including any books and music you buy or movies you rent. If you do not already have a Google account, go to https://accounts.google.com on your desktop computer and sign up for one.

1. Press and hold the Power button until you see the animation start playing.

2. Tap to change your language if needed.

3. Tap Start.

4. Tap a Wi-Fi network you want to connect to during setup. If you'd rather not connect to a Wi-Fi network, tap Next and continue at step 8.

Why Use Wi-Fi During Setup

As you go through the first-time setup of your Note 4, you may choose to restore a backup of a previous device to your Note 4, and at the end of the device setup, a number of apps may need to be updated. Both of these activities can use a lot of data. Using Wi-Fi speeds up these activities as well as saves you the cost of the cellular data charges. Therefore, although you do not have to connect to a Wi-Fi network for device setup, it is advisable.

5. Enter the password for the Wi-Fi network using the onscreen keyboard.

6. Tap Connect. Your Galaxy Note 4 connects to the Wi-Fi network.

Tap to skip and use cellular data.

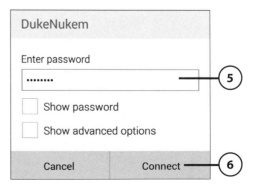

7. Tap Next.

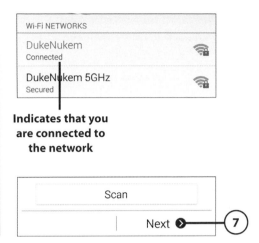

Indicates that you
are connected to
the network

>>>*Go Further*

SMART NETWORK SWITCH

Smart network switch is a feature that, once enabled, allows your Note 4 to seamlessly switch between the two Wi-Fi bands (2.4GHz and 5GHz) and cellular data to maintain a stable Internet connection. Your Note 4 constantly analyzes its connection to the Internet and switches between Wi-Fi networks operating on 2.4GHz and 5GHz to provide the best connection, and if the Wi-Fi connectivity becomes poor, it switches to the cellular data network. Bear in mind that with this option enabled you might start seeing higher cellular data usage, especially in areas where Wi-Fi is unstable, slow, or overcrowded.

8. Tap to check the box after you have read and understood the End User License Agreement (EULA).

9. Decide whether you would like Samsung to collect diagnostic and usage data from your Note 4.

10. Tap Next.

11. Tap Yes to log in to your Google account.

12. Enter your Google account email address (your Gmail address).

13. Enter your Google account password.

14. Tap the right arrow to continue.

15. Check this box to keep data on your Galaxy Note 4 backed up to the Google cloud and restore settings previously saved in the Google cloud to your new Galaxy Note 4 before continuing.

Beware of the Restore

Be careful leaving the Backup & Restore box checked in step 15. If you are switching from a non-Samsung Android device, leaving this box checked will restore original Android apps such as Calendar. Because Samsung rewrites many standard Android apps, if you leave this box checked you may end up with two of certain apps such as Calendar.

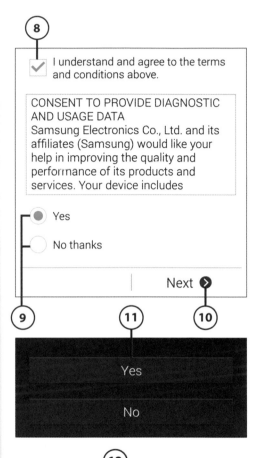

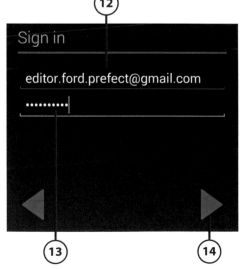

16. Check this box if you are okay with Google collecting information about your geographic location at any time. Although this information is kept safe, if you are concerned about privacy rights, uncheck this box.

17. Check this box if you are okay with Google using your geographic location for Google searches and other Google services.

18. Tap the right arrow to continue.

19. Change your name if needed.

20. Tap the right arrow to continue.

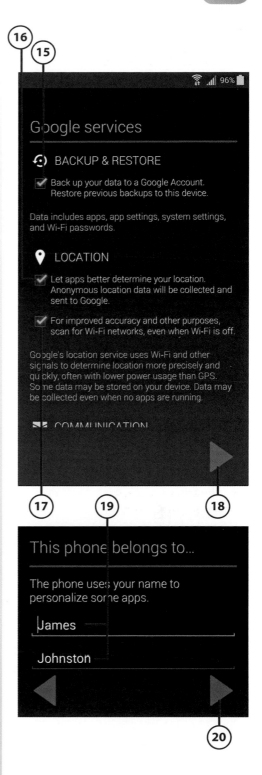

21. Touch to sign in to your Samsung account if you have one, or tap Skip and jump to step 28.

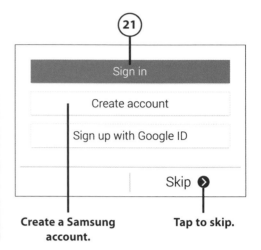

Create a Samsung account.

Tap to skip.

>>>Go Further

DO I NEED A SAMSUNG ACCOUNT?

Android was designed to be used with a Google account. That Google account enables you to access the Google ecosystem of Android apps, music, movies, and books; plus, your phone's settings are backed up to the Google cloud. If you change devices, your new device reverts to the way you had your old device set up. A Samsung account does a similar thing, but it uses the Samsung ecosystem. Technically, you don't really need a Samsung account because a Google account provides everything you need. However, Samsung has its own app store and typically puts Samsung-specific apps in there first before they show up in the Google Play Store, so if you can't stand waiting for apps, you should sign up for a Samsung account.

22. Enter the email address you used for your Samsung account.

23. Enter your Samsung account password.

24. Tap Sign In.

25. Check the box to enable automatically backing up your data to your Samsung account.

26. Check the box to first restore data previously backed up in the Samsung cloud to your Galaxy Note 4 after you have completed the device setup.

27. Tap Next.

28. Enter a name for your Note 4. This name is used whenever you are connecting to other devices.

29. Check the box if you want your Note 4 to use Easy mode. Easy mode uses a simplified Home screen layout, plus enlarges the text and size of the app icons. You can always disable Easy mode later if you decide it's not for you.

30. Tap Finish.

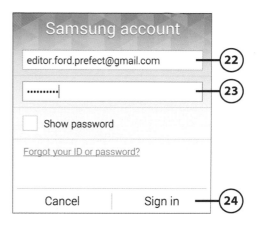

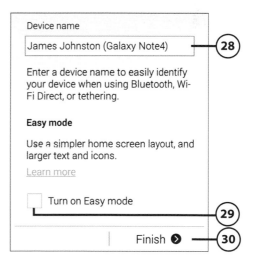

Fundamentals of Android 4.4 and TouchWiz

Your Galaxy Note 4 is run by an operating system called Android. Android was created by Google to run on any smartphone, and your Galaxy Note 4 uses a version called Android 4.4 (or KitKat). Samsung has made many changes to this version of Android by adding extra components and modifying many standard Android features. They call this customization TouchWiz.

The Lock Screen

If you haven't used your Galaxy Note 4 for a while, the screen goes blank to conserve battery power. This task explains how to interact with the Lock screen.

1. Press the Power button or Home button to wake up your Galaxy Note 4.

2. Slide your finger across the screen in any direction to unlock your Galaxy Note 4.

3. Tap the Missed Call or Missed Text Message notification and then swipe the screen to unlock and go directly to the call log.

4. Swipe up from the Camera icon to launch the Camera.

Other notifications

6:06 AM Wed, November 5

Missed call
Craig James Johnston   6:03 AM
                              Clear

Swipe screen to unlock
T-Mobile

Working with Notifications and Settings on the Lock Screen

You can work with notifications and settings right on the Lock screen. If you see notifications in the Notification bar, pull down the Notification bar to view and clear them. Touching a notification takes you straight to the app that created it. Read more about the Notification bar later in this section.

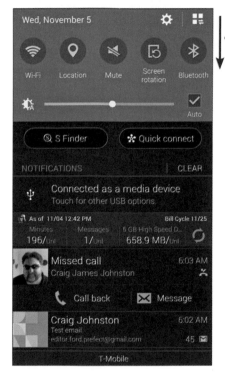

Swipe down to see notifications and settings.

Answering a Call from the Lock Screen

If your Galaxy Note 4 is locked when a call comes in, you have three choices: Drag the green icon to answer the incoming call; drag the red icon to reject the incoming call and send it straight to voicemail; or drag up from the bottom of the screen to reject the call and send a preset text message (SMS) to the caller.

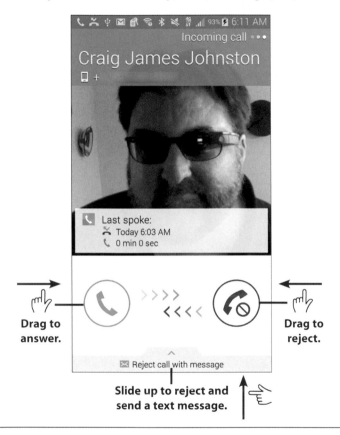

Drag to answer.

Drag to reject.

Slide up to reject and send a text message.

The Home Screen

After you unlock your Galaxy Note 4, you are presented with the Home screen. Your Galaxy Note 4 has four Home screen panes (although you can create more). The Home screen panes contain application shortcuts, a Launcher icon, Notification bar, Shortcuts, Favorites Tray, and widgets.

- **Notification bar**—The Notification bar shows information about Bluetooth, Wi-Fi, and cellular coverage, as well as the battery level and time. The Notification bar also serves as a place where apps can alert or notify you using notification icons.

- **Notification icons**—Notification icons appear in the Notification bar when an app needs to alert or notify you of something. For example, the Phone app can show the Missed Calls icon, indicating that you missed a call.

- **Widget**—Widgets are applications that run directly on the Home screens. They are specially designed to provide functionality and real-time information. An example of a widget is one that shows the current weather or provides a search capability. Widgets can be moved and sometimes resized.

- **App shortcut**—When you tap an app shortcut, the associated app launches.

- **App folders**—You can group apps together in a folder as a way to organize your apps and declutter your screen.

- **Favorites Tray**—The Favorites Tray is visible on all Home screen panes. You can drag apps to the Favorites Tray so that they are available no matter which Home screen pane you are looking at. Apps in the Favorites Tray can be rearranged and removed.

- **Launcher icon**—Tap to show application icons for all applications that you have installed on your Galaxy Note 4.

Work with Notifications

To interact with notifications that appear in the Notification bar, place your finger above the top of the screen and drag to pull down the Notification bar and reveal the notifications. Swipe individual notifications off the screen to the left or right to clear them one by one, or tap Clear to clear all of them at once. The Notification bar also includes Quick Settings such as the ability to turn on or off Wi-Fi or Bluetooth.

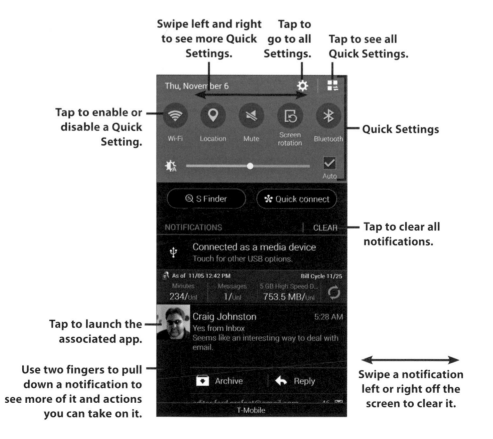

What Are Quick Settings?

Quick Settings are icons that allow quick on/off actions. Examples are turning Wi-Fi on or off and turning Bluetooth on or off. You cannot change the settings for items, just turn them on or off. To change the settings for these items you need to tap the cog icon to go to the full Settings screen.

Create App Shortcuts

Tap the Launcher icon to see all of your apps. Touch and hold on the app you want to make a shortcut for. After the Home screen appears, drag the app shortcut to the location you want the shortcut to be on the Home screen, drag it to an app folder, or drag it left or right off the screen to move between Home screen panes. Release the icon to place it.

Touch and hold an app icon.

Drag to where you want it and release it.

Drag between Home screen panes.

Create App Folders

To create a new app folder, touch and hold the first app shortcut you want in your folder. When the Create Folder icon appears, drag the app shortcut to that icon and release it. After you give your app folder a name, the folder displays on your Home screen. Now you can drag other app shortcuts into that folder. To open the folder, touch it to reveal the shortcuts in that folder.

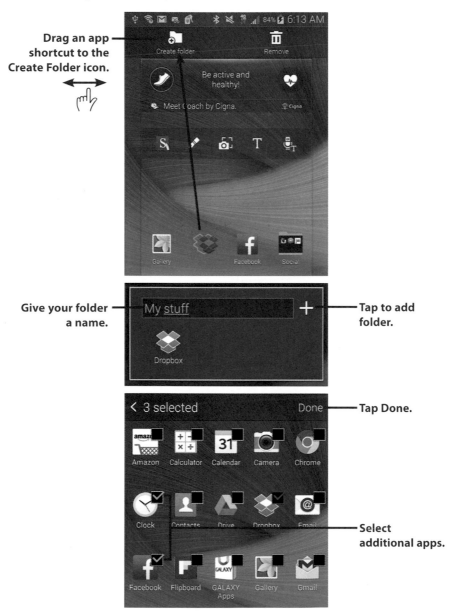

Drag an app shortcut to the Create Folder icon.

Give your folder a name.

Tap to add folder.

Tap Done.

Select additional apps.

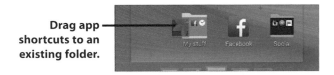

Drag app shortcuts to an existing folder.

Create a New Home Screen Pane and Remove an App Shortcut

If you want to create a new Home screen pane, touch and hold an app shortcut icon. Drag your app shortcut icon to the Create Page icon, and the shortcut is placed on a brand-new Home screen pane. To remove an app shortcut icon, drag it to the Remove icon.

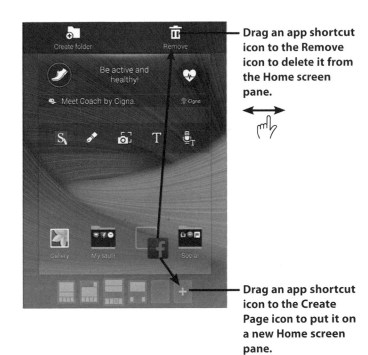

Drag an app shortcut icon to the Remove icon to delete it from the Home screen pane.

Drag an app shortcut icon to the Create Page icon to put it on a new Home screen pane.

Use the Touchscreen

You interact with your Galaxy Note 4 mostly by touching the screen, which is known as making gestures on the screen. You can tap, swipe, pinch, touch and hold, double-tap, and type.

 • **Tap**—To start an application, tap its icon. Tap a menu item to select it. Tap the letters of the onscreen keyboard to type.

 • **Touch and hold**—Touch and hold to interact with an object. For example, if you touch and hold a blank area of the Home screen, a menu pops up. If you touch and hold an icon, you can reposition it with your finger.

 • **Drag**—Dragging always starts with a touch and hold. For example, if you touch the Notification bar, you can drag it down to read all of the notification messages.

 • **Swipe or slide**—Swipe or slide the screen to scroll quickly. To swipe or slide, move your finger across the screen quickly. Be careful not to touch and hold before you swipe or you will reposition something. You can also swipe to clear notifications or close apps when viewing the recent apps.

 • **Double-tap**—Double-tapping is like double-clicking a mouse on a desktop computer. Tap the screen twice in quick succession. For example, you can double-tap a web page to zoom in to part of that page.

 • **Pinch**—To zoom in and out of images and pages, place your thumb and forefinger on the screen. Pinch them together to zoom out or spread them apart to zoom in (unpinching). Applications such as Browser, Gallery, and Maps support pinching.

 • **Rotate the screen**—If you rotate your Galaxy Note 4 from an upright position to being on its left or right side, the screen switches from Portrait view to Landscape view. Most applications honor the screen orientation. The Home screens and Launcher do not.

Use the Keyboard

Your Galaxy Note 4 has a virtual or onscreen keyboard for those times when you need to enter text. You might be a little wary of a keyboard that has no physical keys, but you will be pleasantly surprised at how well it works.

Most applications automatically show the keyboard when you need to enter text. If the keyboard does not appear, tap the area where you want to type and the keyboard slides up, ready for use.

Tap to capitalize the next character. Double-tap to engage CAPS Lock.

Tap for numbers and symbols.

Tap to speak the text.

Using the virtual keyboard as you type, your Galaxy Note 4 makes word suggestions. Think of this as similar to the spell checker you would see in a word processor. Your Galaxy Note 4 uses a dictionary of words to guess what you are typing. If the word you were going to type is highlighted, tap space or period to select it. If you can see the word in the list but it is not highlighted, tap the word to select it.

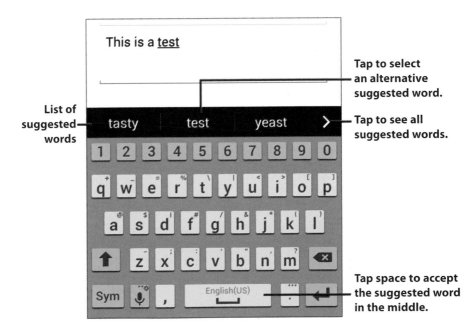

Tap to select an alternative suggested word.

List of suggested words

Tap to see all suggested words.

Tap space to accept the suggested word in the middle.

>>>Go Further
NEXT WORD SUGGESTION

When you are between typing words, the keyboard tries to predict the next word you want to type. (In this example I typed "This is a test"; the keyboard is suggesting that the most obvious word I want to type next is "drive," but it is also showing that I might want to type "of" or end the sentence with a period.) All you need to do is tap the correct word, and the keyboard types it for you. If the keyboard is not showing a word that you want to use, simply continue typing. The more you type, the more the keyboard learns how you write and the better it will become at suggesting the next words you are likely to type.

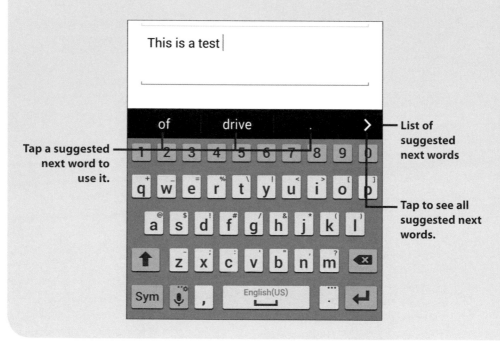

Tap a suggested next word to use it.

List of suggested next words

Tap to see all suggested next words.

To make the next letter you type a capital letter, tap the Shift key. To make all letters capitals (or CAPS), double-tap the Shift key to engage CAPS Lock. Tap Shift again to disengage CAPS Lock.

To type numbers or symbols, tap the Symbols key. When on the Numbers and Symbols screen, tap the Symbols key to see extra symbols. There are two screens of symbols. Tap the ABC key to return to the regular keyboard.

Tap to see more symbols.

Tap to return to letters.

Quick Access to Symbols

If you want to type commonly used symbols, touch and hold the period key. A small window opens with those common symbols. Tap a symbol to type it or tap the Sym icon to see all symbols.

Touch and hold to see common symbols.

To enter an accented character, touch and hold any vowel or the C, N, or S key. A small window opens enabling you to select an accented or alternative character. Slide your finger over the accented character and lift your finger to type it.

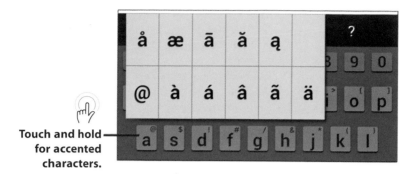

Touch and hold for accented characters.

To reveal other alternative characters, touch and hold any other letter, number, or symbol.

Want a Larger Keyboard?

Turn your Galaxy Note 4 sideways to switch to a landscape keyboard. The landscape keyboard has larger keys and is easier to type on.

Swipe to Type

Instead of typing on the keyboard in the traditional way by tapping each letter individually, you can swipe over the letters in one continuous movement. This is called Swiftkey Flow. It is enabled by default; to use it, just start swiping your finger over the letters of the word you want to type. Lift your finger after each word. No need to worry about spaces because your Galaxy Note 4 adds them for you. To type a double letter (as in the word *pool*), loop around that letter on the keyboard. As you swipe, a blue line trails your finger.

Dictation—Speak Instead of Type

Your Galaxy Note 4 can turn your voice into text. It uses Google's speech recognition service, which means you must have a connection to the cellular network or a Wi-Fi network to use it.

1. Tap the microphone key.

2. Wait until you see Speak Now and start speaking what you want to be typed. You can speak the punctuation by saying "comma," "question mark," "exclamation mark," or "exclamation point."

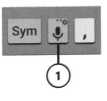

Tap to select a different dictation language.

Edit Text

After you enter text, you can edit it by cutting, copying, or pasting the text. This task describes how to select and cut text so you can paste over a word with the cut text.

1. While you are typing, touch and hold a word you want to copy.

2. Slide the blue end markers until you have selected all of the text you want to copy.

3. Tap to cut the text. Cutting text places it in the Clipboard, just like a Copy action would do.

4. Touch and hold the word you want to paste over.

5. Tap to paste what you cut earlier.

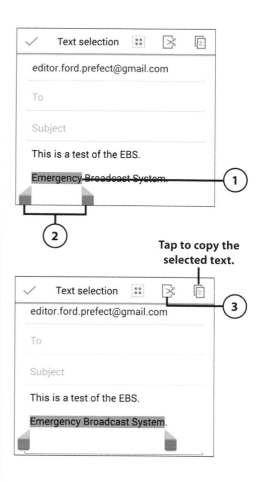

Tap to copy the selected text.

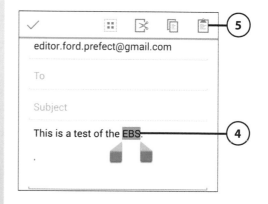

Placing a Cursor

You can also simply place a cursor on the screen and move it around to do manual text editing, such as backspace to delete letters or manually insert a new word. To do this, tap the screen in the text area. A single blue marker displays; drag that marker to the point in the text you want to make changes to. Now start typing or tap backspace, and the action occurs at the cursor position.

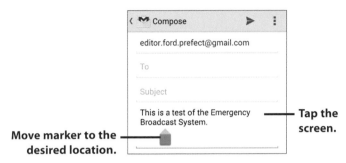

Move marker to the desired location.

Tap the screen.

Writing Instead of Typing

As discussed earlier in this chapter, your Galaxy Note 4 comes with the S Pen stylus. Instead of typing on the keyboard, you can use handwriting recognition to write. To enable Handwriting mode, pull out the S Pen from its holder and tap the Back key to dismiss the Air Command window. Then hover the S Pen over the screen in the text area until you see the handwriting icon. Tap the icon with your S Pen. Any text you have typed appears to be in handwriting. Now write in your own handwriting on the screen and it is turned into text. Tap Done to return to typing.

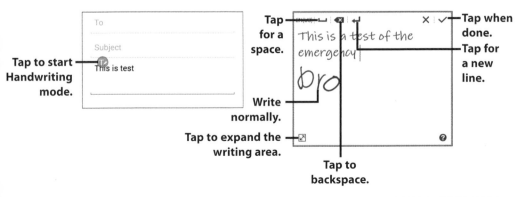

Tap to start Handwriting mode.

Tap for a space.

Write normally.

Tap to expand the writing area.

Tap to backspace.

Tap when done.

Tap for a new line.

Keyboard Tricks

You can write instead of typing, use emoticons (smiley faces), and enable a one-handed keyboard.

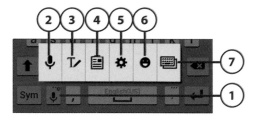

1. Touch and hold the microphone key (to the right of the Sym key).

2. Tap to use dictation.

3. Tap to use Handwriting mode.

4. Tap to see everything you have previously copied to the clipboard. If there is text, you can touch it to paste it at the cursor position.

5. Tap to change keyboard settings, including choosing a new keyboard.

6. Tap to type emoticons (smiley faces).

7. Tap to choose a one-handed keyboard.

>>>*Go Further*

ONE-HANDED TYPING

Your Galaxy Note 4 is a pretty large phone and unlike smaller phones that have 4-inch or 4.7-inch screens, you cannot type with one hand on your Galaxy Note 4. Samsung addresses this by enabling you to put the keyboard into one-handed typing mode. This mode squashes the keyboard so that you can type with one thumb. To enable one-handed mode, follow steps 1 and 7 in the "Keyboard Tricks" task. Drag the shrunken keyboard anywhere on the screen where it is comfortable for you to type with one hand. Repeat steps 1 and 7 in the "Keyboard Tricks" task to revert to the normal keyboard.

Drag the
keyboard.

Menus

Your Galaxy Note 4 has two types of menus: app menus and context menus.
All applications use an app menu. To see the app menu, tap the Menu icon,
which is normally on the top-right of the screen. As an alternative (but slower)
method, you can touch and hold the Recents button to see the app menu.

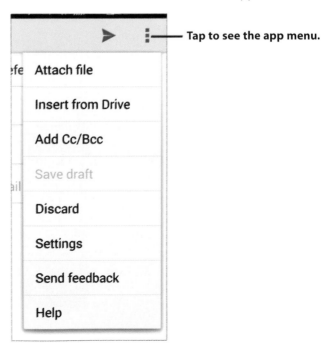

Tap to see the app menu.

A context menu applies to an item on the screen. If you touch and hold something on the screen (in this example, a link on a web page), a context menu appears. The items on the context menu differ based on the type of object you touched.

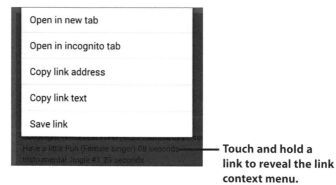

Open in new tab

Open in incognito tab

Copy link address

Copy link text

Save link

— **Touch and hold a link to reveal the link context menu.**

Switch Between Apps

You can switch between running apps as well as close apps using the multitasking feature.

1. Tap the Recents button (to the left of the Home button).

2. Scroll up and down the list of running apps.

3. Tap an app to switch to it.

4. Tap to see memory and processor usage for each active app.

5. Swipe an app left or right off the screen to close it.

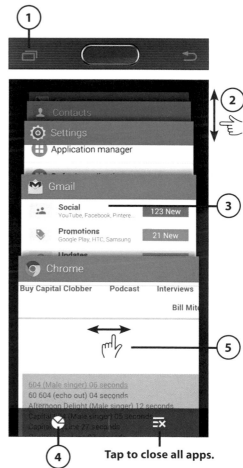

Tap to close all apps.

Run Multiple Apps on the Screen at the Same Time

Your Galaxy Note 4 has a feature called Multi Window that allows certain apps to run on the same screen at the same time. They can either run in a split-screen configuration, in multiple separate small windows, or a combination of both.

Make sure this is green.

Make Sure Multi Window Is Enabled

Before you start this section, make sure that Multi Window is enabled in the Quick Settings.

Two Apps Together on a Split-Screen

This section explains how to run two apps at the same time in a split-screen configuration.

1. Touch and hold the Back button to see apps that support Multi Window.

2. Drag an app onto the screen and release it. Because this is the first app you are choosing, it fills the screen. The first app in this example is the S Note app.

Scroll up and down to see all apps.

Tap to choose which page of a multipage app to use.

Some Apps Want to Be Pop-up Apps

When you drag an app onto the screen in step 2, the app may only want to be a pop-up app. Pop-up apps start by running in a small separate window on the screen instead of either filling the top or bottom of the screen. Unfortunately it is not clear which apps always want to start in pop-up mode and which always start in split-screen mode. You can read more about pop-up apps in the next section.

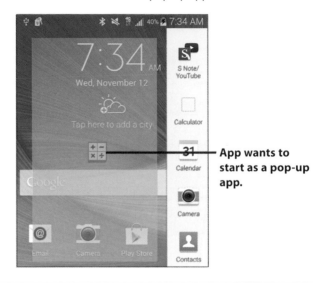

App wants to start as a pop-up app.

Multipage Apps

Some of the app icons have a small left arrow next to them. This indicates that the app is already running and has multiple pages open. An example of this is a web browser such as Chrome. You may have many different websites open, each in its own tab. If you tap the little arrow, you are able to choose which open pages you want to drag onto the multiwindow screen.

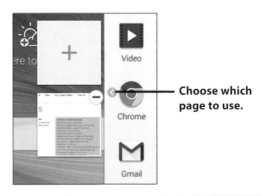

Choose which page to use.

It's Not All Good

Not All Apps Support Multi Window

Apps must be specially written to take advantage of Multi Window mode. This means that you might not see the apps you are looking for until the developer updates the app to support Samsung's Multi Window mode.

3. Drag another app to either the top or bottom half of the screen and release it. If the Multi Window pane on the right of the screen disappears before you do step 3, touch and hold the Back button to see it again.

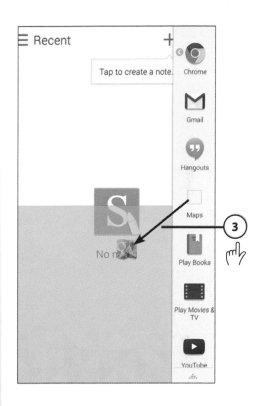

4. Drag the circle up or down to give more or less room to each app.

5. Tap the circle to reveal extra Multi Window features.

6. Tap to swap the position of the apps on the screen.

7. Tap to enable dragging content (such as text or an image) between windows.

8. Tap to minimize the selected app to a small draggable circle on the screen.

9. Tap to maximize the selected app to full screen.

10. Tap to close the app in the selected window.

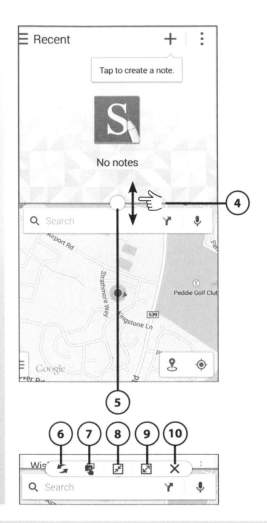

>>>Go Further
MINIMIZED APPS

When you choose to minimize an app as shown in step 8, the app shrinks to a small circle on the screen. You can drag the minimized app anywhere on the screen. If you touch and hold the app, a trash can icon appears; drag the app to the trash can to close the app. If you tap the minimized app, it enlarges to a pop-up window instead of maximizing back to its original window in the split screen. You can then continue working on the app in its small window. Minimized apps continue to be shown no matter what screen you are on and what app you are running.

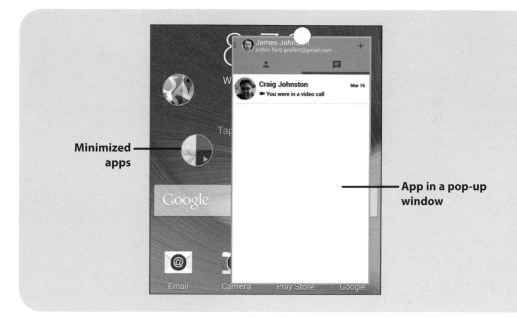

Minimized apps

App in a pop-up window

More Than One App in Each Window

When you use Multi Window, the screen is split into two windows—one at the top and one at the bottom. As previously shown, you can drag an app to either the top or bottom window. You can actually drag more than one app into each window. Follow steps 1–3 and simply drag the new app on top of the one that's already there. The only downside to this is that you can only work with the last app that was dragged to the window. Even though the previous apps are there and running, you cannot switch to them. Your only course of action is to close the app on top and continue working on the previous app in the same window.

>>>Go Further

PRESETTING PAIRS OF APPS

You can create preset pairs of apps. This enables you to quickly open two apps on the screen without first dragging them onto the screen manually each time you open Multi Window. To do this, open the two apps that you want to work with (if you have more than one app in each window, only the one visible is added to the pair). Tap the Multi Window up arrow and tap Create. A new icon is added to the list of Multi Window apps with the name of both apps. In the future when you open the Multi Window list, your preset app pairs will be right at the top.

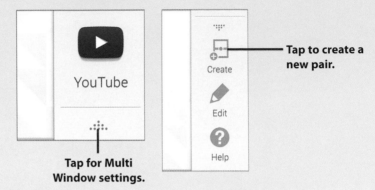

Tap to create a new pair.

Tap for Multi Window settings.

Installing Synchronization Software

Because your Galaxy Note 4 is tightly integrated with Google and its services, all media that you purchase on your phone is stored in the Google cloud and accessible anywhere, anytime. However, you might have a lot of music on your computer and need to copy that to your Google cloud. To do that, you need to install the Google Music Manager software or the Android File Transfer app for your Mac to copy any files back and forth.

Install Android File Transfer (Apple Mac OS X)

You only need the Android File Transfer app when using a Samsung Android phone (such as your Galaxy Note 4) on an Apple Mac running OS X.

1. From your Mac, browse to http://www.android.com/filetransfer/ and download the Android File Transfer app.

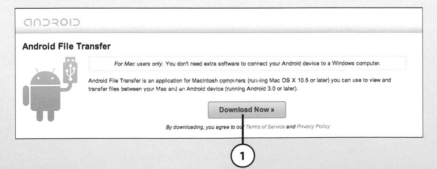

2. Click the Downloads icon.

3. Double-click the app in your Safari Downloads.

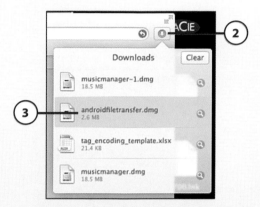

4. Drag the green Android to the Applications shortcut to install the app.

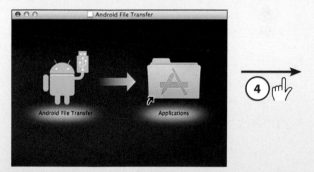

Install Google Music Manager (Apple Mac)

Don't install Google Music Manager unless you plan to upload files from your computer to the Google Music cloud.

1. Visit https://music.google.com/music/listen#manager_pl from your desktop web browser and log in to your Google account if you're prompted.

2. Click to download Music Manager.

3. Click the Downloads icon.

4. Double-click the app in your Safari Downloads.

5. Drag the Music Manager icon to the Applications shortcut to install the app.

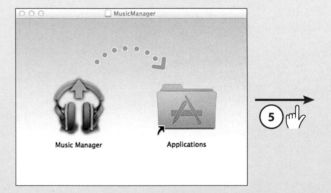

6. Double-click the Music Manager icon in the Applications folder.

7. Skip to the "Configure Music Manager" section to complete the installation.

Install Google Music Manager (Windows)

Don't install Google Music Manager unless you plan to upload files from your computer to the Google Music cloud.

1. Visit https://music.google.com/music/listen#manager_pl from your desktop web browser and log in to your Google account if you're prompted.

2. Click to download Music Manager.

4. Skip to the "Configure Music Manager" section to complete the installation.

3. Double-click the app in your Downloads folder.

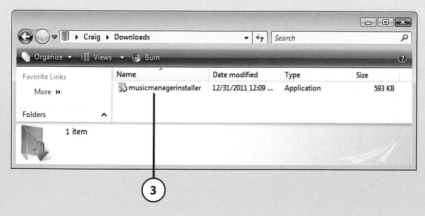

4. Skip to the "Configure Music Manager" section to complete the installation.

Configure Music Manager (Windows and Apple Mac)

1. Click Continue.

2. Enter your Google (Gmail) email address.

3. Enter your Google (Gmail) password.

4. Click Continue.

5. Choose where you keep your music.

6. Click Continue.

Welcome to Google Music

Music Manager will help you add your personal collection to your Music library. In a few minutes you'll be able to start listening on any connected computer or Android device running 2.2 or higher.

Important: By uploading your music, you represent that you will use Google Music only for personal use with your legally acquired music.

Continue

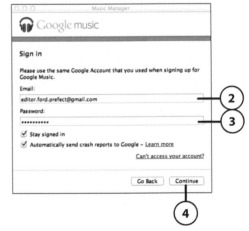

Sign In

Please use the same Google Account that you used when signing up for Google Music.

Email:
editor.ford.prefect@gmail.com

Password:
....

☑ Stay signed in
☑ Automatically send crash reports to Google – Learn more

Can't access your account?

Go Back   Continue

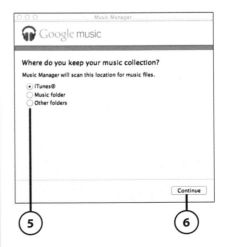

Where do you keep your music collection?

Music Manager will scan this location for music files.

⦿ iTunes®
◯ Music folder
◯ Other folders

Continue

7. Choose whether to upload all of your music or just some of your playlists. Remember that you can only upload 20,000 songs for free. Skip to step 12 if you chose to upload all music.

8. Check if you want to also upload podcasts.

9. Click Continue.

10. Select one or more playlists of music.

11. Click Continue.

12. Choose whether you want to automatically upload any new music that is added to your computer.

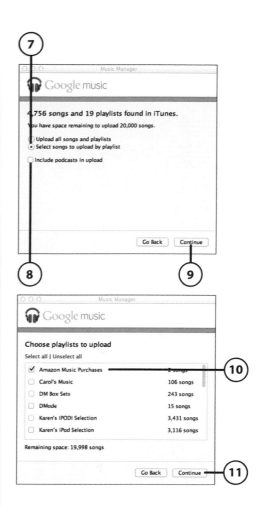

13. Click Continue.

14. Click Close.

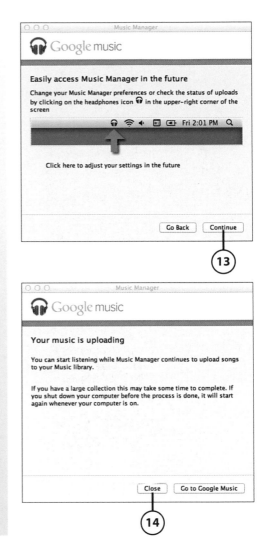

Freeing Up Memory

If you have installed a Secure Digital card (SD card), then you have the ability to move media and parts of some apps to the SD card to free up memory on your Note 4.

Move Apps

Not all apps support being moved
to the SD card (external memory),
and even apps that do support this
feature only move part of themselves
to the SD card.

1. Touch and hold an app you want
   to move to the SD Card.

2. Drag the app to the App Info icon.

3. Tap Move to SD card.

Application	29.36MB
SD card app	0.00B
Data	0.00B
SD card data	0.00B
Move to SD card	Clear data
CACHE	

Move Media

Using the My Files app, you can
move audio, photos, and video to the
SD card to free up memory on your
Note 4.

1. Tap the My Files app icon.

2. Tap the media type that you want to move. This example uses Images.

3. Tap the Menu icon.

4. Tap Select.

5. Select one or more files.

6. Tap the Menu icon.

7. Tap Move.

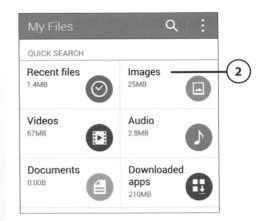

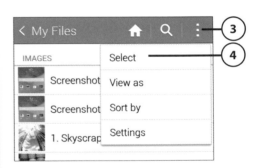

8. Tap SD Card.

9. Tap Create Folder to create a new folder to store your images.

10. Enter a name for the new folder.

11. Tap Create.

12. Tap the new folder you just created.

13. Tap Move Here.

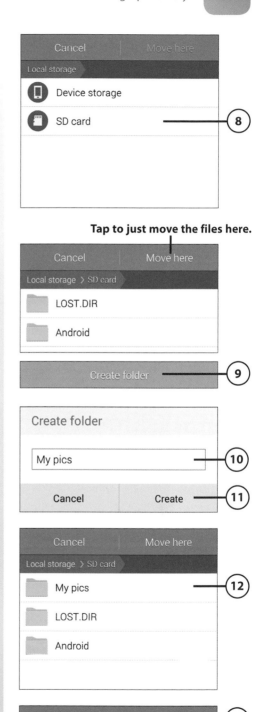

Tap to just move the files here.

Tap to turn Wi-Fi on or off.

Tap to turn Bluetooth on or off.

Tap to turn all radios on or off.

Tap to turn NFC on or off.

In this chapter, you discover the connectivity capabilities of your Galaxy Note 4, including Bluetooth, Wi-Fi, VPN, and NFC. Topics include the following:

→ Pairing with Bluetooth devices

→ Connecting to Wi-Fi networks

→ Working with virtual private networks (VPNs)

→ Using your Galaxy Note 4 as a Wi-Fi hotspot

→ Using Near Field Communications (NFC) and beaming

Connecting to Bluetooth, Wi-Fi, and VPNs

Your Galaxy Note 4 can connect to Bluetooth devices, such as headsets, computers, and car in-dash systems, as well as to Wi-Fi networks and 2G, 3G, and 4G cellular networks. It has all the connectivity you should expect on a great smartphone. Your Galaxy Note 4 can also connect to virtual private networks (VPNs) for access to secure networks. Your Galaxy Note 4 can even share its cellular data connection with other devices over Wi-Fi.

Connecting to Bluetooth Devices

Bluetooth is a great personal area network (PAN) technology that allows for short-distance wireless access to all sorts of devices, such as headsets, other phones, computers, smartwatches, Google Glass, and even car in-dash systems for hands-free calling and playing music. The following tasks walk you through pairing your Galaxy Note 4 to your device and configuring options.

Pair with a New Bluetooth Device

Before you can take advantage of Bluetooth, you need to connect your Galaxy Note 4 with that device, which is called *pairing*. After you pair your Galaxy Note 4 with a Bluetooth device, the two devices can connect to each other automatically in the future.

Putting the Bluetooth Device into Pairing Mode First

Before you pair a Bluetooth device to your Galaxy Note 4, you must first put it into Pairing mode. If you are pairing with a Bluetooth headset, you normally have to hold the button on the headset for a certain period of time. Consult your Bluetooth device's manual to find out how to put that device into Pairing mode.

Your Galaxy Note 4's Bluetooth name

Discovered Bluetooth devices

1. Pull down the Notification bar.

2. Touch and hold the Bluetooth icon to configure Bluetooth.

3. Tap to turn the Bluetooth radio on, if it is not already on.

4. Tap Scan if you don't see the device you want to connect to in the list of discovered devices.

5. Tap the Bluetooth device you want to connect to. This example uses a Plantronics Bluetooth headset, the PLT_M165.

6. If all went well, your Galaxy Note 4 should now be paired with the new Bluetooth device.

Successfully paired

Bluetooth Passkey

If you are pairing with a device that requires a passkey, such as a car in-dash system, smartwatch, other smartphone, or a computer, the screen shows a passkey. Make sure the passkey is the same on your Galaxy Note 4 and on the device you are pairing with. Tap OK on your Galaxy Note 4 and confirm the passkey on the device you are pairing with.

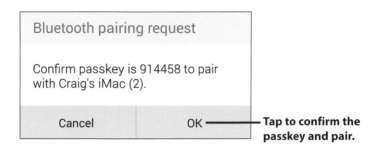

Tap to confirm the passkey and pair.

All Zeros

If you are pairing with an older Bluetooth headset, you might be prompted to enter the passkey. Try using four zeros; it normally works. If the zeros don't work, refer to the headset's manual.

>>>Go Further
REVERSE PAIRING

The steps in this section describe how to pair your Galaxy Note 4 with a Bluetooth device that is in Pairing mode, listening for an incoming pairing command. You can pair Bluetooth another way in which you put your Galaxy Note 4 in Discovery mode. To do this, tap the Bluetooth name of your Galaxy Note 4 on the screen (this is normally "Note 4" unless you have changed it). Your Galaxy Note 4 goes into Pairing mode for two minutes.

MY DEVICE

☐ James Johnston (Galaxy Not..
Visible to all nearby Bluetooth devices ✓ ——— **Tap to make your**
(1:55)   **Galaxy Note 4**
                                                    visible for pairing.

Set Extra Bluetooth Options

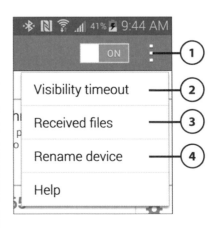

1. Tap the Menu icon.

2. Tap to change how long your Galaxy Note 4 stays visible when pairing.

3. Tap to see any files people have sent you over the Bluetooth network.

4. Tap to rename your Galaxy Note 4. This name is used to identify your device when you connect to other devices over Bluetooth and Wi-Fi. Use a friendly name, such as "Ford's Note 4."

* N 🛜 ⏹ 41% 🔋 9:44 AM

ON ⋮ ——— ①

Visibility timeout ——— ②

Received files ——— ③

Rename device ——— ④

Help

Change Bluetooth Device Options

After a Bluetooth device is paired to your Note 4, you might be able to change a few options for it. The number of options depends on the Bluetooth device you are connecting to. Some have more features than others.

1. Tap the Settings icon to the right of the Bluetooth device.

2. Tap to rename the Bluetooth device to something more descriptive.

3. Tap to disconnect and unpair the Galaxy Note 4 from the Bluetooth device. If you do this, you won't be able to use the Bluetooth device again until you redo the pairing as described in the "Pair with a New Bluetooth Device" task.

4. Tap to use or not use the device's features. Sometimes Bluetooth devices have more than one profile. You can use this screen to select which ones you want to use.

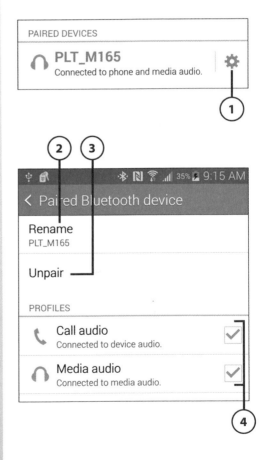

Bluetooth Profiles

Each Bluetooth device can have one or more Bluetooth profiles. Each Bluetooth profile describes certain features of the device. This tells your Galaxy Note 4 what it can do when connected to the device. A Bluetooth headset normally only has one profile, such as Phone Audio (or Call Audio). This tells your Galaxy Note 4 that it can only use the device for phone call audio. Some devices might have this profile but also provide other features such as a Phone Book Access profile, which would allow it to synchronize with your Galaxy Note 4's address book. The latter is typical for a car's in-dash Bluetooth device. The example shown in step 4 of the "Change Bluetooth Device Options" task is a Plantronics Bluetooth headset that has two Bluetooth profiles: Call Audio and Media Audio. Media Audio allows your Galaxy Note 4 to play media such as sounds your Note 4 makes and other media such as music, audio from a video, and so on. You might decide that you only want to use the headset for phone calls (Call Audio) and would prefer the media audio to continue to be directed to your Note 4's built-in speaker. In that case, you would uncheck Media Audio.

Quick Disconnect

To quickly disconnect from a Bluetooth device, tap the device on the Bluetooth Settings screen and then tap OK.

Wi-Fi

Wi-Fi (Wireless Fidelity) networks are wireless networks that run within free radio bands around the world. Your local coffee shop probably has free Wi-Fi, and so do many other places, such as airports, train stations, malls, and other public areas. Your Galaxy Note 4 can connect to any Wi-Fi network and provide you faster Internet access speeds than the cellular network.

Connect to Wi-Fi

The following steps explain how to find and connect to Wi-Fi networks. After you have connected your Galaxy Note 4 to a Wi-Fi network, you automatically are connected to it the next time you are in range of that network.

1. Pull down the Notification bar.

2. Touch and hold the Wi-Fi icon.

3. Tap to turn Wi-Fi on if the slider is in the off position.

4. Tap the name of the Wi-Fi network you want to connect to. If the network does not use any security, you can skip to step 10.

You Are Prompted to Log In

If you are in a hotel, on a plane, or in some other place that provides Wi-Fi, many times even though the Wi-Fi network does not use any security, right after step 4, you are redirected to a login page. The login page is typically there for you to charge the cost of the Wi-Fi usage to your hotel room or some other account. Sometimes it is just to display a terms of use message for you to accept. If the login page is not displayed and you find that your Internet access is not working, open a web browser (Chrome or the default Internet browser) and type any website (such as abc.com). This should prompt the Wi-Fi network to display the login page.

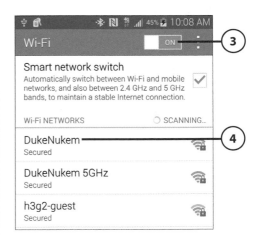

5. Enter the Wi-Fi network password.

6. Tap to configure advanced options such as to use a specific web browsing proxy server or to use static IP settings. If you don't need to configure advanced options, skip to step 9.

7. Tap to use a special web browsing proxy server while connected to this Wi-Fi network.

8. Tap to decide whether to let the Wi-Fi network router provide you with an IP address and IP settings or to use a static IP address and enter your own IP settings.

9. Tap to connect to the Wi-Fi network.

Tap to show the password if you think you might be typing it incorrectly.

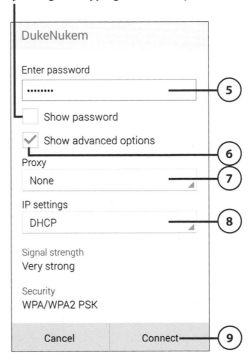

Adding a Hidden Network

If the network you want to connect to is not listed on the screen, it might be purposely hidden. Hidden networks do not broadcast their name—which is known as their Service Set Identifier (SSID). You need to scroll down to the bottom of the listed Wi-Fi networks and tap Add Wi-Fi Network, type in the SSID, and choose the type of security that the network uses. You need to get this information from the network administrator before you try to connect.

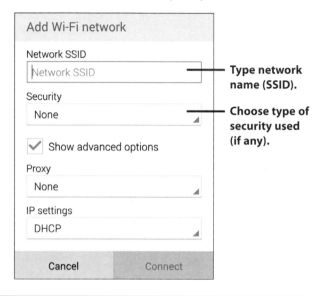

Type network name (SSID).

Choose type of security used (if any).

10. If all goes well, you see the Wi-Fi network in the list with the word "Connected" under it.

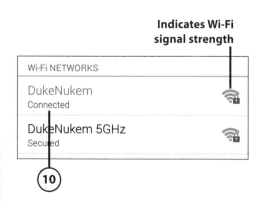

Indicates Wi-Fi signal strength

Configure Wi-Fi Network Options

1. Tap a Wi-Fi network to reveal a pop-up that shows information about your connection to that network.

2. Tap Forget to tell your Galaxy Note 4 to not connect to this network in the future.

3. Touch and hold on a Wi-Fi network to reveal two actions.

4. Tap to forget the Wi-Fi network and no longer connect to it.

5. Tap to change the Wi-Fi network password or encryption key that your Galaxy Note 4 uses to connect to the network.

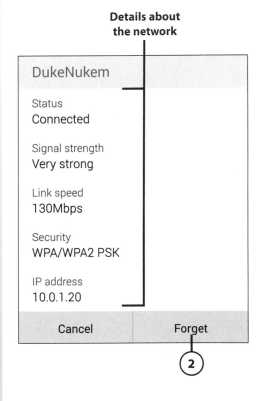

Details about the network

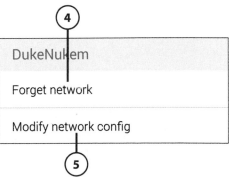

Configure Advanced Wi-Fi Options

Your Galaxy Note 4 enables you to configure a few advanced Wi-Fi settings that can actually help preserve your battery life.

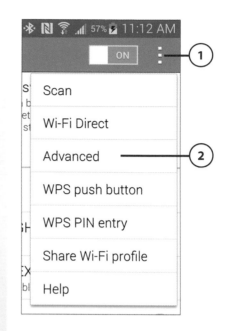

1. Tap the Menu button.

2. Tap Advanced.

3. Tap to enable or disable the ability for your Galaxy Note 4 to automatically notify you when it detects a new Wi-Fi network.

4. Tap to let your Note 4 automatically connect to Wi-Fi networks that support Passpoint.

5. Tap to change the sort order of Wi-Fi networks. By default they are sorted alphabetically.

6. Tap to change the Wi-Fi sleep policy. This enables you to choose if your Galaxy Note 4 should keep its connection to Wi-Fi when it goes to sleep.

7. Tap to choose whether to allow Google and apps running on your Note 4 to scan for Wi-Fi networks, even if you have turned Wi-Fi off.

8. Tap to install certificates for authentication onto Wi-Fi networks that are provided by your administrator, and that you earlier stored on the SD card (external memory).

Should You Keep Wi-Fi on During Sleep?

In step 6 of the "Configure Advanced Wi-Fi Options" task, you can choose how your Galaxy Note 4 handles its connection to Wi-Fi when it goes to sleep. Because Wi-Fi is much faster and more efficient than 3G or 4G, and is free, you should keep this set to Always. However, battery usage can be affected by always being connected to Wi-Fi, so you might want to set this to Only When Plugged In, which means that if your Galaxy Note 4 is not charging, and it goes to sleep, it switches to the cellular network for data; when the Galaxy Note 4 is charging and it goes to sleep, it stays connected to Wi-Fi. If you choose Never for this setting, when your Galaxy Note 4 goes to sleep, it switches to using the cellular network for all data. This can lead to more data being used out of your cellular data bundle, which might cost extra, so be careful.

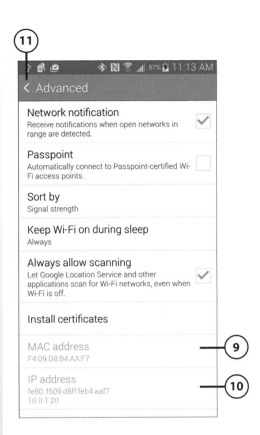

9. Use this Wi-Fi MAC address if you need to provide a network administrator with your MAC address in order to be able to use a Wi-Fi network.

10. This shows the IP address that has been assigned to your Galaxy Note 4 when it connected to the Wi-Fi network.

11. Tap to save your changes and return to the previous screen.

>>>*Go Further*

WHAT ARE IP AND MAC ADDRESSES?

A Media Access Control (MAC) address is a number burned into your Galaxy Note 4 that identifies its Wi-Fi adapter. This is called the *Physical Layer address* because it is a physical adapter. An Internet Protocol (IP) address is a secondary way to identify your Galaxy Note 4. Unlike a Physical Layer address or MAC address, the IP address can be changed at any time. Modern networks use the IP address when they need to deliver some data to you. Typically when you connect to a network, a device on the network assigns a new IP address. On home networks, this is typically your Wi-Fi router.

Some network administrators use a security feature to limit who can connect to their Wi-Fi network. They set up their network to only allow connections from Wi-Fi devices with specific MAC addresses. If you are trying to connect to such a network, you will have to give the network administrator your MAC address, and he will add it to the allowed list.

>>>*Go Further*

WHAT IS PASSPOINT?

Passpoint is a technology that is being used increasingly by operators of Wi-Fi hotspots, and its purpose is to let your Note 4 (and other Passpoint-enabled smartphones and tablets) to automatically roam onto the hotspots with no need for you to search for them or log in to them using the typical hotspot login web page. Simply based on the SIM card in your Note 4, you are automatically authenticated onto these hotspots and provided a secure encrypted connection.

Wi-Fi Direct

Wi-Fi Direct is a feature that allows two Android devices running version 4.1 (Jelly Bean) or later to connect to each other using Wi-Fi so they can exchange files. Because Wi-Fi is much faster than Bluetooth, if you are sending large files, using Wi-Fi Direct makes sense. You do not need to be attached to an existing Wi-Fi network to use Wi-Fi Direct.

It's Not All Good

Wi-Fi Direct Is Not Working

At the time of writing, Wi-Fi Direct was not working on the Galaxy Note 4. I made several attempts to send files to a number of different Android devices that were running different versions of Android, and the sending always failed. If you search for Wi-Fi Direct in the Google Play Store, you can find a number of third-party solutions that use Wi-Fi Direct but make the connections between devices themselves instead of relying on Android to do it.

Send a File Using Wi-Fi Direct

Follow these steps to connect to an Android device running version 4.1 (Jelly Bean) or later via Wi-Fi Direct and send it files from your Note 4.

1. Ask the other person to enable Wi-Fi Direct on his Android device. The Wi-Fi Direct screen is normally under the Wi-Fi Settings or Wi-Fi Advanced Settings.

2. Tap the Share icon for the item you want to send. This can be a picture in the Gallery app, for example.

3. Tap the Wi-Fi Direct icon.

4. Tap the other user's device name to invite it to connect with your Galaxy Note 4 via Wi-Fi Direct and send the file to that device.

5. Ask the other person to tap Accept or Connect on the device you are inviting.

6. If the Wi-Fi Direct connection is made successfully, the file is sent to the other device.

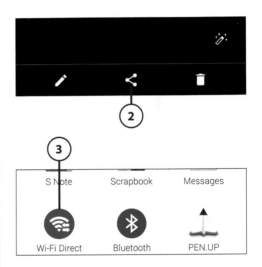

Receive a File Using Wi-Fi Direct

Follow these steps to receive files from an Android device running 4.1 (Jelly Bean) or later.

1.   Pull down the Notification bar.

2.   Touch and hold the Wi-Fi icon.

3.   Tap the Menu icon.

4.   Tap Wi-Fi Direct and wait for the other person to invite you.

5.   Tap Connect when the other person invites you to connect using Wi-Fi Direct. One or more files should now start copying to your Note 4.

Does Wi-Fi Direct Work for All Android Devices?

Theoretically, all Android devices running version 4.1 should be able to send or receive files via Wi-Fi Direct; however, some devices do have reported issues.

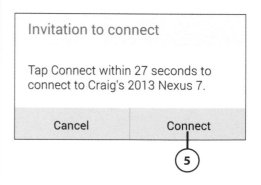

Near Field Communications (NFC)

Your Galaxy Note 4 has the ability to swap data via its NFC radio with other phones that use NFC or read data that is stored on NFC tags. You can also use NFC to pay for items you have purchased. Android Beam and Samsung S Beam also use NFC to send files between Android devices by setting up the sending process automatically via NFC and then continuing it via Bluetooth or Wi-Fi Direct.

Enable NFC, Android Beam, and S Beam

To get the full benefit from NFC, you need to enable the NFC radio. You should also enable Android Beam and S Beam.

1. Pull down the Notification bar.

2. Tap the Settings icon.

3. Tap NFC under the Connect and Share section.

4. Tap to enable NFC if the switch isn't already in the On position.

5. Tap to enable Android Beam. (See the next section for more about Android Beam.)

6. Tap to enable S Beam. (See the "What Is Samsung's S Beam?" note later in this chapter for more information.)

7. Tap to save your changes and go back to the main Settings screen.

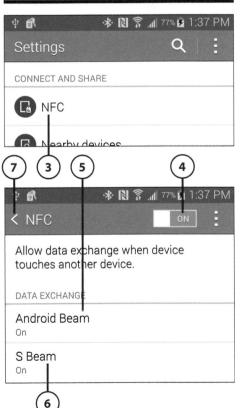

>>>Go Further
WHAT IS ANDROID BEAM?

All Android devices running version 4.0 (Ice Cream Sandwich) or later have a feature called Android Beam. This feature sends small bits of data via NFC (such as links to YouTube videos or links to apps in Google Play) to enable you to effectively share content, but it also automates sending actual files (such as pictures and videos) between devices via Bluetooth.

Use Android Beam to Send Links to Content

You can use Android Beam to send links to content—such as apps, music, and video in the Google Play Store or website links—to another device. Android Beam only works between devices that are both running Android 4.0 (Ice Cream Sandwich) or later. The following example shows you how to send a website link.

1. Open a website that you'd like to share the link to. Put the back of your Galaxy Note 4 about 1" from the back of another NFC-enabled device. You know that the two devices have successfully connected when the web page zooms out.

2. Tap the web page after it zooms out.

3. The browser on the other device opens and immediately loads the link you shared.

Beam Google Play Content and YouTube Videos

If you like a song, movie, book, or app that is in the Google Play Store, you can beam it to someone. Simply open the song, movie, book, or app in Google Play, tap your devices together, and tap to beam. To beam a YouTube video, open the video in the YouTube app, tap the devices together, and tap to beam. The other device opens YouTube and jumps directly to the video.

Use Android Beam to Send Real Files

You can also use Android Beam to send real content such as pictures, music, and video that's stored on your Galaxy Note 4. Sending real files using Android Beam only works between devices that are running Android 4.1 (Jelly Bean) or later. This task describes how to beam a picture.

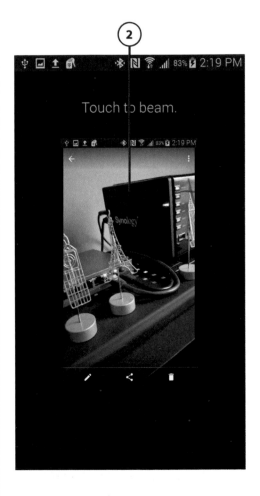

1. Open the picture you want to beam. (Note that the picture must reside on your Galaxy Note 4 and not in the Google cloud.) Then put the back of your Galaxy Note 4 about 1" from the back of another NFC-enabled phone. You know that the two devices have successfully connected when the picture zooms out.

2. Tap the picture after it zooms out.

3. Pull down the Notification bar to see the progress of the file transfer.

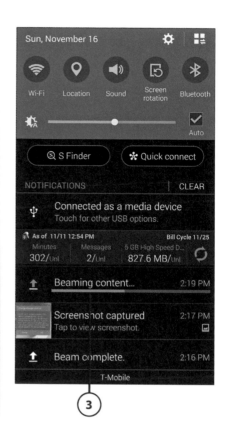

What Is Samsung's S Beam?

When you try to beam something between two Samsung devices, they automatically use S Beam instead of Android Beam. The process you use to do the beaming is identical (bring the two devices together and tap the object to beam it), but S Beam transfers files using Wi-Fi Direct, which is much faster than how it is done using Android Beam, which uses Bluetooth.

>>>Go Further

SHARE YOUR FILES USING NEARBY DEVICES

Digital Living Network Alliance (DLNA) is a technology that allows devices to share multimedia with each other. It has been around for many years. It allows one device to make its pictures, audio, and movies available on a network to be used by other devices. For example, you may configure your storage device to share its content via DLNA, and your DLNA-compatible TV will be able to browse the content and stream it. Your Note 4 uses another name for DLNA; it calls it "Nearby Devices." While in the Settings screen, scroll down and tap Nearby Devices. From the screen that opens, choose what content you want to share and enable Nearby Devices. Other devices on the network that support DLNA are able to browse your Note 4 and stream the media from it, including movies, videos, pictures, and audio.

Cellular Networks

Your Galaxy Note 4 can connect to many different cellular networks around the world. The exact networks that it can connect to are determined by the variant of Galaxy Note 4 you have because not all carriers use the same technology. To complicate things even more, many network carriers use different frequencies from one another.

Change Mobile Settings

Your Galaxy Note 4 has a few options when it comes to connecting to cellular (or mobile) networks.

1. Pull down the Notification bar.

2. Tap the Settings icon.

3. Tap More Networks in the Network Connections section.

4. Tap to enable or disable Wi-Fi Calling.

5. Tap Mobile Networks.

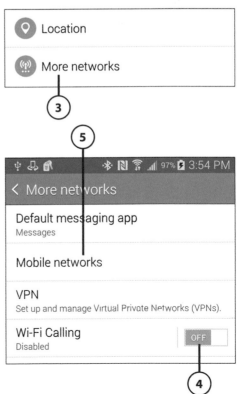

What Is Wi-Fi Calling?

Wi-Fi Calling, also known as Universal Mobile Access (UMA), is provided by some cellular carriers both to augment their coverage and to provide free calls over Wi-Fi. This is not Voice over IP (VoIP) calling but a regular GSM voice call, routed via a Wi-Fi hotspot, over the Internet, to your carrier. Because the call is not using the cellular network infrastructure, the calls are free, and because of the speeds at which Wi-Fi networks operate, the call quality is much higher because much less compression is needed. To read more about UMA, try this online article: http://crackberry.com/saving-call-charges-recession-your-blackberry.

6. Tap to enable or disable cellular data. If this option is unchecked, your Galaxy Note 4 is able to use only Wi-Fi networks for data.

7. Tap to enable or disable cellular data roaming. If this is unchecked, your Galaxy Note 4 does not attempt to use data while you roam away from your home cellular network.

8. Tap to view, edit, and add APNs. It is unlikely that you need to make any APN changes.

9. Tap to change the network mode. This setting enables you to choose to force your Note 4 to connect to a slower 2G network (GSM Only) to save battery, but it also allows you to manually select whether you want your Note 4 to only connect to 3G networks (WCDMA Only), automatically select between 3G and 2G (WCDMA/GSM Auto Connect), or let your Note 4 automatically select between 4G, 3G, and 2G networks (LTE/WCDMA/GSM Auto Connect).

10. Tap to view and choose mobile operators to use manually.

11. Tap to save your changes and return to the previous screen.

What Is an APN?

APN stands for Access Point Name. You normally don't have to make changes to APNs, but sometimes you need to enter them manually to access certain features. For example, if you need to use tethering, which is where you connect your laptop to your Galaxy Note 4, and your Galaxy Note 4 provides Internet connectivity for your laptop, you might be asked by your carrier to use a specific APN. Think of an APN as a gateway to a service.

Can I Disable Mobile Data?

If you disable mobile data, you can save on battery life; however, you effectively kill the functionality of any app that needs to be connected all the time, such as instant messaging apps (Yahoo! or Google Talk) or apps such as Skype. You also stop receiving email in real time. When this feature is disabled, about 5 minutes after your Galaxy Note 4 goes to sleep, it disconnects from the mobile data network; however, it remains connected to the mobile voice network.

>>>Go Further

WHY SELECT OPERATORS MANUALLY?

When you are roaming in your home country, your Galaxy Note 4 automatically selects your home cellular provider. When you are roaming outside your home country, your Galaxy Note 4 registers on a cellular provider based on its name and how it scores alphabetically. The lowest score always wins. For example, a carrier whose name starts with a number is always chosen over carriers whose names start with letters. A carrier whose name starts with the letter *A* is chosen over a carrier whose name starts with the letter *B*, and so on. As you roam, your home carrier might not have a good roaming relationship with a carrier that your Galaxy Note 4 has chosen based on its name, so it's better for you to choose the carrier manually to ensure the best roaming rates and, many times, basic connectivity. You will notice that sometimes carriers are represented not by their names but by their operator codes (or Public Land Mobile Network [PLMN] number). For example, 53024 is actually 2Degrees in New Zealand, and 53005 is Telecom New Zealand.

>>>Go Further
BOOST YOUR DOWNLOAD SPEEDS

Your Galaxy Note 4 has a feature called Download Booster. When you enable it, it allows your Galaxy Note 4 to download content over both the cellular data and Wi-Fi networks at the same time. Because the downloads are transferring over both networks, the time it takes to download content is faster, sometimes double the speed of just Wi-Fi, depending on circumstances. Of course, if you have a limited cellular data plan, you might want to be cautious using this feature, or keep it disabled. To enable Download Booster, pull down the Notification bar and swipe from left to right across the Quick Settings icons to see more icons. Tap the Download Booster icon and make sure it turns green.

Virtual Private Networks (VPNs)

Your Galaxy Note 4 can connect to virtual private networks (VPNs), which are normally used by companies to provide a secure connection to their inside networks or intranets.

Add a VPN

Before you add a VPN, you must first have all the information needed to set it up on your Galaxy Note 4. Speak to your network administrator to get this information ahead of time (and save yourself some frustration). The information you need includes the type of VPN protocol used, the type of encryption used, and the name of the host to which you are connecting.

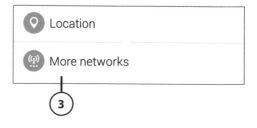

1. Pull down the Notification bar.

2. Tap the Settings icon.

3. Tap More Networks in the Network Connections section.

4. Tap VPN.

5. Tap Basic VPN or Advanced IPsec VPN. The one you choose is based on what your network administrator tells you to use. The steps to set up either type of VPN are the same. This example sets up a basic VPN. If you already have a screen lock PIN, pattern, or password, you can skip to step 8.

6. Tap OK to set up a screen lock PIN, pattern, or password. If you already have a screen lock PIN or password, you won't be prompted at this point, and you can proceed to step 8.

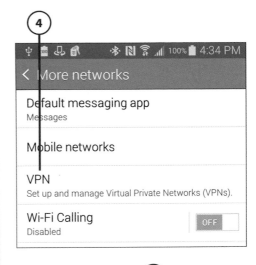

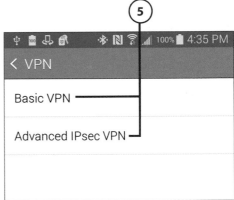

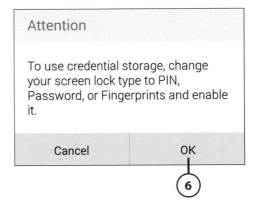

7. Choose the method you want to use to unlock your Galaxy Note 4 and follow the steps to create it. After you have set up your device unlock method, you are directed back to the VPN screen.

Why Do You Need to Set a PIN or Password?

If you don't already have a screen lock PIN, password, or pattern set up before you create your first VPN network connection, you are prompted to create one. This is a security measure that ensures your Galaxy Note 4 must first be unlocked before anyone can access a stored VPN connection. Because VPN connections are usually used to access company data, this is a good idea.

8. Tap the plus icon to add a new VPN network.

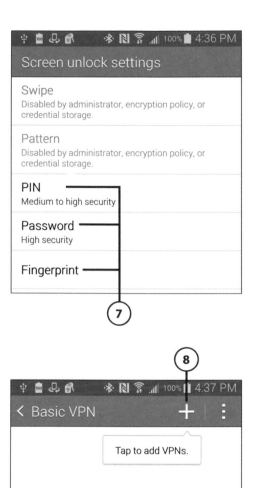

9. Enter a name for your VPN network. You can call it anything, such as Work VPN, or the name of the provider, such as Public VPN.

10. Tap to choose the type of technology used to create the VPN.

11. Enter the remaining parameters that your network administrator has provided.

12. Tap Save.

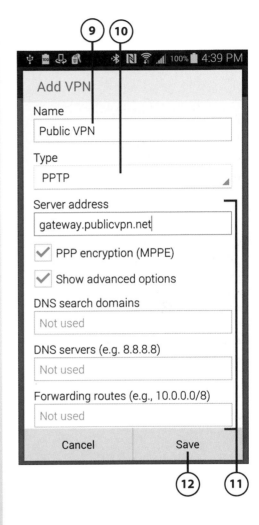

Connect to a VPN

After you have created one or more VPN connections, you can connect to them when the need arises.

1. Pull down the Notification bar.

2. Tap the Settings icon.

3. Tap More Networks on the Network Connections tab.

4. Tap VPN.

5. Tap either Basic VPN or Advanced IPsec VPN, depending on the type of preconfigured VPN you need to use. This example uses the basic VPN set up in the preceding task.

6. Tap a preconfigured VPN connection.

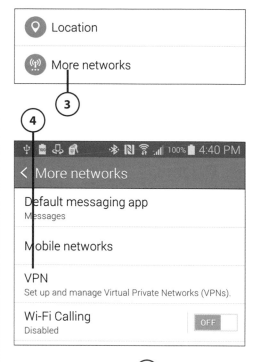

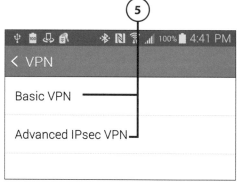

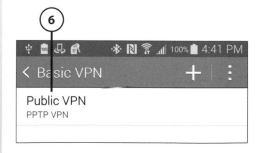

7. Enter the VPN username.

8. Enter the VPN password.

9. Tap Connect. After you're connected to the VPN, you can use your web browser and other applications normally, but you now have access to resources at the other end of the VPN tunnel, such as company web servers or even your company email.

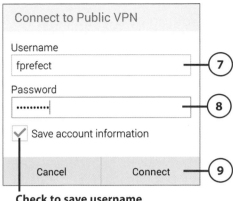

Connect to Public VPN

Username

fprefect — 7

Password

•••••••• — 8

☑ Save account information

Cancel   Connect — 9

Check to save username and password.

>>>Go Further

HOW CAN YOU TELL IF YOU ARE CONNECTED?

After your Galaxy Note 4 successfully connects to a VPN network, you see a key icon in the Notification bar. This indicates that you are connected. If you pull down the Notification bar, you can tap the icon to see information about the connection and to disconnect from the VPN.

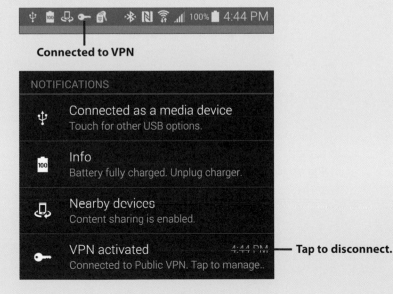

Connected to VPN

NOTIFICATIONS

Connected as a media device
Touch for other USB options.

Info
Battery fully charged. Unplug charger.

Nearby devices
Content sharing is enabled.

VPN activated   4:44 PM — **Tap to disconnect.**
Connected to Public VPN. Tap to manage..

Editing or Deleting a VPN

You can edit an existing VPN or delete it by touching and holding the name of the VPN. A window pops up with a list of options.

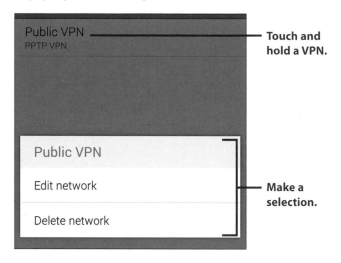

Public VPN — Touch and hold a VPN.
PPTP VPN

Public VPN

Edit network — Make a selection.

Delete network

It's Not All Good

No Quick Way to Start a VPN Connection

Unlike many other Android phones, the Galaxy Note 4 does not have a way to add a shortcut to your Home screen to jump straight to the VPN screen. There may be third-party solutions in the form of apps you can install that will add this functionality. Check the Google Play Store.

Mobile Wi-Fi Hotspot

Your Galaxy Note 4 has the ability to share its cellular data connection with up to eight devices over Wi-Fi. Before you use this feature, you normally need to sign up for a tethering or hotspot plan with your cellular provider, which is normally an extra monthly cost.

Start Your Mobile Wi-Fi Hotspot

After your Wi-Fi hotspot is set up the way you want it, you can start it and begin sharing your Internet connection.

1. Pull down the Notification bar.

2. Tap the Settings icon.

3. Tap Tethering and Mobile HotSpot in the Network Connections section.

4. Tap to adjust the range of your hotspot. If you need people who are not in your immediate vicinity to be able to connect to your hotspot, set this to High.

5. Tap Mobile HotSpot to configure and start your hotspot.

What Is USB Tethering?

USB tethering is a feature that enables you to share your Note 4's Internet connection with a computer via the USB port. To use this, connect your Note 4 to the computer using the supplied USB cable and enable USB tethering. On the computer there will be some extra setup to do, which includes choosing your Note 4 as an Internet access point. (And on older Windows computers you might need to install a device driver. Be sure to consult the computer's manual for instructions.)

Tap to enable USB tethering.

6. Tap the Menu icon to preconfigure your hotspot before starting it. If you would rather just start the hotspot now, skip to step 19.

7. Tap Configure.

8. Choose a network name (also known as the SSID) for your mobile hotspot. You can leave it set to the auto-generated name or change it to something more friendly.

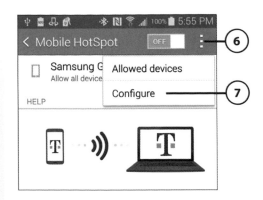

9. Tap to enable or disable broadcasting your hotspot's network name (its SSID). If you choose not to broadcast it, your network will be hidden, but it requires more steps to connect to it.

10. Tap to choose the type of security to use for your mobile hotspot or choose Open to use no security.

11. Enter a password for your portable hotspot if you chose to use a security method in step 10.

12. Tap to show advanced options for your hotspot.

13. Choose either the 2.4GHz or 5GHz radio bands for your hotspot. Because the 2.4GHz bands can be overcrowded, choosing the 5GHz bands can help with performance.

14. Tap if you want to manually select the channels that your hotspot uses.

15. Scroll down for more options.

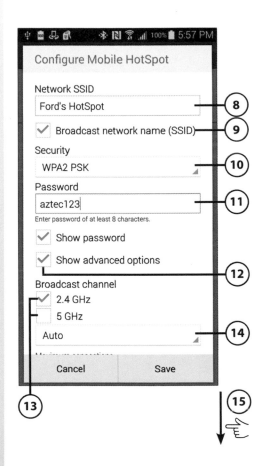

16. Tap to change the maximum number of people who can connect to your hotspot. Because Wi-Fi is a shared network, fewer people normally means faster performance for everyone.

17. Tap to change the number of minutes of inactivity that must pass before the hotspot turns itself off.

18. Tap to save your hotspot settings.

19. Tap to turn your hotspot on. Provide the hotspot connection information at the bottom of the screen to people you want to connect to your hotspot.

Limit Who Can Connect

People can only connect to your hotspot after you give them the connection information; however, you can further limit who can connect to your hotspot by allowing devices that have specific MAC addresses.

1. Tap to add an already connected device to the allowed devices list. Because the devices are already connected, your Note 4 already knows its MAC address.

2. Tap the Menu icon and Allowed Devices to add devices to the allowed list manually. You need to ask the device owner for her MAC address.

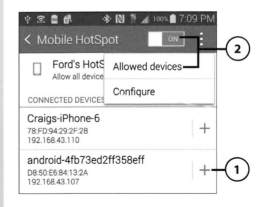

3. Tap the name of the hotspot to choose what devices are allowed to connect to your hotspot.

4. Tap Allowed Devices Only to limit the devices to the ones on the allowed list.

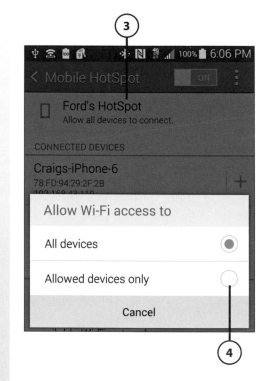

Tap to choose where
to use the wallpaper.

Tap to choose a
new wallpaper.

In this chapter, you find out how to customize your Galaxy Note 4 to suit your needs and lifestyle. Topics include the following:

→ Using wallpapers and live wallpapers
→ Replacing the keyboard
→ Adjusting sound and display settings
→ Setting the region and language
→ Using the fingerprint scanner

2

Customizing Your Galaxy Note 4

Your Galaxy Note 4 arrives preconfigured to appeal to most buyers; however, you might want to change the way some of the features work, or even personalize it to fit your mood or lifestyle. Luckily, your Galaxy Note 4 is customizable.

Changing Your Wallpaper

Your Galaxy Note 4 comes preloaded with a cool wallpaper. You can install other wallpapers, use live wallpapers that animate, and even use pictures in the Gallery application as your wallpaper.

1. Touch and hold in an open area on the Home screen.

2. Tap Wallpapers.

3. Tap to select where you want to change the wallpaper. You can choose a new wallpaper for the Home screen only or the Lock screen only, or you can use the same new wallpaper for both the Home and Lock screens.

4. Use the steps in one of the following three sections to choose the type of wallpaper to use as well as to select your new wallpaper.

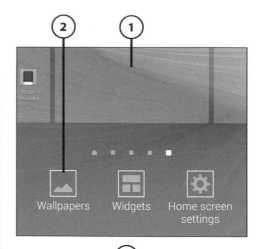

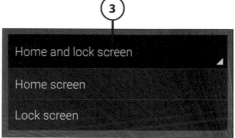

Set Up Wallpaper from Gallery Pictures

You can use any picture in your Gallery as a wallpaper.

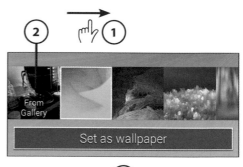

1. Swipe from left to right over the wallpaper thumbnails until you see one labeled From Gallery.

2. Tap From Gallery.

3. Navigate your photo albums and tap a photo you want to use for your wallpaper.

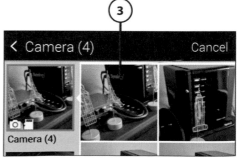

4. Move the crop box by dragging it to the part of the photo you want to use.

5. Adjust the size of the crop box to include the part of the photo you want to use. The crop box indicates what part of the photo will be used when the device is in portrait and landscape orientation.

6. Zoom in and out of the picture using the pinch gesture. Sometimes if the photo you have chosen is very large, you will not be able to zoom in or out.

7. Tap Save to use the cropped portion of the photo as your wallpaper. If you chose to use this new wallpaper on both your Home and Lock screens, you see a reminder dialog box. Tap OK to continue.

Set Up Live Wallpaper

Live wallpaper is wallpaper with some intelligence behind it. It can be a cool animation or even an animation that keys off things such as the music you are playing on your Galaxy Note 4, or it can be something simple such as the time. There are some very cool live wallpapers in Google Play that you can install and use.

1. Swipe from left to right over the wallpaper thumbnails until you see the Bubbles and Phase Beam options. Live wallpapers are kept on the right side of the wallpaper thumbnails.

2. Tap the live wallpaper you want to use.

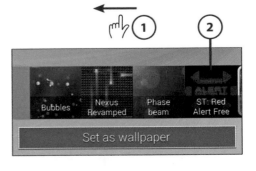

3. Tap Settings to change the way the live wallpaper works. (Not all live wallpapers will have settings that you can adjust.)

4. Tap Set as Wallpaper to use the live wallpaper.

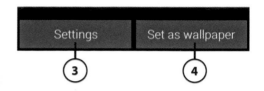

Finding More Wallpaper

You can find wallpaper or live wallpaper in the Google Play Store. Open the Google Play Store app and search for "wallpaper" or "live wallpaper." Read more on how to use the Google Play Store in Chapter 11, "Working with Android Apps."

Set Up Wallpaper

Choose a static wallpaper that is pre-loaded and sized correctly for your screen.

1. Swipe left and right over the wallpaper thumbnails to see static wallpaper options. Static wall-papers are in between the From Gallery option and the live wall-papers.

2. Tap a wallpaper to preview it.

3. Tap Set as Wallpaper to use the wallpaper.

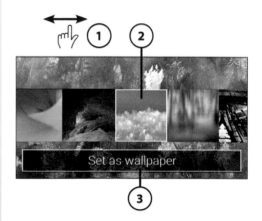

Changing Your Keyboard

If you find it hard to type on the standard Galaxy Note 4 keyboard, or you just want to make it look better, you can install replacement keyboards. You can download free or purchase replacement keyboards from the Google Play Store. Most if not all keyboards come with their own installation wizard that walks you through adding and activating a keyboard, but if the one you installed does not have a wizard, or when you want to manually switch keyboards in the future, you need to use these steps.

1. Pull down the Notification bar and tap the Settings icon.

2. Tap Language and Input.

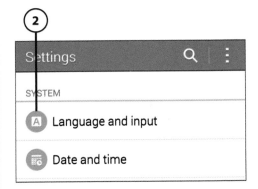

3. Check the box next to a keyboard you have previously installed from the Google Play Store (this example uses SwiftKey Keyboard) to make that keyboard available for use.

4. Tap OK to change the input method.

Doing Your Research

When you choose a different keyboard in step 3, the Galaxy Note 4 gives you a warning telling you that nonstandard keyboards have the potential for capturing everything you type. Do your research on any keyboards before you download and install them.

5. Tap Default to change the default keyboard to the one you have just enabled.

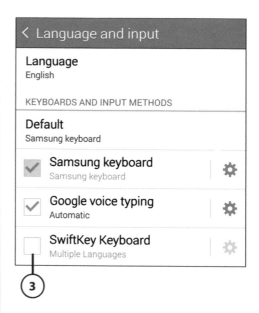

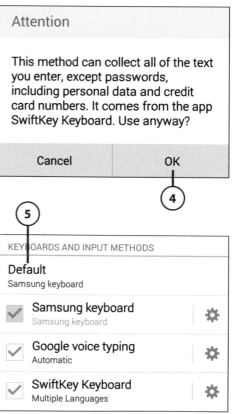

6. Tap the name of your new keyboard to select it to be the default.

What Can You Do with Your New Keyboard?

Keyboards you buy in the Google Play Store can do many things. They can change the key layout, change the color and style of the keys, offer different methods of text input, and even enable you to use an old T9 predictive input keyboard that you might have become used to when using an old "dumb phone" that had only a numeric keypad.

7. Tap the Settings icon for a keyboard to make changes, including customizing it. Sometimes tapping this icon launches the keyboard's customization wizard.

8. Tap to save your changes.

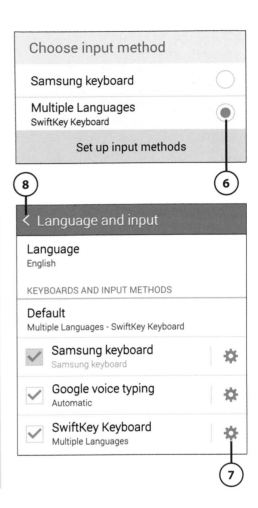

Adding Widgets to Your Home Screens

Some applications that you install come with widgets that you can place on your Home screen panes. These widgets normally display real-time information, such as stocks, weather, time, and Facebook feeds. Your Galaxy Note 4 also comes preinstalled with some widgets. Here is how to add and manage widgets.

Add a Widget

Your Galaxy Note 4 should come preinstalled with some widgets, but you might also have some extra ones that have been added when you installed applications. Here is how to add those widgets to your Home screen panes.

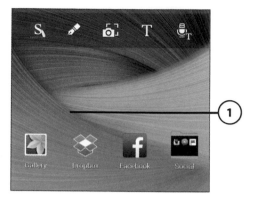

1. Touch and hold an open area on the Home screen.

2. Tap Widgets.

3. Touch and hold a widget to move it to a Home screen pane. Keep holding the widget as you move to step 4. This example uses the Alarm widget.

How Many Widgets Can I Fit?

Each part of the Home screen is divided into four blocks across and four blocks down. In the figure for step 3, notice that some widgets show their size in blocks across and down (such as 4×1). From that, you can judge if a widget is going to fit on the screen you want it to be on, but it also helps you position it in step 4.

Widget's size

Tap to see all widgets in a group.   Scroll left and right to see all widgets.

4. Position the widget where you want it on the Home screen pane.

5. Drag the widget to different Home screen panes if you want to place it on a different pane, or drag it to the plus symbol to create a new Home screen pane and place the widget on the new pane.

6. Release your finger to place the widget. Some widgets might prompt you with a few questions after they are positioned to help them get set up.

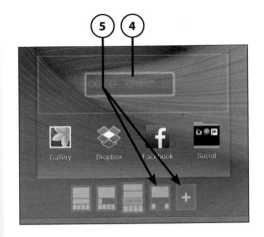

Resizing Widgets

Some (not all) widgets can be resized. To resize a widget, touch and hold the widget until you see an outline and then release it. If the widget can be resized, you see the resizing borders. Drag them to resize the widget. Tap anywhere on the screen to stop resizing.

Drag to resize the widget.

Remove and Move a Widget

Sometimes you want to remove a widget, resize it, or move it around.

1. Touch and hold the widget until the widget zooms out, but continue to hold it.

2. Drag the widget to the word Remove to remove it.

3. Drag the widget around the screen or drag it to one of the Home screen pane thumbnails to reposition it.

4. Release the widget.

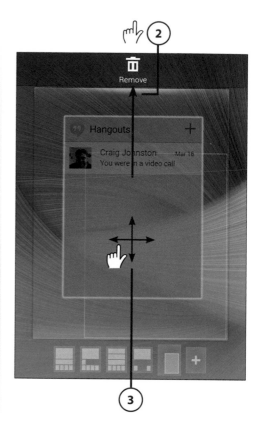

Setting the Language

If you move to another country or want to change the language used by your Galaxy Note 4, you can do so with a few taps.

1. Pull down the Notification bar and tap the Settings icon.

2. Tap Language and Input under the System section.

3. Tap Language.

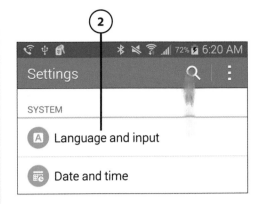

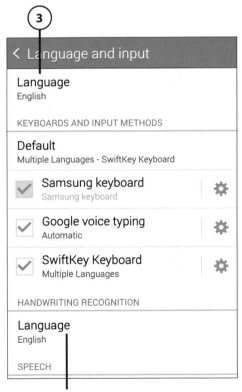

Tap to set the handwriting language.

4. Tap the language you want to switch to. The language is changed, and you are returned to the previous screen automatically.

What Obeys the Language Setting?

When you switch your Galaxy Note 4 to use a different language, you immediately notice that all standard applications and the Galaxy Note 4 menus switch to the new language. Even some third-party applications honor the language switch. However, many third-party applications ignore the language setting on the Galaxy Note 4. Therefore, you might open a third-party application and find that all its menus are still in English.

Changing Accessibility Settings

Your Galaxy Note 4 includes built-in settings to assist people who might otherwise have difficulty using some features of the device. The Galaxy Note 4 has the ability to provide alternative feedback, such as vibration and sound. It can even read menu items aloud to you.

1. Pull down the Notification bar and tap the Settings icon.

2. Tap Accessibility under the Personalization section.

3. Tap one of the categories on the Accessibility screen and use the following sections to change the settings in the different categories.

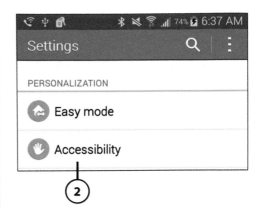

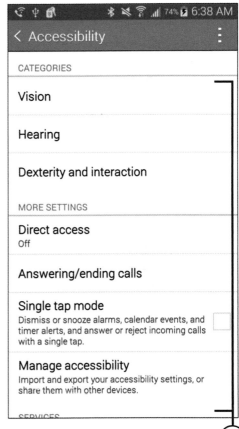

Vision

1. Tap to enable or disable TalkBack and change the TalkBack settings. When enabled, TalkBack speaks everything, including menus, but it also has other features, such as requiring that you double-tap something to select it instead of single tapping.

2. Tap to enable the Dark Screen feature. Once this feature is enabled, you double-press the Power key to enable and disable it. When you have it enabled, your screen remains off for privacy.

3. Tap to enable the Rapid Key Input feature. When enabled, it overrides the TalkBack requirement of having to double-tap each key while typing.

4. Tap to enable Speak Passwords. When this feature is enabled, TalkBack speaks each character of your password as you type it.

5. Tap to set the font size used on your Galaxy Note 4. You can choose sizes ranging from tiny to huge.

6. Tap to enable or disable magnification gestures, which include the ability to magnify any screen by double-tapping it. When a screen is magnified, you can pan around it.

7. Tap to enable or disable the Hover Zoom feature. When this feature is enabled, hovering your S Pen over anything on the screen magnifies it.

8. Tap to enable or disable the notification reminder that beeps to remind you that you have unread notifications (such as a new email notification).

9. Scroll down for more settings.

10. Tap to enable or disable the Negative Colors feature, which makes all colors displayed on your Galaxy Note 4 reversed. (For example, black text on a white background instead appears as white text on a black background.)

11. Tap to enable the Color Adjustment Wizard, which helps you adjust the screen colors if you have difficulty seeing it.

12. Tap to enable or disable the Accessibility shortcut. When it's enabled, you can access accessibility features by performing certain gestures.

13. Tap to change the settings for the text-to-speech service provided by Samsung or to switch to the Google text-to-speech service.

14. Tap to save your changes and return to the previous screen.

Hearing

1. Tap to enable or disable making your Note 4 light up the camera flash when you have a new notification.

2. Tap to turn off all sounds.

3. Tap to enable or disable improving the sound quality if you use a hearing aid.

4. Tap to enable video subtitles provided by Samsung, and adjust how the subtitles appear on the screen.

5. Tap to enable or disable video subtitles provided by Google, and adjust how the subtitles appear on the screen.

6. Tap to adjust the balance of audio played when wearing earphones.

7. Tap to use mono audio when wearing one earphone.

8. Tap to enable or disable an option that makes your Note 4 vibrate when it detects a baby crying or a doorbell ringing.

9. Scroll down for more settings.

10. Tap to enable or disable a feature that causes your Note 4 to vibrate in time to music being played, a video being watched, or a game being played.

11. Tap to save your changes and return to the previous screen.

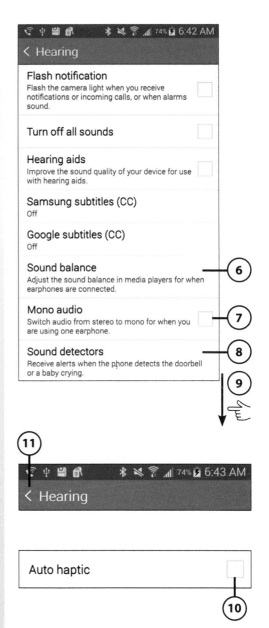

Dexterity and Interaction

1. Tap to enable or disable the Assistant menu. Once it is enabled, you can set your dominant hand, reorder the menu items, and adjust the level of zoom. The Assistant menu appears as a small gray box on your screen at all times. When you tap it, it provides quick access to common device functions.

2. Tap to enable or disable the Air Wake Up feature. When this feature is enabled, you can wave your hand over the front of the device while it lies on a flat surface to wake it up.

3. Tap to adjust the press and hold delay (also known as touch and hold).

4. Tap to enable or disable interaction control, which includes blocking areas of the screen so they do not respond to taps.

5. Tap to save your changes and return to the previous screen.

Direct Access

1. Tap to enable or disable direct access to certain accessibility settings. When this feature is enabled, press the Home button three times in quick succession to see the direct access menu.

2. Choose which accessibility settings you want direct access to.

3. Tap to save your changes and return to the previous screen.

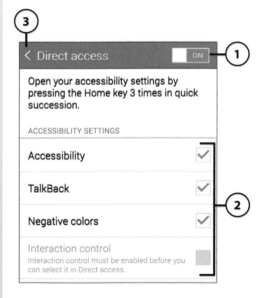

Answering/Ending Calls

1. Tap to enable or disable answering a call by pressing the Home button.

2. Tap to enable or disable using voice commands to answer or reject calls. When enabled, just say "Answer" or "Reject."

3. Tap to enable or disable ending a call by pressing the Power button.

4. Tap to save your changes and return to the previous screen.

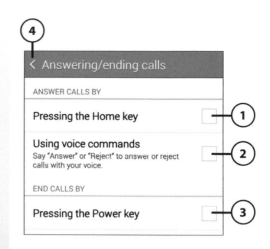

Manage Accessibility

1. Tap to import accessibility settings that someone has shared with you or to export your settings.

2. Tap to share your accessibility settings with friends. You must first export your settings as discussed in step 1.

3. Tap to return to the previous screen.

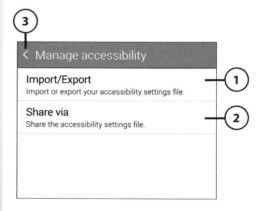

More About Text-to-Speech

By default, your Galaxy Note 4 uses the Samsung Text-to-Speech service with an option to use the Samsung service to speak any text you need to read. You can install other text-to-speech software by searching for it in the Google Play Store. After you've installed the software, you'll have multiple choices.

Adjusting Sound Settings

You can change the volume for games, ringtones, and alarms, change the default ringtone and notification sound, plus control what system sounds are used.

1. Pull down the Notification bar and tap the Settings icon.

2. Tap Sound in the Sound and Display section.

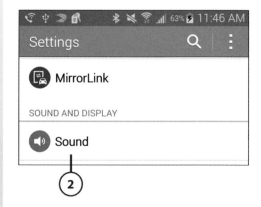

3. Tap to change the sound mode between Sound (play all sounds), Vibrate (vibrate instead of playing sounds), or Mute (silence all sounds and vibrations).

4. Tap to change the volume for ringtones, music, video games, and other media, notifications, and system alerts.

5. Tap to choose the intensity of vibrations for incoming calls, notifications, and haptic feedback.

6. Tap to choose the default notification ringtone or add new ones. Before adding new ringtones, you must first copy the audio files to the Ringtones folder while your Note 4 is connected to your computer. See the Prologue for instructions on moving files to your Note 4.

7. Tap to choose the vibration pattern used for notifications or create your own.

8. Tap to choose the sound that plays for notifications.

9. Tap to enable or disable playing a sound and vibration when being notified. This option is only available when you have selected the Sound option in step 3.

10. Tap to enable or disable playing tap-tone sounds when typing numbers on the phone keypad.

11. Scroll down for more settings.

12. Tap to enable or disable the touch sounds that play when you tap something on the screen or a menu.

13. Tap to enable or disable the screen lock sound that plays when your Galaxy Note 4 locks the screen after the inactivity timeout.

14. Tap to enable or disable haptic feedback, which is a vibration that indicates that you have successfully tapped the Menu and Back keys.

15. Tap to save your changes and return to the previous screen.

Creating Your Own Vibration Patterns

In step 7, you can choose the vibration pattern to be used when you are notified, but you can also create your own. Tap Create. On the next screen, tap in the area where it reads Tap to Create, and then tap out your vibration pattern on the screen using short taps for short vibrations and long taps for longer vibrations. The example in the figure uses Morse Code for SOS. You can create any vibration pattern you want.

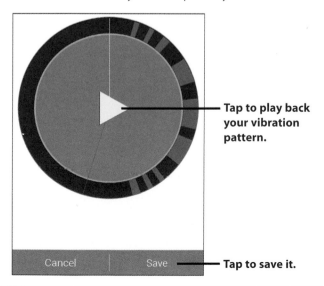

Tap to play back your vibration pattern.

Tap to save it.

Modifying Display Settings

You can change many display settings, the screen mode, the wait time before your Galaxy Note 4 goes to sleep, the size of the font used, and the Pulse notification light settings.

1. Pull down the Notification bar and tap the Settings icon.

2. Tap Display in the Sound and Display section.

3. Tap to change the screen brightness manually or set it to automatic. When on automatic, your Galaxy Note 4 uses the built-in light sensor to adjust the brightness based on the light levels in the room.

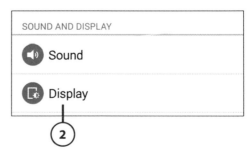

4. Tap to change the system font and how large the font style is. The system font is used for all menus, notifications, alerts, and warnings on your Note 4.

5. Tap to enable or disable screen rotation. When this setting is enabled, the screen automatically rotates based on the orientation in which you are holding your Note 4.

6. Tap to enable Smart Stay. When this feature is enabled, your Note 4 uses the front-facing camera to look for your eyes. It keeps the screen on as long as it detects that you are looking at the screen.

7. Tap to choose how many minutes of inactivity must pass before your Galaxy Note 4 puts the screen to sleep.

8. Tap to choose the Screen mode, which is how the screen represents colors. You can manually choose Cinema, Photo, and Basic, or leave it set to Adaptive Display, which means your Note 4 chooses the best settings based on usage.

9. Tap to enable or disable automatically adjusting the tone of the screen based on the kinds of images being shown. Adjusting the screen tone is done to conserve battery power; however, it may degrade the appearance of the image.

10. Tap to enable or disable Daydream mode, decide what must be displayed when day-dreaming, and when to day-dream. Daydream mode is essen-tially a screensaver.

11. Tap to choose whether your Note 4 should use the LED indi-cator to alert you of any device changes, notifications, or when voice recording is in progress, even if the screen is turned off.

12. Scroll down for more settings.

13. Tap to set how long the backlight behind the Menu and Back tap keys remains illuminated after you either tap the screen or tap one of the Touch keys.

14. Tap to choose whether you want to increase the screen's touch sen-sitivity. This can be useful if you are wearing gloves.

15. Tap to save your changes and return to the previous screen.

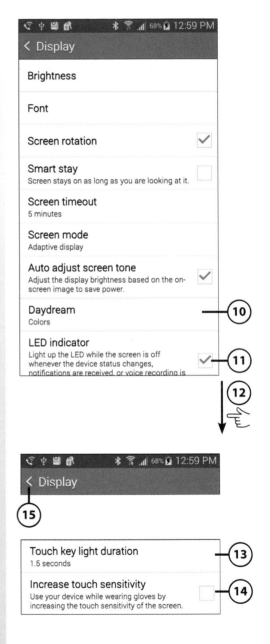

Is Adaptive Display Mode Good?

If you leave your screen mode set to Adaptive Display, you should know that your Note 4 adjusts the color range, saturation, and sharpness of the screen for the Gallery, Camera, Internet Web Browser, Samsung Video, Samsung Smart Remote, and Google Play Books apps only. All other system apps and apps that you install are not optimized. With this in mind, you might prefer to manually select an appropriate screen mode in step 8.

Aren't Screensaver's Obsolete?

In step 10 you can enable and manage the Daydream mode, which is essentially a screensaver, as you might remember them from desktop computers. For many years now, screen savers have not been needed because we no longer use Cathode Ray Tube (CRT) monitors and screens. In the days when we used CRTs, if an image remained in one spot for a long time, it would be burned into the front of the screen. Having a screensaver on a CRT monitor made sense because the images were moving and changing constantly. Screen savers continue to be used because people like seeing the patterns and images in the screensavers. This is why Daydream mode is on your Note 4. Once activated, it can display your photos or cool color patterns after a period of inactivity, when you plug your Note 4 into a dock, or when it is charging.

Adjusting Samsung-Specific Settings

On top of the regular Android features, Samsung has added some features that work only on Samsung phones. Here is how to set these features. For this section, assume that all screens start on the Settings screen.

Multi Window Mode

When Multi Window mode is enabled, you can use two apps at the same time on the same screen. You can read more about Multi Window mode in the Prologue.

1. Tap the Multi Window setting.

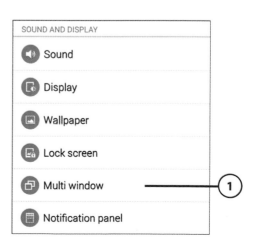

2. Tap to enable or disable Multi Window mode.

3. Tap to choose whether you want to have apps that support Multi Window mode to always open in Multi Window mode.

4. Tap to choose whether you want to minimize an app into a small pop-up window by swiping down diagonally.

5. Tap to save your changes and return to the previous screen.

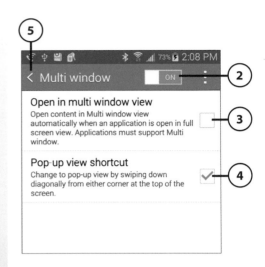

Notification Panel

Control what Quick Settings are shown when you pull down the Notification panel.

1. Tap Notification Panel.

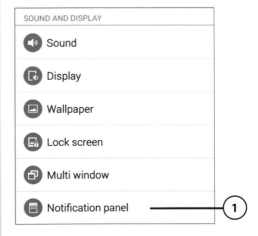

2. Drag icons from the Active Buttons section to the Available Buttons section to remove them.

3. Drag icons from the Available Buttons section to the Active Buttons section to add them.

4. Tap to save your changes and return to the previous screen.

One-Handed Operation

These settings, when enabled, help you use your Note 4 with only one hand.

1. Tap One-Handed Operation.

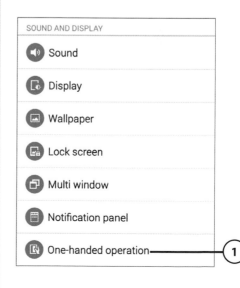

2. Tap to enable a feature that lets you use a sliding gesture to make the screen small and shifted to the side of the device.

3. Tap to enable or disable a reduced-sized keyboard and numeric keypad. When this feature is enabled, any time you see a numeric keypad or full keyboard, it will be small and shifted to one side of the screen.

4. Tap to choose whether you want to have an onscreen side panel that contains the physical Recent Apps, Home, and Back buttons, plus some other virtual buttons.

5. Tap to save your changes and return to the previous screen.

Easy Home Screen Mode

You can choose to use the Standard mode Home screen or the Easy mode Home screen. When you select Easy mode, all the text on your Note 4 is enlarged for easier reading, icons are enlarged, and the screen layouts are simplified for novice smartphone users.

1. Tap Easy Mode in the Personalization section.

2. Tap to enable Easy mode.

3. Scroll down to select which apps you want to have shortcuts to on your Home screen.

4. Tap Done to save your changes and return to the previous screen.

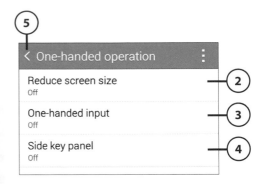

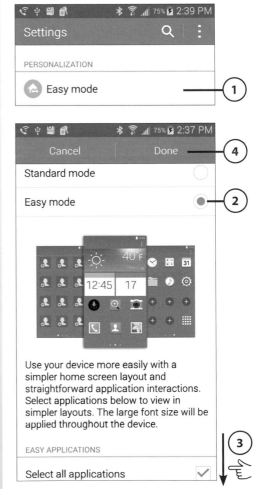

Use your device more easily with a simpler home screen layout and straightforward application interactions. Select applications below to view in simpler layouts. The large font size will be applied throughout the device.

Blocking Mode

Blocking mode enables you to choose a time period when notifications are blocked. This would normally be while you are asleep, but it could be any time you choose. Think of Blocking mode as "Do Not Disturb" mode.

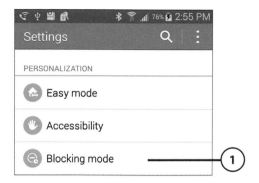

1. Tap Blocking Mode.

2. Tap to enable or disable Blocking mode.

3. Tap to enable or disable blocking all incoming calls while in Blocking mode.

4. Tap to enable or disable blocking all notifications while in Blocking mode.

5. Tap to enable or disable blocking all alarms and timers while in Blocking mode.

6. Tap to set Blocking mode to Always. Uncheck to set it for a specific period (see step 7).

7. Set the period of time when Blocking mode is automatically enabled and disabled.

8. Tap to configure which contact's calls will get through when Blocking mode is enabled.

9. Tap to save your changes and return to the previous screen.

Private Mode

While Private mode is enabled, you can move content from certain apps to a secret area on your Note 4. When Private mode is disabled, the content is invisible unless you come back into Settings and enable it again.

1. Tap Private Mode.

2. Choose a method for securing Private mode. The method you use here is in addition to the method you already use for unlocking your Note 4. You only need to do this the first time you want to enable Private mode.

3. Tap to enable or disable Private mode.

4. Tap to change the method for securing Private mode.

5. Tap to enable or disable automatically disabling Private mode when the screen turns off. This is recommended.

6. Tap to save your changes and return to the previous screen.

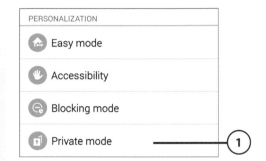

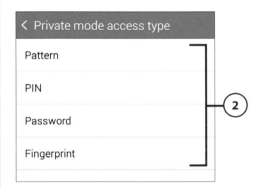

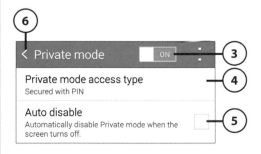

>>>*Go Further*

USING PRIVATE MODE

Private mode is a confusing feature. Essentially when Private mode is enabled, you can move content from certain apps to a secret, hidden area on your Note 4. You can also see content that you previously moved to this secret area. When Private mode is disabled, anything in the secret area becomes unavailable and invisible. When you enable Private mode again, you have to use a password, PIN, pattern, or your fingerprint. Private mode only works with the following apps (that Samsung has heavily modified): Gallery, Video, Music, Voice Recorder, My Files, and S Note. When Private mode is enabled, tapping the Menu icon reveals a new menu item called Move to Private.

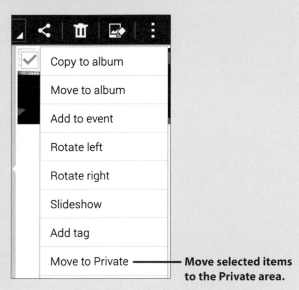

Move to Private ——————— **Move selected items to the Private area.**

Finger Scanner

Finger Scanner (or the fingerprint reader) allows you to register one or more thumb or fingerprints with your Note 4 and set when to use them. The most common use is to unlock your Note 4. The fingerprint reader/scanner is built in to the Home button.

1. Tap Finger Scanner.

2. Tap to manage your fingerprints. You can add or remove fingerprints.

3. Tap to change the backup password that must be entered if your Note 4 cannot read your fingerprint.

4. Choose when your fingerprint should be used.

5. Tap to save your changes and return to the previous screen.

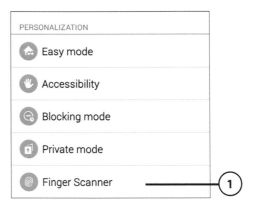

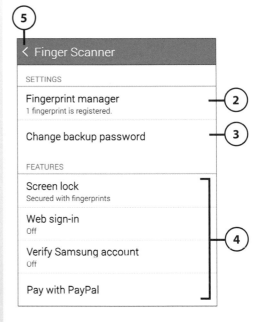

Motions and Gestures

Your Note 4 has a number of Motion Control features that enable you to use hand movements and phone movements to show information and perform certain functions.

1. Tap Motions and Gestures.

2. Direct Call enables you to lift the phone to your ear to automatically place a call to a contact whose phone number is on the screen.

3. Smart Alert vibrates the phone as you pick it up if you have missed any calls or messages.

4. Mute/Pause allows you to mute the audio or pause a video or song by turning your Note 4 face down on a surface, or by placing your palm over the screen.

5. Tap to enable or disable the ability to capture what is on the screen by swiping your palm across the screen at a 90 degree angle to the screen.

6. Tap to save your changes and return to the previous screen.

S Pen

The S Pen Settings screen enables you to configure how your S Pen behaves and even makes it possible for your Galaxy Note 4 to alert you if you leave your S Pen on the desk and walk away.

1. Tap S Pen.

2. Tap to enable Air Command to launch when you hover your S Pen over the screen and press the S Pen button.

3. Tap to enable or disable Air View. When this feature is enabled, if you hover your S Pen over an item such as an icon, image, or link, you see a preview of that item.

4. Tap to enable or disable showing a pointer on the screen marking where the S Pen is hovering.

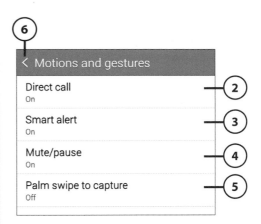

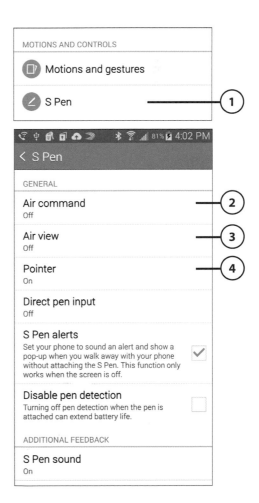

5. Tap to enable or disable a feature that allows you to hover your S Pen over text and press the S Pen button to switch to hand-writing mode.

6. Tap to enable or disable S Pen alerts. When this feature is enabled, you are alerted if you walk away carrying your Note 4 but leave your S Pen lying on the desk.

7. Tap to disable S Pen detection, which saves the battery. S Pen detection enables your Galaxy Note 4 to detect when you remove the S Pen from its holder.

8. Scroll down for more options.

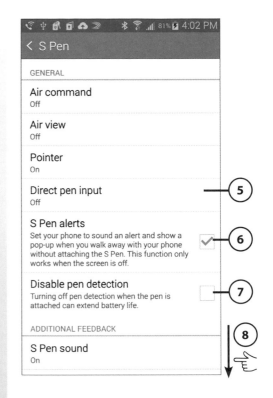

9. Tap to play a sound when you activate Air Command, Air View, or Handwriting mode.

10. Tap to choose whether you want S Pen vibration feedback when you activate Air Command, Air View, Handwriting mode, or use S Pen gestures.

11. Tap to choose what happens when you detach your S Pen. You can choose to have nothing happen, or you can automatically launch the Action memo or Air Command.

12. Tap to choose the sound that plays when you detach and attach your S Pen.

13. Tap to choose whether you want to feel a vibration when you detach or attach your S Pen.

14. Tap to save your changes and return to the previous screen.

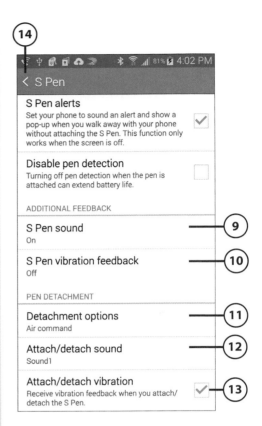

Browse without leaving
traces using the
Incognito feature.

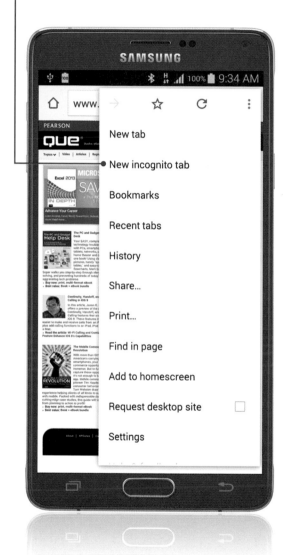

In this chapter, you discover how to browse the World Wide Web using the Chrome browser app that comes with your Galaxy Note 4. Topics include the following:

→ Bookmarking websites

→ Using tricks to browse quickly

→ Keeping track of websites you have visited

→ Configuring Chrome to work your way

Browsing the Web

Your Galaxy Note 4 comes with not one but two web browsers to enable you to explore the Web on its large screen. This chapter shows you how to use Chrome, a browser developed by Google. Your Galaxy Note 4 also includes the browser usually called simply Internet, but sometimes called (arguably even more simply) Browser, which is developed by Samsung.

Chrome is fast and easy to use. You can bookmark sites you want to revisit, hold your Galaxy Note 4 in landscape orientation so you can see more on the screen, and optionally share your GPS location with sites.

Navigating with Chrome

The Chrome browser app enables you to access sites quickly, bookmark them for future use, and return instantly to the sites you visit most frequently. You can even sync your open Chrome tabs among your Galaxy Note 4, your other portable devices, and your computer.

Go to a Web Page by Typing Its Address

1. Touch the Chrome icon on the Apps screen. Alternatively, if the Chrome icon appears on the Home screen, touch it there; it might be in the Google folder on the Home screen. Chrome opens and displays either your home page (as in the example shown here) or the last page you visited.

2. Touch the omnibox—a combined address box and search box—to select its contents. If the website has moved the previous page up so that the omnibox is hidden, drag the web page down so that the omnibox appears again.

3. Type the web address, such as **android.com**. Chrome displays any matching results.

4. Tap the result for the web page you want to display. The web page appears.

5. Tap Home to go back to your home page.

6. Tap the Menu button to display the menu, which contains many commands. The next section explains these commands.

7. Tap the Tabs button to display the Tabs screen. You use this screen to open new tabs, switch among open tabs, and close tabs you no longer need.

8. If the square green icon bearing a white padlock appears, tap it to display the security information for the website. See the nearby sidebar for more details.

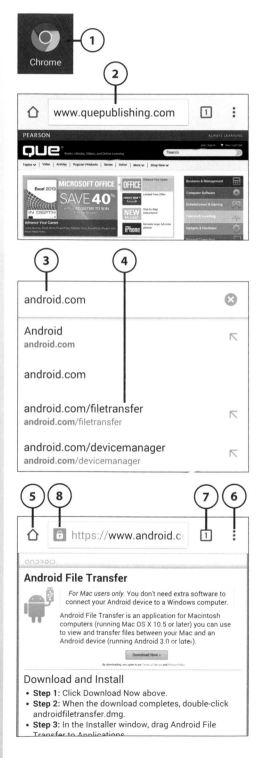

What Does the Green Icon with the White Padlock Mean?

The green icon with the white padlock appears when Chrome has established a secure connection to the website. The omnibox shows the address here starting with https:// to indicate that the connection uses Hypertext Transfer Protocol Secure (HTTPS) instead of regular Hypertext Transfer Protocol (HTTP), which is not secure. Chrome uses technologies called Secure Sockets Layer (SSL) and Transport Layer Security (TLS) to secure the connection using encryption.

When you connect to any site with which you will exchange private or sensitive information, it is best to make sure that the padlock icon appears. But because of the recent furor over government surveillance of the Internet, more and more websites are using encryption as a matter of course, so don't be surprised to see the padlock icon for "regular" websites.

You can tap the padlock icon to display a pop-up window containing details about the website's identity and the security of your connection to it.

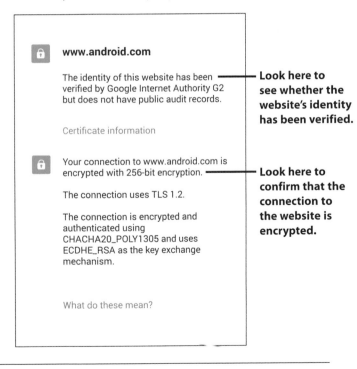

Web Page Options

While a web page is open, you have a number of options, such as opening a new tab, creating a bookmark for the page, and finding text on the page.

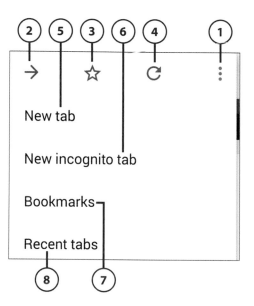

New tab

New incognito tab

Bookmarks

Recent tabs

1. Tap the Menu button to display the menu.

2. Tap the Forward button to return to the previous web page from which you have gone back on this tab. The Forward button is available only when you have visited multiple pages on this tab and gone back from at least the last page, by tapping the Back button, to an earlier page.

3. Tap the Bookmark star to add a bookmark for this page.

4. Tap the Refresh icon to refresh the display of the current web page. You'd normally do this either if a page failed to load completely or to load updated information, such as fresh news.

5. Tap New Tab to open a new tab.

6. Tap New Incognito Tab to open a new Incognito tab for private browsing. Incognito tabs are covered later in this chapter.

7. Tap Bookmarks to display your bookmarks.

8. Tap Recent Tabs to display your Recent Tabs list. This list includes the Other Devices list, which gives you access to recent tabs on other devices with which you sign in to the same Chrome account.

9. Tap History to display the History screen, which contains a list of the pages you have visited on your Galaxy Note 4.

10. Tap Share to share this web page with other people using apps such as Email, Gmail, Facebook, Messaging, and Twitter. The Share Via dialog shows all the apps you can use to share the web page.

11. Tap Print to start the process of printing the current page.

12. Tap Find in Page to search this page for specific text you type.

13. Tap Add to Homescreen to display the Add to Homescreen dialog. You can then type the name to give the icon that Android adds to the Home screen. You can then tap this icon to go straight to the website in your default browser, such as Chrome.

14. Tap Request Desktop Site to enable or disable forcing websites to show the regular view of a web page designed for full-size screens instead of a mobile view designed for small screens. When you change this setting, Chrome reloads the page, displaying the desktop version if it is available.

15. Tap Settings to change the settings for the Chrome browser.

16. Tap Help & Feedback to get help or to vent your frustrations with Chrome.

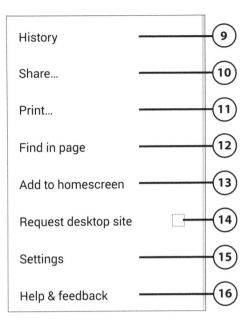

History — 9

Share... — 10

Print... — 11

Find in page — 12

Add to homescreen — 13

Request desktop site — 14

Settings — 15

Help & feedback — 16

Browser Tricks

The Chrome browser app has some neat tricks to help you browse regular websites comfortably on your Galaxy Note 4's screen.

1. Rotate your Galaxy Note 4 so that its long edge is sideways. This puts the screen into what's called *landscape orientation*. Your Galaxy Note 4 automatically switches the screen to landscape mode.

Why Won't My Screen Rotate?

If Chrome does not switch to landscape mode when you rotate the Galaxy Note 4, you need to turn on screen rotation. Pull down the Notifications panel and tap the Screen Rotation icon in the Quick Settings bar, turning the arrow green.

2. If necessary, double-tap the screen to zoom in and out. You can also place your thumb and forefinger on the screen and spread them apart to zoom in or pinch them together to zoom out.

Portrait

www.quepublishing.com/

Your Definitive Guide to Profiting from Mobile Commerce

With more than 60% of Americans carrying smartphones, your mobile commerce opportunities are immense: not someday, right now. But, to fully capture those opportunities, it's not enough to build an app. You need to know how mobile is transforming your customers' behavior, your organization, and your competitive environment. You need to assess and apply a wide spectrum of strategies, tactics, and technologies: from responsive web design and location-based tactics to mobile payment systems. You need to change your processes and your culture. The Mobile Commerce Revolution covers all this and more. Mobile commerce pioneer Tim Hayden and consumer behavior expert Tom Webster draw on their experience helping clients of all kinds to succeed with mobile— from startups to the world's top

Landscape

Your Definitive Guide to Profiting from Mobile Commerce

With more than 60% of Americans carrying smartphones, your mobile commerce opportunities are immense: not someday, right now. But, to fully capture those opportunities, it's not enough to build an app. You need to know how mobile is transforming your customers' behavior, your organization, and your competitive environment. You need to assess and apply a wide spectrum of strategies, tactics, and technologies: from responsive web design and location-based tactics to mobile payment systems. You need to change your processes and your culture. The Mobile Commerce Revolution covers all this and more. Mobile commerce pioneer Tim Hayden and consumer behavior expert Tom Webster draw on their experience helping clients of all kinds to succeed with mobile— from startups to the world's top brands. Packed with indispensable data and cutting-edge case studies, this guide will take you from planning to action to profit!

- Discover how customer mobile behavior is radically maturing and shifting
- Weave mobility throughout your marketing mix and business operations
- Prepare for the instant and impulse when your customer wants to buy
- Identify mobile tactics that are actually influencing purchases
- Earn confidence from customers that you will protect their privacy

Using Bookmarks, Recent Tabs, and History

Chrome enables you to bookmark your favorite websites for quick access, but it also keeps a list of the sites you visit most often so you can return to them at the tap of an icon. Chrome also syncs your recent tabs among your devices that run Chrome and sign in to the same Google account, so you can quickly pick up browsing on your Galaxy Note 4 exactly where you left it on your desktop computer, laptop, or tablet—or vice versa.

Manage Bookmarks

1. Tap the Menu button.

2. Tap Bookmarks. Normally, the Mobile Bookmarks folder opens. If not, you can navigate to it manually.

3. Tap Bookmarks to display the main Bookmarks folder. From there, you can tap a bookmark it contains or another bookmarks folder.

4. Tap a bookmarks folder to display the bookmarks it contains.

5. Tap a bookmark to display the web page it marks.

6. Tap and hold a bookmark to display a menu of extra actions you can take with it.

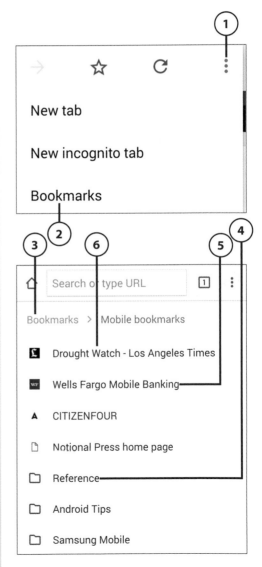

7. Tap Open in New Tab to open the bookmarked web page in a new tab.

8. Tap Open in Incognito Tab to open the bookmark in an Incognito tab.

9. Tap Edit Bookmark to edit the bookmark. For example, you can change the bookmark's name or move it to a different folder.

10. Tap Delete Bookmark to delete the bookmark.

Create a Bookmark

1. Navigate to the page you want to bookmark.

2. Tap the Menu button to open the menu.

3. Tap the Bookmark star to start creating a new bookmark.

4. Change the bookmark name if you want to. The default is the web page's title; you might prefer a shorter name.

5. Edit the address if necessary. If you went to the right page in step 1, you do not need to change the address.

6. Select the folder in which to save the bookmark. You can create new folders as needed by tapping New Folder on the Choose a Folder screen.

7. Tap Save.

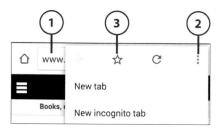

Go to a Web Page Using the Recent Tabs List

Chrome's Recent Tabs list enables you to go back to web pages that you have opened recently on either your Galaxy Note 4 or any other device on which you log Chrome in to the same Google account, such as your Android tablet or your PC or Mac.

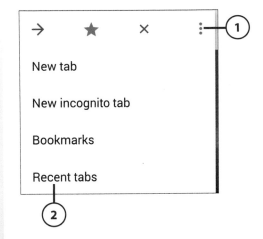

1. Tap the Menu button.

2. Tap Recent Tabs to display the Recent Tabs screen.

3. Look at the Recently Closed list to see tabs you've recently closed on your Galaxy Note 4.

4. Tap a sideways caret on a heading to expand the list of tabs the computer or device contains.

5. Tap a downward caret on a heading to collapse the list of tabs.

6. Tap Show Full History to display the full history of Chrome browsing on your Galaxy Note 4.

7. Tap a tab to display the web page.

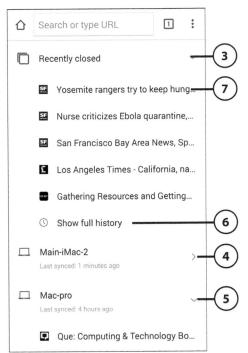

Go to a Web Page Using Your History

Chrome's History list enables you to go back to web pages that you have opened in Chrome on your Galaxy Note 4. The History list contains both pages you have bookmarked and pages you have not bookmarked.

1. Tap the Menu button.

2. Tap History to display the History screen.

3. Tap Search History to search through your history using keywords.

4. Tap the button for the page you want to display.

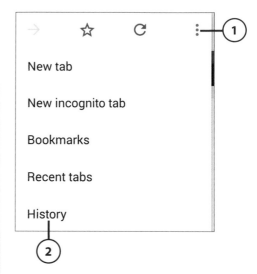

New tab

New incognito tab

Bookmarks

Recent tabs

History

Tap × to delete a history item.

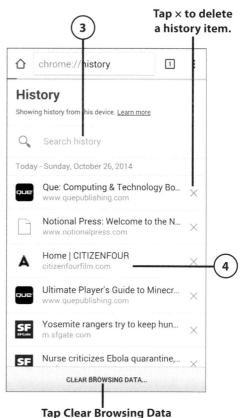

chrome://history

History

Showing history from this device. Learn more

Search history

Today - Sunday, October 26, 2014

Que: Computing & Technology Bo...
www.quepublishing.com

Notional Press: Welcome to the N...
www.notionalpress.com

Home | CITIZENFOUR
citizenfourfilm.com

Ultimate Player's Guide to Minecr...
www.quepublishing.com

Yosemite rangers try to keep hun...
m.sfgate.com

Nurse criticizes Ebola quarantine,...

CLEAR BROWSING DATA...

Tap Clear Browsing Data to clear all your history.

Delete Individual History Items—or All History Items

Given the nature of the Web, it's easy enough to browse to a site that you don't want to keep in your history. When this happens, tap the Menu button, tap History, and then tap the × icon on the right side of the button for the item you want to remove.

Clear browsing data	
Clear browsing history	☑
Clear the cache	☐
Clear cookies, site data	☐
Clear saved passwords	☐
Clear autofill data	☐
You won't be signed out of your Google Accounts	
Cancel	Clear

Check the Clear Browsing History box.

Then tap Clear.

If you want to get rid of all your history items, tap Clear Browsing Data to open the Clear Browsing Data screen. Check the Clear Browsing History box and tap Clear to delete your history. From the Clear Browsing Data screen, you can also clear other browsing data than your history; we'll look at your options later in this chapter.

Browsing with Multiple Tabs

Chrome can have multiple web pages open at the same time, each in a different tab. This enables you to open multiple web pages at once and switch between them.

1. Tap the Tabs icon to display the Tabs screen.

2. Tap New Tab (+) to open a new tab displaying the New Tab screen.

3. Tap the Menu button to navigate to a web page via the menu. For example, you may want to tap History on the menu so that you can navigate to a web page you visited earlier.

4. Tap Home to display your home page in the new tab.

5. Tap Search or Type URL to search using the search engine shown.

6. Tap the microphone icon to perform a voice search.

7. Tap one of the Most Visited site thumbnails to visit that site's default page.

8. Tap the Bookmarks star to display the Bookmarks screen, from which you can go to a bookmark.

9. Tap the Recent Tabs icon to display the Recent Tabs screen, from which you can go to a web page you have visited recently in Chrome using this Google account.

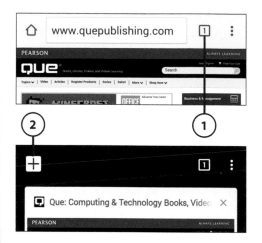

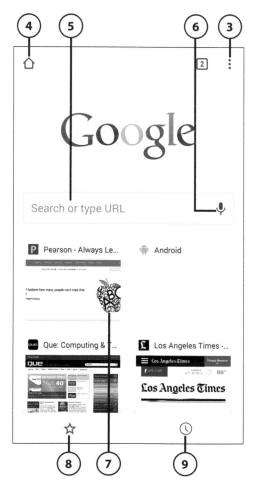

10. After opening multiple tabs, tap the Tabs icon to display the Tabs screen.

11. Tap × to close a tab.

12. Swipe a tab left or right off the list to close it.

13. Tap and pull down or up to display more or less of the tabs. You can also tap and hold a tab to display more of the tab.

14. Tap the tab you want to display.

Browsing in Secret with Incognito Tabs

If you want to visit a website in secret, you can use Incognito tabs. Incognito is a special mode that means that the web pages you visit don't appear in your browser history or search history and do not leave traces on your Galaxy Note 4 unless you create bookmarks for the pages or download files from them.

1. Tap the Menu button.

2. Tap New Incognito Tab. Chrome displays the Incognito screen for new tabs, which shows the "You've gone incognito" message.

3. Navigate to the web page using normal means. For example, tap Search or Type URL and type your search terms; then tap the appropriate search result.

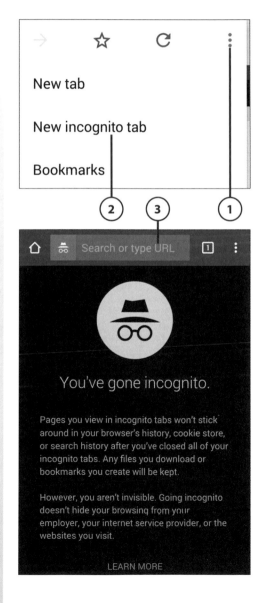

4. When you want to switch tabs, tap the Tabs icon to display the Tabs screen.

5. Tap and drag the border between the gray Incognito tabs and the light-shaded regular tabs to switch from your Incognito tabs to your regular tabs.

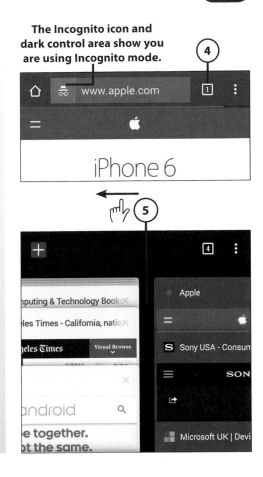

The Incognito icon and dark control area show you are using Incognito mode.

It's Not All Good

Incognito Mode Doesn't Make You Anonymous

If you use Incognito mode, it's important you understand its limitations. Incognito mode keeps the web pages you visit out of your browser history and search history so they don't appear either on your Galaxy Note 4 or on other devices on which you use Chrome with the same Google account.

However, Incognito mode doesn't make you anonymous on the Web. Your ISP can still see, and may well store, the details of your web browsing in Incognito mode. Worse, government agencies may be able to extract this information from your ISP.

Customizing Browser Settings

You can customize Chrome to make it behave the way you want. Chrome has a wide range of settings, which it breaks up into the categories Basics and Advanced. Chrome also enables you to choose settings for syncing your data among the computers and devices that log in to your Google account.

Choose Sync Settings

1. Tap the Menu button.

2. Tap Settings to display the Settings screen.

3. Tap your Google account name.

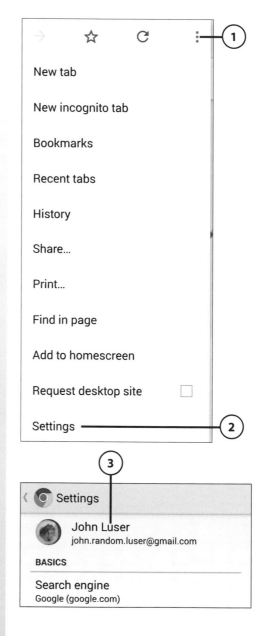

4. Move the Accounts switch to On if you want to sign in to your account or to Off if you don't want to sign in.

5. Tap your Google account's email address to display the Sync screen.

6. Move the Sync switch to On or Off, as needed. To get the most out of Chrome, set the switch to On, as in this example, and then choose which items to sync.

7. Check the Sync Everything box if you want to sync all the available items. Otherwise, check the Autofill box, the Bookmarks box, the History box, the Passwords box, and the Open Tabs box as needed.

8. Tap Encryption to display the Encryption dialog.

Tap Manage Synced Data to display the Chrome Sync page of configuration options.

9. Tap the Encrypt All with Passphrase radio button and then enter the passphrase when prompted. Make sure your password is strong enough by using at least eight characters (preferably 12 to 20), combining uppercase and lowercase letters with numbers and symbols (such as $ or %), and avoiding any word or misspelling of a word in any language.

10. Tap Sync or the Back button to return to the account screen.

11. Tap your name or the Back button to return to the Settings screen.

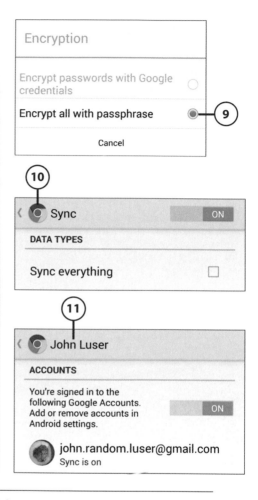

Why (and How) You Should Encrypt Your Chrome Sync Data

Browsing the Web often involves private or sensitive data, even when you don't buy anything or do anything embarrassing. So it is a good idea to encrypt your Chrome sync data to prevent others from being able to read it if they intercept it.

The Encryption dialog contains two options: the Encrypt Passwords with Google Credentials radio button and the Encrypt All with Passphrase radio button. At this writing, the Encrypt Passwords with Google Credentials radio button is not usually available, so your only choice is the Encrypt All with Passphrase radio button. This is the better choice anyway, because it encrypts all the data that Chrome syncs instead of encrypting only the passwords.

Choose Basic Settings

Chrome's basic settings include choosing your search engine and home page, deciding whether to use the Autofill Forms feature, and managing your saved passwords.

1. From the Settings screen, tap Search Engine to display the Search Engine screen.

2. Tap the search engine you want to use.

3. Tap Search Engine or the Back button to return to the Settings screen.

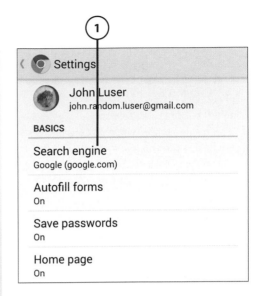

4. Tap Autofill Forms to display the Autofill Forms screen.

5. Set the Autofill Forms switch to On to enable the use of Autofill Forms.

6. Tap Add Profile to display the Add Profile screen, where you enter the name and address details you want Autofill Forms to use.

7. Tap Add Credit Card to display the Add Credit Card screen, where you enter the details of the credit cards you want to use.

8. Tap Autofill Forms or the Back button to return to the Settings screen.

9. Tap Save Passwords to display the Save Passwords screen. Here, you can move the Save Passwords switch to On or Off to enable or disable Chrome's ability to save your passwords so it can enter them for you. You can also manage the passwords on the Saved Passwords list and the Never Saved List.

10. Tap Home Page to display the Home Page screen.

11. Set the Home Page switch to On if you want to use a home page. If you don't want a home page, set this switch to Off; this makes Chrome remove the Home Page icon from the area to the left of the omnibox.

12. Type or paste the address of the page you want to use as your home page.

13. Check the Default box if you want to use the default home page instead of a page you specify. The default home page is usually a page set by your Galaxy Note 4's carrier.

14. Tap Home Page or the Back button to return to the Settings screen.

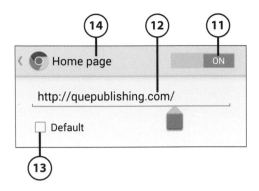

Choose Advanced Settings

In the Advanced section of the Settings screen in Chrome, you can choose settings in three categories: Privacy, Accessibility, and Content Settings. You can also turn on or off the Reduce Data Usage feature and view the About Chrome information, which may be useful for trouble-shooting problems.

1. On the Settings screen, tap Privacy to display the Privacy screen.

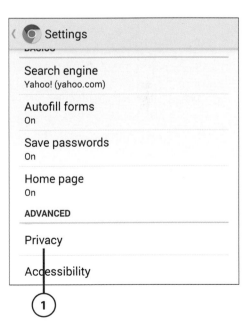

2. Tap Navigation Error Suggestions to enable or disable showing suggestions for web addresses that you enter incorrectly or that Chrome cannot locate.

3. Tap Search and URL Suggestions to enable or disable showing related queries and popular websites similar to those you type in the omnibox.

4. Tap Network Action Predictions to display the Network Action Predictions dialog.

5. Tap the Always radio button, the Only on Wi-Fi radio button, or the Never radio button, as needed. See the "What Are Network Action Predictions?" sidebar for details.

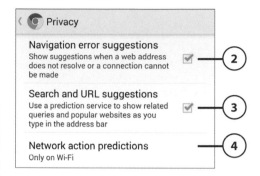

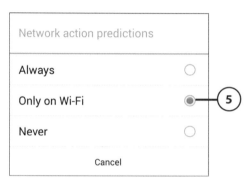

>>>Go Further

WHAT ARE NETWORK ACTION PREDICTIONS?

Network Action Predictions is a feature that allows the Chrome app to preload web pages you are likely to want to load. The app does this in two ways. First, when you start typing an address in the omnibox, the Chrome app preloads a matching web page if it has high confidence that you will want it—for example, because you have visited that page before. Second, when you are on a particular web page, the app might preload the pages whose links you are most likely to click—for example, the top few search results.

If Chrome has predicted correctly and loaded the correct pages into memory, when you tap a link, that page renders straight from your Galaxy Note 4's memory instead of first loading over the network. Although this can be a timesaver, it means that your Galaxy Note 4 might preload pages that you will not look at, which can lead to wasted data usage. If you decide to use Network Action Predictions, it is normally best to choose the Only on Wi-Fi radio button to allow the Chrome app to preload pages only when your Galaxy Note 4 is connected to Wi-Fi, not when it's connected via a cellular data connection (as it does if you select the Always radio button).

6. Tap Usage and Crash Reports to display the Usage and Crash Reports dialog.

7. Tap the Always Send radio button, the Only Send on Wi-Fi radio button, or the Never Send radio button. If you are happy to provide usage and crash data, choosing Only Send on Wi-Fi is usually the best choice because it prevents the reports from consuming your cellular data allowance.

8. Tap 'Do Not Track' to display the Do Not Track screen, where you can choose whether to turn on the Do Not Track feature. This feature requests that the websites you visit not track you, but websites are not bound to honor the request.

9. Tap Clear Browsing Data to display the Clear Browsing Data screen.

10. Tap Clear Browsing History to enable or disable clearing your browsing history. This clears the history of websites you have visited using the Chrome app on your Galaxy Note 4.

11. Tap Clear the Cache to enable or disable clearing the cache (data that Chrome stores so that it can redisplay web pages more quickly when you visit them again).

12. Tap Clear Cookies, Site Data to enable or disable clearing your cookies and website data. Browser cookies are used by websites to personalize your visit by storing information specific to you in the cookies.

13. Tap Clear Saved Passwords to enable or disable clearing your saved passwords.

14. Tap Clear Autofill Data to enable or disable clearing your Autofill data.

15. Tap Clear to clear the items whose boxes you checked in the Clear Browsing Data dialog.

16. Tap Privacy or the Back button to return to the Settings screen.

17. Tap Accessibility to display the Accessibility screen.

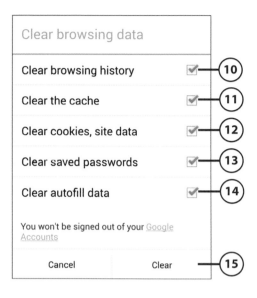

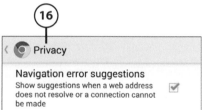

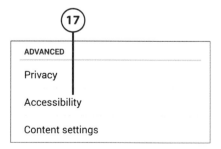

18. Drag the Text Scaling slider to make the text in the Preview box appear at a comfortable size for reading. This is the minimum size to which the Chrome app zooms the text when you double-tap a paragraph.

What Is Text Scaling?

When you use text scaling, you instruct your Galaxy Note 4 to always increase or decrease the font sizes used on a web page by a specific percentage. For example, you can automatically make all text 150% larger than was originally intended.

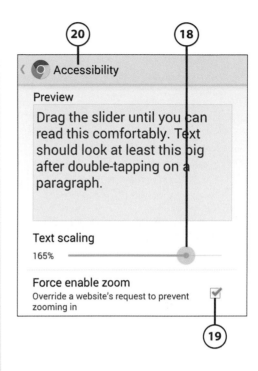

19. Tap Force Enable Zoom to turn on or off Chrome's ability to zoom in on a website that prevents zooming. Some websites turn off zooming because their creators consider design to be more important than readability.

20. Tap Accessibility or the Back button to return to the Settings screen.

21. Tap Content Settings to display the Content Settings screen.

22. Tap Accept Cookies to enable or disable accepting cookies. Browser cookies are used by websites to personalize your visit by storing information specific to you in the cookies.

23. Tap Enable JavaScript to enable or disable JavaScript. JavaScript is used on many web pages for formatting and other functions, so you might want to leave this enabled.

24. Tap Block Pop-Ups to enable or disable blocking pop-up windows. Pop-up windows are almost always advertisements, so keeping this enabled is a good idea; however, some websites might not work correctly if pop-up blocking is on.

25. Tap Protected Content to display the Protected Content screen, where you can set the Protected Content switch to On to allow websites to authenticate your Galaxy Note 4 to verify it is authorized to play premium videos.

26. Tap Google Translate to display the Google Translate page, where you can enable or disable the Google Translate service for translating web pages.

27. Tap Location Settings to allow or disallow websites access to your GPS information. Providing your location to websites is helpful when you need information related to where you are, but at other times, you might prefer to keep your location private.

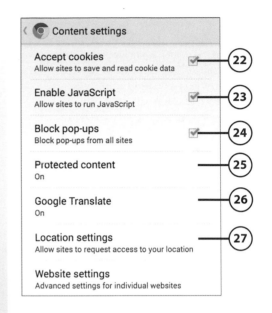

28. Tap Website Settings to view the list of websites that are storing data on your Galaxy Note 4. You can then clear the data for a specific website if necessary.

29. Tap Content Settings or the Back button to return to the Settings screen.

30. Tap Reduce Data Usage to display the Reduce Data Usage screen.

31. Set the Reduce Data Usage switch to On if you want Chrome to use Google's servers to compress web pages other than pages you load via secure HTTP or in Incognito tabs.

32. After turning on Reduce Data Usage and doing some browsing, you can look at the Data Savings histogram to see how much data the compression has saved you.

33. Tap Reduce Data Usage or the Back button to return to the Settings screen.

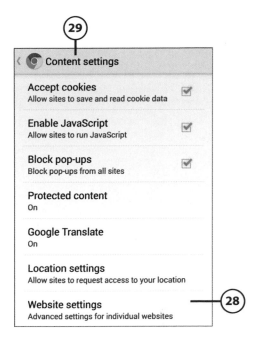

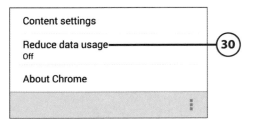

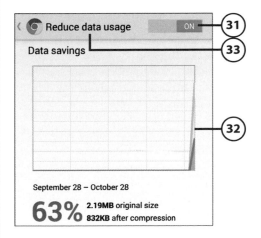

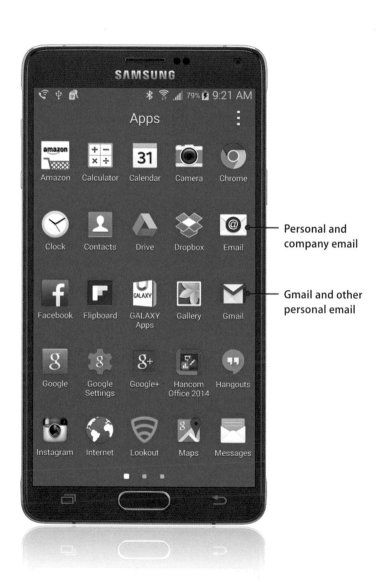

Personal and company email

Gmail and other personal email

In this chapter, you discover your Galaxy Note 4's email applications for Gmail and other accounts, such as POP3, IMAP, and even Microsoft Exchange. Topics include the following:

→ Sending and receiving email
→ Working with attachments
→ Working with Gmail labels
→ Changing settings

Email

Your Galaxy Note 4 has two email programs: the Gmail app, which works with Gmail, POP3, and IMAP email accounts, and the Email app that works with POP3, IMAP, and Microsoft Exchange (corporate email) accounts.

Gmail

When you first set up your Galaxy Note 4, you set up a Gmail account. The Gmail application enables you to have multiple Gmail accounts, which is useful if you have a business account and a personal account. If you don't want to add a second Gmail account, you can skip this section.

Add a Google Account

When you first set up your Galaxy Note 4, you added your first Google (Gmail) account, but you might have other Gmail accounts that you'd also like to access through your Galaxy Note 4. The following steps describe how to add a second account.

1. Pull down the Notification bar and tap the Settings icon.

2. Tap Accounts under the User and Backup section.

3. Tap Add Account.

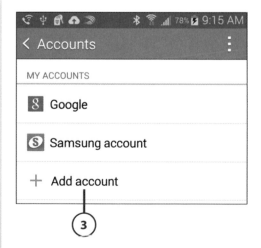

4. Tap Google.

5. Tap Existing if you already have a Google account.

6. Enter your existing Google account name. This is your Gmail address.

What If I Don't Have a Second Google Account?

If you don't already have a second Google account but want to set one up, in step 5, tap New. Your Galaxy Note 4 walks you through the steps of creating a new Google account.

7. Enter your existing Google password.

8. Tap the right arrow to move to the next screen.

Tap to get a new Google account.

9. Tap to allow or disallow Google from emailing you news and offers from Google Play and then tap the right-pointing arrow at the bottom of the screen (not shown).

10. Tap Skip to bypass setting up payment information for Google Wallet for this Google account. Right now you just want to set up the email account.

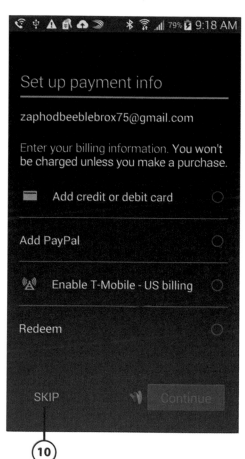

11. Select what components of your Google account you want to synchronize with your Galaxy Note 4.

12. Tap the right-arrow to finish the Google account setup.

Why Multiple Google Accounts?

You are probably wondering why you would want multiple Google accounts. Isn't one good enough? Actually, it is not that uncommon to have multiple Google accounts. It can be a way to compartmentalize your life between work and play. You might run a small business using one account, but email only friends with another. Your Galaxy Note 4 supports multiple accounts, but still enables you to interact with them in one place.

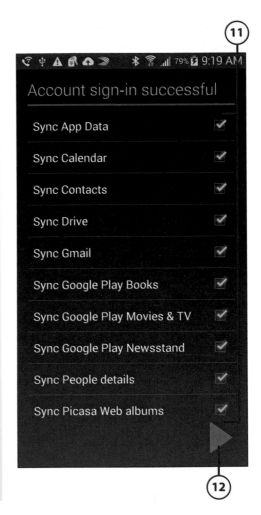

Add a POP3/IMAP Account

Unlike previous versions of the Gmail app, the latest version supports the non-Gmail account types of POP3 and IMAP. If you don't want to add a POP3 or IMAP account to the Gmail app, you can skip this section.

>>>*Go Further*

GMAIL APP SUPPORTING NON-GMAIL ACCOUNT TYPES

Although your Note 4 is still running Android KitKat, the Gmail app supports Gmail, POP3, and IMAP account types. When your Note 4 updates to Android Lollipop (Android 5.0), the Gmail app will also support the Microsoft Exchange (corporate mail) account type. When that happens, the Email app will become a dummy icon and the Gmail app will handle all email on your Note 4.

1. Pull down the Notification bar and tap the Settings icon.

2. Tap Accounts under the User and Backup section.

3. Tap Add Account.

4. Tap Personal (IMAP) or Personal (POP3). This example uses an IMAP account type. However, the steps are the same for a POP3 account type.

5. Enter your IMAP account's email address.

6. Tap Next.

What Is Manual Setup?

If you are using an email service provider that is not well known, or you are using email from your personal domain, the Gmail app may not be able to automatically work out the server settings. In that situation you might want to tap Manual Setup, which enables you to enter all information manually.

7. Enter the password for the email account you are adding.

8. Tap Next.

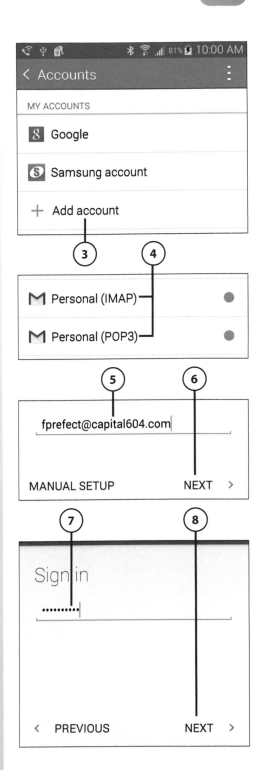

9. Verify the incoming server name and change if needed.

10. Verify the port number and change if needed.

11. Verify the security type and change if needed.

12. Tap Next.

13. Verify the outgoing server name and change if needed.

14. Verify the port number and change if needed.

15. Verify the security type and change if needed.

16. Check the box if your email provider requires that you use your username and password when sending email. This is almost always the case.

17. Tap Next.

Carried over from previous screens

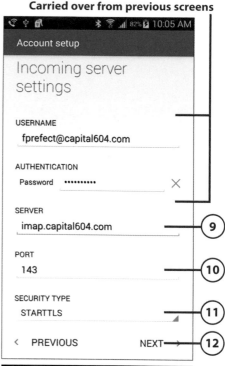

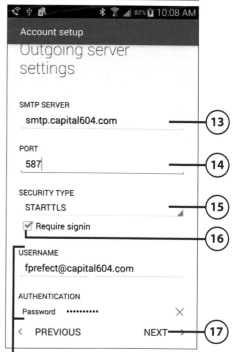

Carried over from previous screens

18. Tap to choose how often the Gmail app automatically looks for and downloads new email in this account. You can also set it to Never, which means that email from this account is only downloaded when you open the Gmail app.

19. Check the box to be notified when new email arrives in this account.

20. Check the box if you want to synchronize mail from this account. Unchecking this box means that you don't want email to synchronize (not common).

21. Check the box if you want the Gmail app to automatically download email attachments when it detects that your Note 4 is connected to a Wi-Fi network.

22. Tap Next.

23. Enter a friendly name for this account.

24. Enter the name you want to use when sending email from this account.

25. Tap Next to complete the setup of the email account.

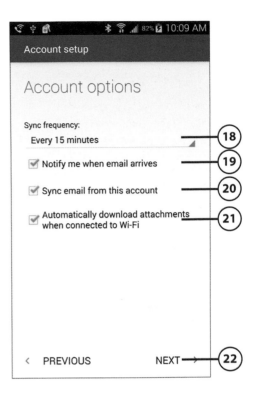

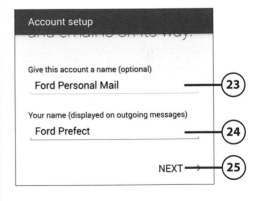

Be Secure If You Can

If your mail provider supports email security such as SSL or TLS, you should strongly consider using it. If you don't, emails you send and receive go over the Internet in plain readable text. Using SSL or TLS encrypts the emails as they travel across the Internet so that nobody can read them. Set this under the Advanced settings for the Incoming and Outgoing Servers.

Navigate the Gmail App

Let's take a quick look at the Gmail app and find out how to navigate the main screen.

1. Tap the Gmail icon to launch the app. Your initial view will be of the Inbox of your primary Google (Gmail) account, which is the account you used when setting up your tablet.

2. Tap to search the current folder for an email.

3. Tap to compose a new email.

4. Tap to see only new messages received from your social networking sites such as Facebook and Google+. When you have tapped it once, the Social option disappears until new social media emails arrive.

5. Tap to see any new emails that are promotions for products. When you have tapped it once, the Promotions option disappears until more promotional emails arrive.

6. Tap to see any new updates. Updates include messages about updating an app, but can also include update email relating to things you have purchased, bills you need to pay, and even updates to meeting invites. After you have tapped Updates once, this option disappears until there are more new updates.

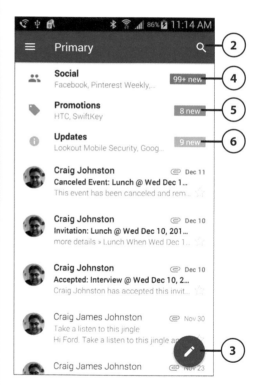

7. Swipe in from the left to reveal the menu.

8. Tap to switch between your email accounts, if you have more than one.

9. Tap to view Social, Promotions, and Updates. These are only visible when viewing Google (Gmail) accounts.

10. Tap to view messages in any forums you are participating in. This is only visible when viewing Google (Gmail) accounts.

11. Tap to switch between your different folders (or *labels,* as the Gmail app calls them).

12. Scroll down to see all of your labels.

13. Swipe the vertical action bar to the left to close the menu.

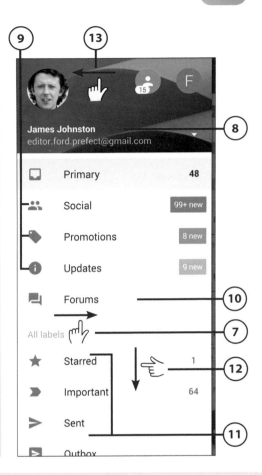

>>>*Go Further*

STARS AND LABELS

In the Gmail app, you use stars and labels to help organize your email. In most email clients you can create folders in your mailbox to help you organize your emails. For example, you might create a folder called "emails from the boss" and move any emails you receive from your boss to that folder. The Gmail app doesn't use the term *folders;* it uses the term *labels* instead. You can create labels in Gmail and choose an email to label. When you label the email, it is actually moved to a folder with that label. Any email that you mark with a star is actually just getting a label called "starred." However, when viewing your Gmail, you see the yellow star next to the email. People normally add a star to an email as a reminder of something important.

Compose an Email

1. Tap the compose icon.

2. Tap to change the email account from which the message is being sent (if you have multiple accounts).

3. Type names in the To field. If the name matches someone in your Contacts, a list of choices is displayed and you can tap a name to select it. If you only know the email address, type it here.

4. Tap to add Carbon Copy (CC) or Blind Carbon Copy (BCC) recipients.

5. Tap the paperclip icon to add one or more attachments or insert links to one or more Google Drive files.

6. Type a subject for your email.

7. Type the body of the email.

8. Tap to save the email as a draft or discard it.

9. Tap to send the email.

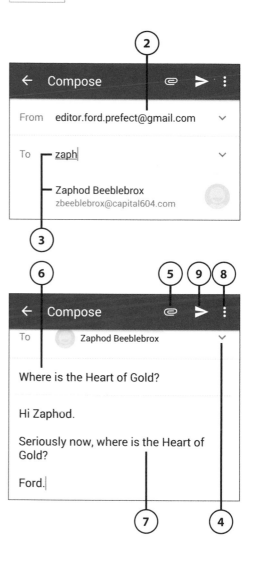

Add Attachments or Insert Drive Links

Before sending an email, you can add one or more attachments or insert links to files you have in your Google Drive account. The Gmail app can attach files that you've saved on your tablet and in your Google Drive account. Here is how to add attachments and link Drive documents.

1. After filling in the fields as described in the "Compose an Email" task, tap the paperclip icon.

2. Tap either Attach File or Insert from Drive. This example uses the Attach File option.

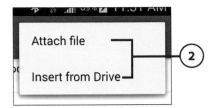

What Is the Difference Between Attaching and Inserting?

When you choose to attach a file to an email, you can choose a file located on your Note 4, in the Photos app, or in your Google Drive account. The file is then copied from that location and attached to the email. If you choose to insert a file from Google Drive, the file you choose is not actually copied out of Google Drive and attached to the email. Instead, a link to that file is placed in the body of the email. The link enables the recipients to tap the link and open the document right in your Google Drive account.

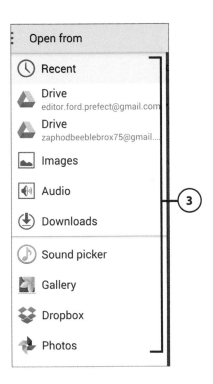

3. Choose where you want to search for the file. This can include your recent downloads, your Google Drive account, the Downloads folder, internal Note 4 storage, or the Photos app.

4. Tap the file to attach it. In this example the attachment is a document in my Google Drive account.

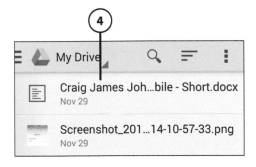

5. Tap Send.

Links to Drive files ⑤

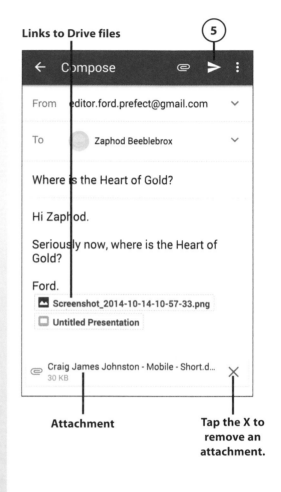

Attachment

Tap the X to remove an attachment.

Read an Email

1. Tap an email to open it. Unread emails are in bold, and emails that you have already read are not bold.

①

2. Tap to mark the email as unread and return to the email list view.

3. Tap to reply to the sender of the email. This does not reply to anyone in the CC field.

4. Tap the Menu icon to reply to the sender of the email and any recipients in the To and CC fields (Reply All). You can also choose to forward the email or print it.

5. Tap to expand the email header to see all recipients and all other email header information.

6. Tap to "star" the message, or move it to the "starred" label.

7. Tap the sender's contact picture to see more contact information about them.

8. Tap to move the email to the Trash folder.

9. Tap to move the email to a different label.

10. Scroll down to see the rest of the email and extra actions you can take.

Rich Text Formatting

A Rich Text Formatting (RTF) message is a message formatted with anything that is not plain text. RTF includes bulleted lists, different fonts, font colors, font sizes, and styles such as bold, italic, and underline. Although you cannot type an email on your Note 4 with the standard keyboard using RTF, when you receive an RTF email, your Note 4 preserves the formatting and displays it correctly.

What Are Conversations?

Conversations are Gmail's version of email threads. When you look at the main view of the Gmail app, you are seeing a list of email conversations. The conversation might have only one email in it, but to Gmail that's a conversation. As you and others reply to that original email, Gmail groups those messages in a thread, or conversation.

11. Tap to reply to the email and all recipients (Reply All).

12. Tap to forward the email.

13. Tap attachments to open them.

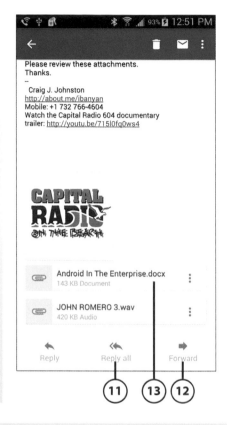

>>>Go Further

GMAILS HAVE EXTRA OPTIONS

If you are receiving email in your Gmail Inbox, you will have a few extra options that are specific to Gmail. You will be able to archive an email as well as send it to Trash. You will also be able to mark an email as important, mute the email conversation, report an email as spam, and report an email as a phishing scam. When you mute a conversation, you will no longer see any emails in that conversation (or email thread). For more information on printing emails, and an explanation on what an important email is, see the notes and Go Further sidebars later in the chapter.

Archive email. ————  ———— Tap for more options.

>>>*Go Further*

HOW DO I PRINT EMAILS?

When you choose to print an email, the print dialog enables you to choose to print the email to a PDF, which turns the email into a Portable Document Format (PDF) file, or to print the email to any printers you have previously connected to Google Cloud Print using your desktop Chrome web browser. To learn more about how to connect your printers to your Google Cloud Print account, look at the instructions at https://support.google.com/chrome/answer/1069693?hl=en.

What Is Important?

Gmail tries to automatically figure out which of the emails you receive are important. As it learns, it might sometimes be wrong. If an email is marked as important but it is not important, you can manually change the status to "not important." Important emails have a yellow arrow whereas emails that are not important have a clear arrow. All emails marked as "important" are also given the Priority Inbox label.

What Happens to Your Spam or Phishing Emails?

When you mark an email in Gmail as spam or as a phishing scam, two things happen. First, it gets a label called Spam. Second, a copy of that email is sent to Gmail's spam servers so that they are now aware of a possible new spam email that is circulating around the Internet. Based on what the servers see for all Gmail users, they block the emails that have been marked as spam and phishing emails from reaching other Gmail users. So the bottom line is that you should always mark spam emails because it helps all of us.

Customize Gmail App Settings

You can customize the way the Gmail app works, and you can also customize how each independent email account functions.

1. Swipe in from the left and tap the current email account to reveal its folders.

2. Tap Settings.

3. Tap General Settings.

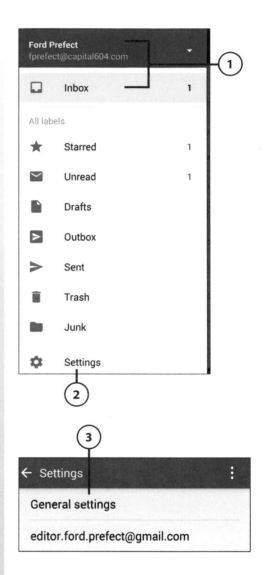

4. Tap to choose what must be shown when you choose to archive or delete a message in Gmail accounts. The choices are Archive and Delete.

5. Check the box to enable the ability to swipe an email left or right to archive it.

6. Check the box to enable showing the email sender's contact image in the conversation list.

7. Check the box to enable making Reply All the default reply action.

8. Tap to enable automatically shrinking the emails to fit on the screen.

9. Tap to choose what happens when you archive or delete a message. Your choices are to show newer messages, older messages, or the conversation list.

10. Choose which actions you want to show a confirmation screen for.

11. Tap to save your changes and return to the main Settings screen.

12. Tap one of your accounts to change settings specific to that account, and then follow the steps in the following sections.

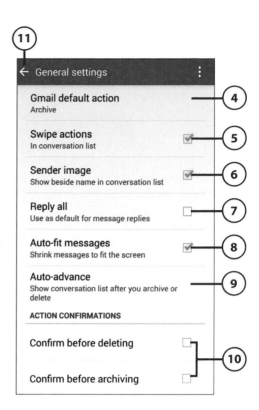

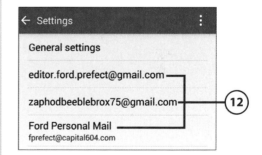

Additional Options in General Settings

While in the General Settings screen, if you tap the Menu icon, you can clear your email search history or your picture approvals. When you clear picture approvals, you are clearing your previous decisions on which emails you wanted to automatically load the images for.

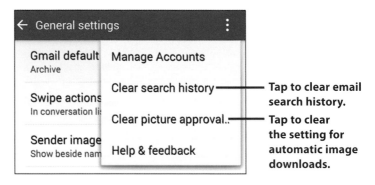

Customize Google Account Settings

1. Tap to choose whether you want to see your Priority Inbox instead of your regular Inbox (Default Inbox) when opening the Gmail app.

2. Tap to choose what Inbox categories will be shown. As shown earlier in the chapter, by default the Social and Promotions categories are displayed. You can also show Updates and Forums.

3. Tap to enable or disable notifications when new email arrives for this Gmail account.

4. Tap to select how to get notified when new email arrives for this account. You can choose a different notification for each label and also decide which labels in addition to the Primary label you will be notified for.

5. Tap to enter a signature to be included at the end of all emails composed using this account.

6. Tap to set your Vacation Responder. This is a message that is automatically sent to people when you are on vacation.

7. Scroll down for more settings.

What Is the Priority Inbox?

Google introduced the Priority Inbox as a way to automatically figure out which emails are important to you and place them in a folder called Priority Inbox. It does this by analyzing which emails you open and reply to. If it makes a mistake, you can mark a message as less important or more important. Over time, Google's handle on which emails are important to you gets more accurate. Because the Priority Inbox probably has the most-important emails, you might want to open it first and then go to the regular Inbox later to handle less-important emails. Read more about the Priority Inbox at http://mail.google.com/mail/help/priority-inbox.html.

Email Signature

An email signature is a bit of text that is automatically added to the bottom of any email you send from your Android tablet. It is added when you compose a new email, reply to an email, or forward an email. A typical use for a signature is to automatically add your name and some contact information at the end of your emails. Email signatures are sometimes referred to as email footers.

8. Tap to choose whether to synchronize Gmail to this tablet. Turning this off stops Gmail from arriving on your tablet.

9. Tap to choose how many days' worth of email to synchronize to your tablet.

10. Touch to manage labels. Labels are like folders. You can choose which labels synchronize to your tablet, how much email synchronizes, and what ringtone to play when new email arrives in that label.

11. Check the box to automatically download attachments to recently received emails while connected to a Wi-Fi network.

12. Tap to choose how images embedded in emails are handled. They can be automatically downloaded, or you can be prompted before they are downloaded for each email.

13. Tap to save your changes and return to the main Settings screen.

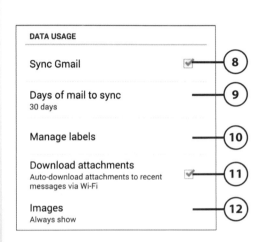

Customize POP/IMAP Account Settings

1. Tap to change the name of your account. This is the friendly name you may have typed when you originally set it up on your tablet.

2. Tap to change the full name you want people to see when you reply to emails using this account.

3. Tap to enter a signature to be included at the end of all emails composed using this account.

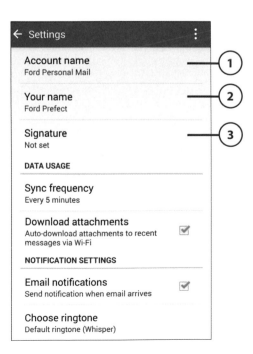

4. Tap to change the frequency with which your tablet checks for new email for this account. You can set it to Never, which means that your tablet only checks for email when you open the Gmail app, or you can set it to automatically check between every 15 minutes to every hour.

5. Check the box to automatically download attachments to recently received emails while connected to a Wi-Fi network.

6. Tap to enable or disable notifications when new email arrives for this email account.

7. Tap to select the ringtone to play when you are notified of new email for this account.

8. Scroll down for more settings.

9. Check the box if you also want to feel a vibration when new email arrives for this account.

10. Tap to change the incoming email server settings for this account.

11. Tap to change the outgoing email server settings for this account.

12. Tap to save your changes and return to the main Settings screen.

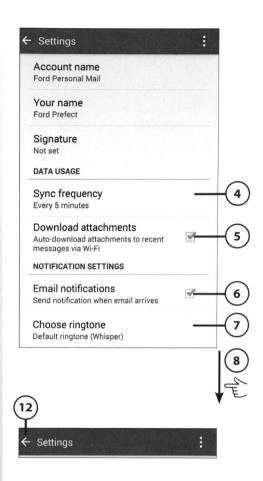

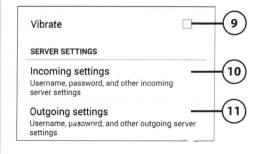

Email Application

The Email application supports all email accounts with the exception of Gmail. This includes any corporate email accounts that use Microsoft Exchange or corporate email systems, such as Lotus Domino/Notes, that have an ActiveSync gateway. In addition to corporate email accounts, the Email application also supports POP3 and IMAP accounts. POP3 and IMAP accounts are also supported by the Gmail app, so this is a duplication of functionality.

Add a Work Email Account

Your Galaxy Note 4 can synchronize your contacts from your work email account as long as your company uses Microsoft Exchange or an email gateway that supports Microsoft ActiveSync (such as Lotus Traveler for Lotus Domino/Notes email systems). It might be useful to be able to keep your work and personal contacts on one mobile device instead of carrying two phones around all day.

1. From the Home screen, pull down the Notification bar and tap the Settings icon.

2. Tap Accounts under the User and Backup section.

3. Tap Add Account.

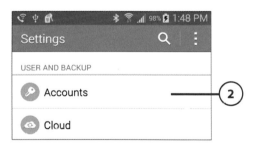

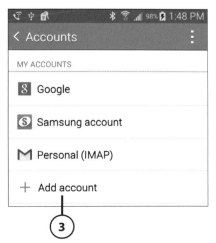

4. Tap Microsoft Exchange ActiveSync.

5. Enter your full corporate email address.

6. Enter your corporate network password.

7. Tap Next.

Error Adding Account? Guess the Server.

Your Galaxy Note 4 tries to work out some information about your company's ActiveSync setup. If it can't, you are prompted to enter the ActiveSync server name manually. If you don't know what it is, you can try guessing it. If, for example, your email address is dsimons@allhitradio.com, the ActiveSync server is most probably webmail.allhitradio.com or autodiscover.allhitradio.com. If options like these don't work, ask your email administrator.

8. Tap to agree that your mail administrator may impose security restrictions on your Galaxy Note 4 if you proceed.

9.   Tap to choose how many days' worth of email to synchronize to your Note 4.

10. Tap to choose how often your corporate email is delivered to your Galaxy Note 4. Push means that as it arrives in your Inbox at work, it is delivered to your phone. You can set it to Manual, which means that your work email is only delivered when you open the Email app on your phone. You can also set the delivery frequency from every 5 minutes to every hour.

11. Tap to choose how often email is synchronized to your Note 4 during the peak schedule.

12. Tap to choose how much of each email is retrieved. You can also set this to have no size limit so that the entire email is downloaded.

13. Tap to choose how many days in the past calendar items are synchronized to your Galaxy Note 4.

14. Tap to enable or disable being notified when new email arrives from your corporate Inbox.

15. Scroll down to see more settings.

16. Tap to enable or disable synchronizing your corporate email to your Galaxy Note 4.

17. Tap to enable or disable synchronizing your corporate contacts to your Galaxy Note 4.

18. Tap to enable or disable synchronizing your corporate calendar to your Galaxy Note 4.

19. Tap to enable or disable synchronizing your corporate tasks to your Galaxy Note 4.

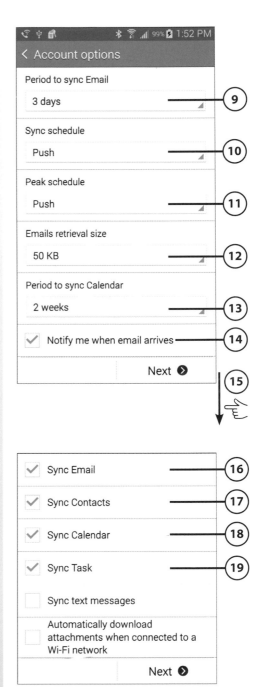

20. Tap to enable or disable synchro-nizing SMS (text) messages you receive on your Galaxy Note 4 to your corporate Inbox.

21. Tap to enable or disable automati-cally downloading email attach-ments when your Galaxy Note 4 is connected to a Wi-Fi network.

22. Tap Next.

23. Tap Activate to allow your compa-ny's mail server to act as a device administrator for your Note 4.

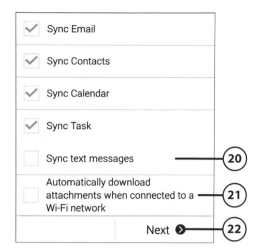

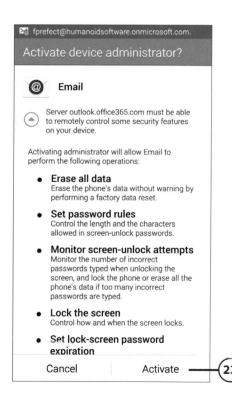

24. Enter a name for this email account. Use something meaningful that describes the purpose of the account, such as Work Email.

25. Tap Done to complete the setup.

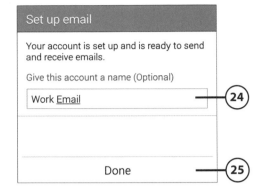

>>>*Go Further*

CAN YOU TRULY KEEP WORK AND PRIVATE DATA SEPARATE?

More and more companies are adopting a Bring Your Own Device (BYOD) policy, which means that they expect you to use your personal phone to get access to company emails, contacts, calendar, and internal apps. As you have seen, your Galaxy Note 4 fully supports accessing your company's email system, but when you activate, you have to agree to allow your administrator control over your phone. This is not ideal because the administrator can see what apps you have installed, and he can send a self-destruct command to your Galaxy Note 4, which means you could lose all your private data and apps. *Dual persona* is fast becoming the way for you to truly keep your private data private and not allow your company to wipe your phone or see what you have installed. A few companies today provide this service, including Enterproid (the product is called Divide, www.divide.com/), Good Technology (the product is called Good, www1.good.com/), and Samsung (the system is called KNOX, www.samsung.com/global/business/mobile/platform/mobile-platform/knox/). The idea is that your Galaxy Note 4 has two personalities—a work persona and a private persona. All work data is kept in its own separate area on your phone, and administrators from your company have no control over the rest of your phone.

Add a New POP3 or IMAP Account

Remember that the Gmail app also supports POP3 and IMAP accounts, so you may not want to use the Email app for this type of account. It is up to you.

1. Pull down the Notification bar and tap the Settings icon.

2. Tap Accounts under the User and Backup section.

3. Tap Add Account.

4. Tap Email.

5. Enter your email address.

6. Enter your password.

7. Tap Next.

Why Manual Setup?

Your Galaxy Note 4 tries to figure out the settings to set up your email account. This works most of the time when you are using common email providers such as Yahoo! and Hotmail. It also works with large ISPs such as Comcast, Road Runner, Optimum Online, and so on. It might not work for smaller ISPs, in smaller countries, or if you have created your own website and set up your own email. In these cases, you need to set up your email manually.

8. Tap POP3 or IMAP. IMAP has more intelligence to it, so select that option when possible.

9. Ensure that the information on the incoming server screen is accurate.

10. Tap Next.

Where Can I Find This Information?

If you need to manually set up your email account, you must have a few pieces of information. Always check your ISP's (or email service provider's) website, and look for instructions on how to set up your email on a computer or smartphone. This is normally under the Support section of the website.

Username and Password

On the Incoming Server and Outgoing Server screens, your username and password should already be filled out because you typed them in earlier. If not, enter them.

11. Ensure that the information on the outgoing server screen is accurate.

12. Tap Next.

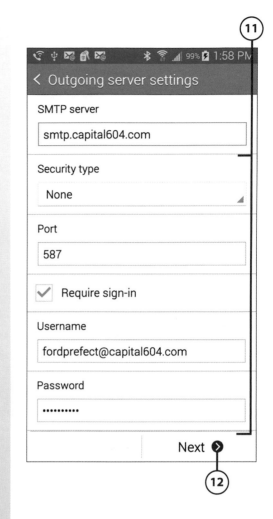

13. Tap to change how far back in the past email must synchronize.

14. Tap to change the frequency with which email from this account synchronizes to your Galaxy Note 4.

15. Tap to change the frequency with which email from this account synchronizes to your Galaxy Note 4 during the peak schedule.

16. Tap to check the box if you want email to synchronize between this account and your Galaxy Note 4.

17. Tap to check the box if you want email to be sent from this account by default.

18. Tap to check the box if you want to be notified when new email arrives into this account.

19. Tap to check the box if you want email to be automatically downloaded when you are connected to a Wi-Fi network.

20. Tap Next.

21. Enter a friendly name for this account, such as Home Email.

22. Enter your full name or the name you want to be displayed when people receive emails sent from this account.

23. Tap Done to save the settings for this account and return to the Add Accounts screen.

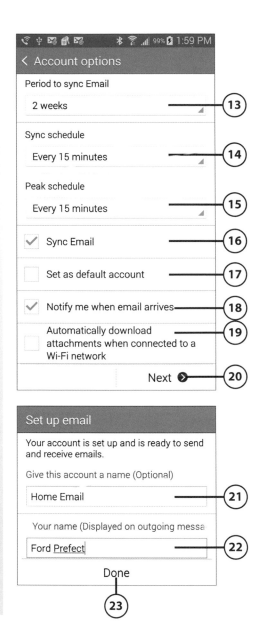

Be Secure If You Can

If your mail provider supports email security, such as Secure Sockets Layer (SSL) or Transport Layer Security (TLS), you should strongly consider using it. If you don't, emails you send and receive go over the Internet in plain readable text. Using SSL or TLS encrypts the emails as they travel across the Internet so nobody can read them. Set this under the Advanced settings for the incoming and outgoing servers.

Working with the Email App

Now that you have added two new accounts, you can start using the Email application. Everything you do in the Email application is the same for every email account. The Email app enables you to work with email accounts either separately or in a combined view.

Navigate the Email Application

Before you learn how to compose or read emails, you should become familiar with the Email application.

1. Tap to launch the Email app.

2. Tap to switch between email accounts or select Combined Inbox, which shows all emails from all accounts.

3. Tap the star to mark a personal account (POP3/IMAP) email as flagged.

4. Each color represents a specific email account.

5. Tap to compose a new email.

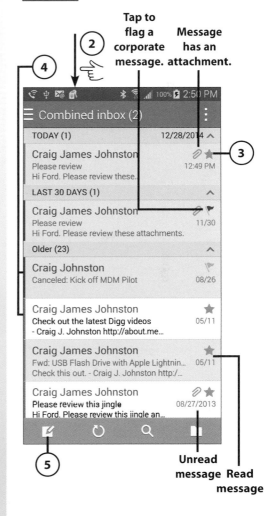

Tap to flag a corporate message.

Message has an attachment.

Unread message Read message

Landscape Mode

Because your Galaxy Note 4 has such a large screen, Samsung rewrote the Email app to support a Landscape mode. If you rotate your Galaxy Note 4 sideways, the Email app reconfigures to show the email list on the left and the actual email you are reading on the right.

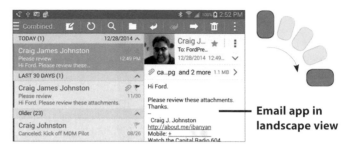

Email app in landscape view

Compose an Email

1. Tap to compose a new email.

2. Enter one or more recipients. As you type, your Galaxy Note 4 tries to guess who you want to address the message to. If you see the correct name, tap it to select it. This includes names stored on your Galaxy Note 4 and in your company's corporate address book.

Tap to change which account you want to send the email from.

3. Enter a subject.

4. Tap to reveal and hide the formatting toolbar. Use the formatting icons to change the font, font size, color, and other properties.

5. Tap to send the message.

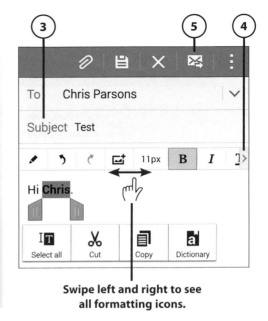

Swipe left and right to see all formatting icons.

Drawing in Your Email

Instead of just typing your email, you can draw in it. Pull out your S Pen and tap the Drawing mode icon. Then draw in the area indicated. Tap the Pen Settings icon to change the style of instrument (brush, pen, and so on) and the color of the ink. Tap the Eraser icon and use the S Pen to erase parts of your drawing. Tap the Insert icon to insert images from the Gallery.

Drawing mode ——→

Add Attachments to a Message

Before you send your message, you might want to add one or more attachments. You can attach any type of file, including pictures, video, audio, contacts, and location.

1. Tap the Attach icon.

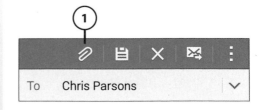

2. Choose the type of attachment.

3. Tap to remove an attachment.

4. Tap to send your email.

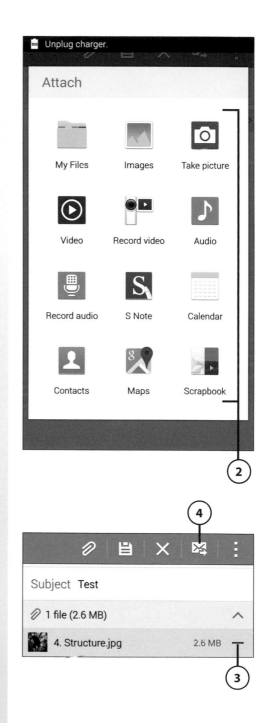

Read Email

Reading messages in the Email application is the same regardless of which account the email has come to.

1. Tap an email to open it.

2. Tap to reply to the sender of the email. This does not reply to anyone in the Cc field.

3. Tap to forward the email.

4. Tap to expand the email header to see all recipients and all other email header information.

5. Tap to mark the message as flagged.

6. Tap to delete the message.

7. Tap to see the attachments on a separate screen.

8. Tap to preview the attachment. In this example it is an audio file.

9. Tap to save the attachment to your phone.

10. Tap to return to the email view.

Tap to reply to Reply All

11. Tap the Menu icon to see more options.

12. Tap to mark the message as unread.

13. Tap to move the message to a different folder.

14. Tap to save the email as a file on your phone (outside the Email app).

15. Tap to mark the message as spam or junk mail.

16. Tap to add the sender to the Priority Sender list. Email from people in the Priority Sender list is displayed in the Priority Sender view.

17. Tap to print the email on a Samsung printer available on the Wi-Fi network.

Change Email App Settings

1. Tap the Menu icon.

2. Tap Settings.

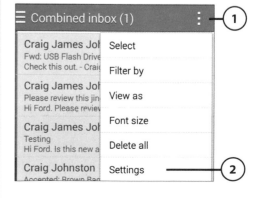

3. Tap to change how many lines of the email are shown in the preview, what shows in the title line, and to enable auto-fit (which shrinks emails so they fit on the screen properly when you read them).

4. Tap to change how auto-advance works. You can choose to either advance to a newer message, older message, or back to the message list.

5. Tap to manage the Priority Sender list.

6. Tap to manage your spam address list.

7. Tap to choose whether you want your email sending to be delayed. When this is enabled, after you tap the Send icon, your email will not be sent right away, allowing you to edit the email or delete it if you need to.

Quick Responses

You can write words, phrases, sentences, or paragraphs of text ahead of time and save them as Quick Responses. While you are composing an email, you can choose to insert one or more of your Quick Responses. The idea is that using Quick Responses saves on typing the same things over and over.

8. Tap to enable or disable Split View mode when you rotate your Galaxy Note 4 on its side.

9. Tap Manage Accounts to manage settings specific to your email accounts. Use the next two sections to change settings per account type.

What Is the Priority Sender List?

Emails received from people whom you have listed in the Priority Sender list are shown in the Priority Sender Inbox as well as in the regular Inbox. Opening the Priority Sender Inbox folder shows only emails from these people, which can be a way of filtering email so that you respond to the important people first and then switch to the regular Inbox and respond to everyone else.

Corporate Account Settings

You are able to change your email signature as well as control what components are synchronized and how often they are synchronized.

1. Tap your corporate email account.

2. Tap to manage synchronization settings, which include the schedule to sync your email, how far back in the past to sync, and the size of the portion of each email to retrieve.

3. Tap to enable or disable using an email signature, add an email signature, or edit a signature.

4. Tap to set whether you are out of the office and your out-of-office message. This synchronizes to the out-of-office feature on your corporate mailbox so your out-of-office messages will be sent by your mail server.

5. Tap to enable or disable using this account as the default account when composing email.

6. Tap to update your password, such as when your company requires you to change your password.

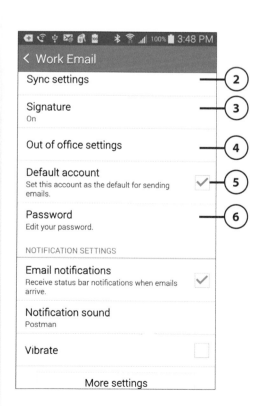

7. Tap to enable or disable being notified when new emails arrive for this account.

8. Tap to select the ringtone that plays when you are notified of new email for this account.

9. Tap to enable or disable vibrating when the notification ringtone plays.

10. Tap for more settings.

11. Tap to change the friendly name for this account.

12. Tap to choose whether to always Bcc or Cc yourself on emails you send.

13. Tap to enable or disable automatically loading embedded images in emails sent to you on this account.

14. Tap to enable or disable automatically downloading email attachments when your Note 4 is connected to Wi-Fi.

15. Tap to choose which folders (excluding Inbox and Outbox) you want to synchronize from your office email account and when they synchronize based on the peak and off-peak schedule.

16. Tap to choose how far back in the past your calendar synchronizes.

17. Tap to empty your Trash folder on the email server back in the office.

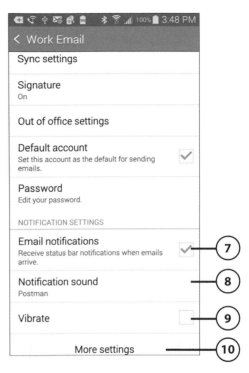

18. Tap to change which device wins if there is a conflict between your phone and your email account back at the office.

Why Empty the Office Trash Folder?

Step 17 describes how you can choose to empty your Trash folder back in the office. This feature is useful because sometimes your email administrator sets a limit on the size of your mailbox, and when you reach that limit, you are unable to send emails. By emptying your Trash folder back at the office, you might be able to clear a little bit of space in your mailbox so you can send that important email.

19. Scroll down for more settings.

How Are There Conflicts?

A conflict can occur if you or someone who has delegate access on your email account makes a change in your mailbox using a desktop email client such as Outlook (for example, your delegate moves an email to a folder) and you then make a change on your Galaxy Note 4 (say, you delete that same email). Now there is a conflict because an email has been both moved and deleted at the same time. If you set the server to have priority, then the conflict is resolved using your rule that the server wins. In this example, the email is not deleted but rather is moved to a folder.

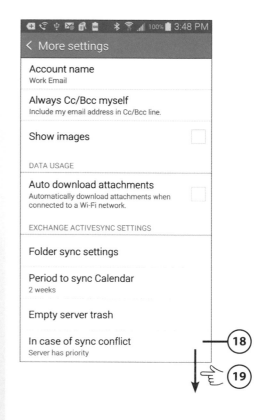

20. Tap to set advanced security options, including whether you want to encrypt your emails, sign emails with an electronic signature, and email certificates to use with S/MIME (if your company supports it).

21. Select what to synchronize between your Note 4 and your office email account.

22. Check the box to include old emails that are part of an email conversation (also known as a *thread*) when synchronizing email.

23. Tap to change the Exchange mail server settings for this account. This includes your account username and password if these have changed.

24. Tap to return to the previous screen.

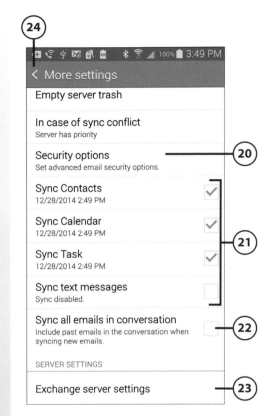

POP/IMAP Account Settings

1. Tap to manage synchronization settings that include the schedule to sync your email, how far back in the past to sync, and the size of the portion of each email to retrieve.

2. Tap to enable or disable using an email signature, add an email signature, or edit a signature.

3. Tap to enable or disable using this account as the default account when composing email.

4. Tap to update your password.

5. Tap to enable or disable being notified when new emails arrive for this account.

6. Tap to select the ringtone that plays when you are notified of new email for this account.

7. Tap to enable or disable vibrating when the notification ringtone plays.

8. Tap for more settings.

9. Tap to change the friendly name for this account.

10. Tap to edit the name that is displayed when you send email to others.

11. Tap to choose whether to always Bcc or Cc yourself on emails you send.

12. Tap to enable or disable automatically loading embedded images in emails sent to you on this account.

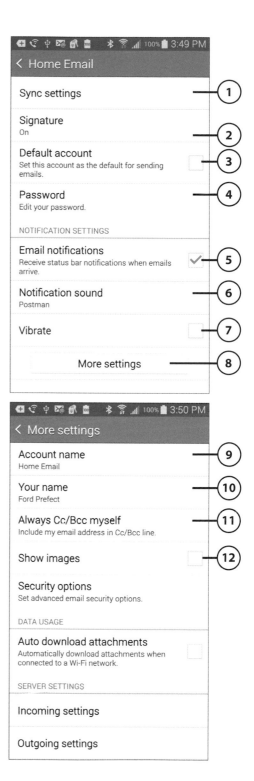

13. Tap to set advanced security settings for this account, including choosing to encrypt emails, sign them with a digital signature, and manage encryption keys on your phone for use with encrypting emails.

14. Tap to enable or disable automatically downloading email attachments when your Note 4 is connected to Wi-Fi.

15. Tap to change the incoming server settings for this account.

16. Tap to change the outgoing server settings for this account.

17. Tap to return to the Settings main screen.

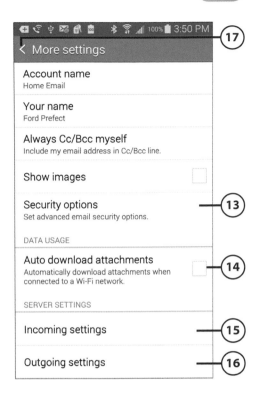

It's Not All Good

Which Email Client Should I Use?

As you have seen in this chapter, the Gmail app and the Email app can both support POP3 and IMAP email accounts (typically used for personal email accounts). In the next version of Android (Lollipop), the Email app will no longer be supported, and the Gmail app will support Gmail, POP3/IMAP, and Exchange ActiveSync email account types. Because we are now in a transition state, the Gmail app running on Android KitKat does not yet support Exchange ActiveSync, so you are forced to use the Email app if you have corporate email. If you don't need Exchange ActiveSync support, you may want to ignore the Email app completely and set up your Gmail and POP3/IMAP accounts in the Gmail app. The possible drawback of this is that unlike with the Email app, you cannot see all accounts on the screen at the same time; instead, you have to switch between them. If you want to be able to use Rich Text Formatting (RTF), you can only do this in the Email app, because the Gmail app doesn't support it. It is a confusing time right now when it comes to email on your Note 4, but hopefully you can make an educated choice based on your needs.

See your
stocks.

Search
Google.

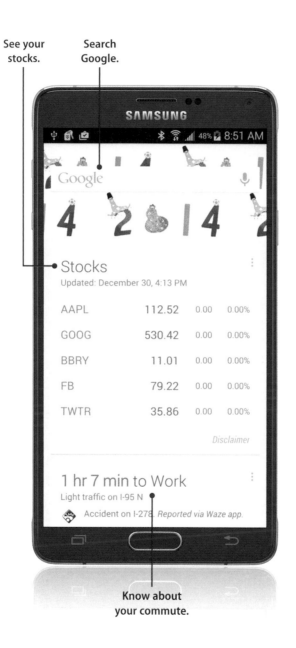

SAMSUNG

Google

Stocks
Updated: December 30, 4:13 PM

AAPL	112.52	0.00	0.00%
GOOG	530.42	0.00	0.00%
BBRY	11.01	0.00	0.00%
FB	79.22	0.00	0.00%
TWTR	35.86	0.00	0.00%

Disclaimer

1 hr 7 min to Work
Light traffic on I-95 N

Accident on I-278. *Reported via Waze app.*

Know about
your commute.

In this chapter, you find out how to use Google Maps, Navigation, and Google Now. Topics include the following:

→ Getting to know Google Now
→ Working with Google Maps
→ Using Google Maps with no data coverage
→ Getting around with Navigation

Google Now and Navigation

Your Galaxy Note 4 can be used as a GPS navigation device while you are walking or driving around. The Galaxy Note 4 also includes a new app called Google Now that offers to provide you all the information you need when you need it.

Google Now

You can access Google Now, which enables you to search the Internet, from any screen. The app also provides you information, such as how long it will take to drive to work and the game scores from your favorite teams.

Accessing Google Now

Access Google Now any time your Note 4 is unlocked by pressing and holding the Home button.

— **Press and hold.**

>>>Go Further
ACCESS GOOGLE NOW FROM THE LOCK SCREEN

You can configure your Note 4 to allow you to say "OK Google" to access Google Now when the screen is off, and even when your Note 4 is locked. To do this, open Settings, tap Language and Input, and then tap Voice Search. On the Voice Search screen tap "OK Google" Detection. Make sure that all three check boxes are checked. You must say "OK Google" four times so that your Note 4 can recognize your voice. However, bear in mind that this is not foolproof, so others may be able to command your Note 4 to do things using their voices, too.

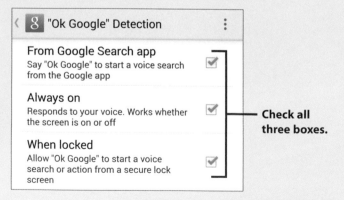

— **Check all three boxes.**

Understand the Google Now Screen

1. Information, in the form of cards, automatically appears based on your settings. Possibilities include sports teams you follow, upcoming meetings, weather where you work, and traffic on the way to work.

2. Tap and speak a request or search. You can also say "OK Google" and then speak your request. Cards relevant to your search or request appear.

Scroll down to see more cards.   **Tap to change card settings.**

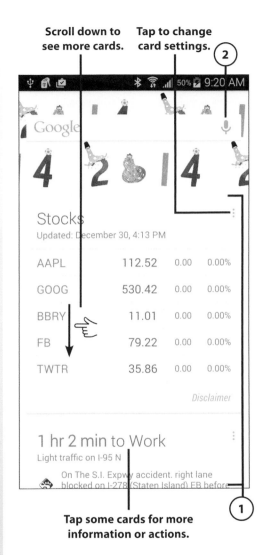

Tap some cards for more information or actions.

Set Up Google Now

1. While you have Google Now open, scroll down to the bottom of the screen.

2. Tap the Menu icon and tap Settings.

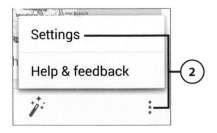

3. Tap to disable or enable Google Now.

4. Tap to choose what Google Now can search for when you conduct a search. You can choose to let it search the names of apps you have installed, bookmarks and web history in Chrome, your contacts, and what books, movies, TV shows, and music you have.

5. Tap Voice.

6. Tap to choose the language that Google Now uses.

7. Tap to set when Google Now speaks the search results. The choices are On, Off, and Only When You Are Using a Hands-free Device.

8. Tap to choose whether your Note 4 listens for you to say "OK Google" to launch Google Now, and when it listens for it.

9. Tap to download speech recognition software so you can do voice searches even when you're not connected to the Internet. You can download multiple languages.

10. Tap to block or allow offensive words. Turning this on causes the Voice Search feature to hide any search results that contain offensive words.

11. Tap to enable or disable Audio History. If you disable this, your voice searches and commands are still sent to the Google servers, but you do not have access to manage them, and Google is not able to personalize your results. In addition, you are no longer able to say "OK Google" from any screen or the lock screen.

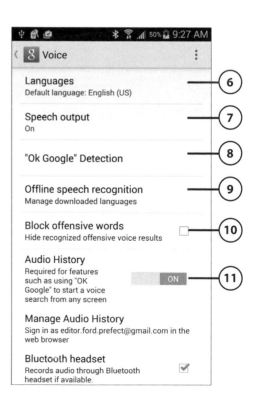

12. Tap to view and manage recordings of your voice that were recorded and sent to Google servers when you said "OK Google" and followed that with some command.

13. Tap to allow Google Now to listen for your voice when you are using a Bluetooth headset. This is very useful to have enabled when you are using your car's built-in Bluetooth connection.

14. Tap to save your changes and return to the main Settings screen.

15. Tap Accounts & Privacy.

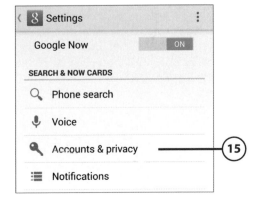

16. Tap to change which Google account you want to use for Google Now.

17. Tap to choose whether you want to share your commuting information with your friends on Google+. They will be able to see when you leave work and when you arrive home.

18. Tap to change or turn Google location on or off. If you turn this off, you severely limit the usefulness of Google Now.

19. Tap to turn off the Web History feature. It is recommended that you leave this turned on for better search results from Google. Also, having it off might disable Google Now.

20. Tap to manage your web history. If you have Web History enabled in step 19, you can manage the history items that have been collected, including deleting them.

21. Tap to allow Google to personalize your search results.

22. Scroll down for more settings.

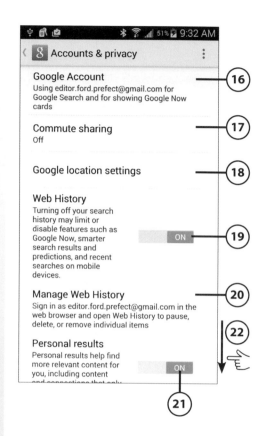

23. Tap to decide whether you want to allow some apps running on your Note 4 to report their history to Google. You can also clear the history provided by these apps.

24. Tap to choose whether you want to have explicit content filtered from your search results.

25. Tap to choose whether you want to let Google keep a copy of your device contacts so it can recognize names when you instruct Google Now to do something involving your contacts (such as send a message).

26. Tap to control how much storage on your device is used for search data by apps running on your Note 4.

27. Tap to save your changes and return to the previous screen.

28. Tap to choose whether you want to see updates from Google Now in your Notification bar, and control what ringtone plays when those notifications are displayed.

29. Tap to save your changes and return to Google Now.

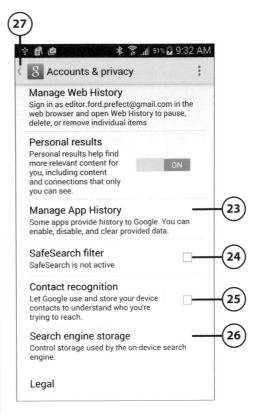

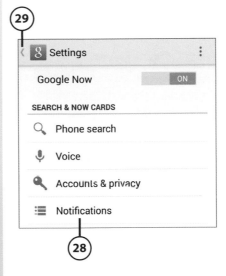

>>>*Go Further*

DOING MORE WITH GOOGLE NOW

In addition to searching the Internet using Google Now, you can command Google Now to do things for you. For example, you can tell Google Now to set an alarm for you, compose a text message, or even send an email. This is just a small list of the types of things you can have Google Now do for you. To see a comprehensive list of commands, visit http://trendblog.net/list-of-google-now-voice-commands-infographic/.

To make Google Now even more effective, configure your work and home addresses in Google Maps. Google Now then uses that information to tell you things such as how long your commute to work will be, whether there is heavy traffic on the route, and so on. See step 4 in the "Configure Google Maps Settings" task later in this chapter to find out how to do that.

Google Maps

Google Maps enables you to see where you are on a map, find points of interest close to you, get driving or walking directions, and review extra layers of information, such as a satellite view.

1. Tap to launch Google Maps.

2. Tap to type a search term, the name of a business, or an address.

3. Tap to speak a search term, the name of a business, or an address.

4. Tap to get walking or driving directions from one location to another. You can also choose to use public transit or biking paths to get to your destination.

5. Swipe in from the left of the screen to reveal the menu.

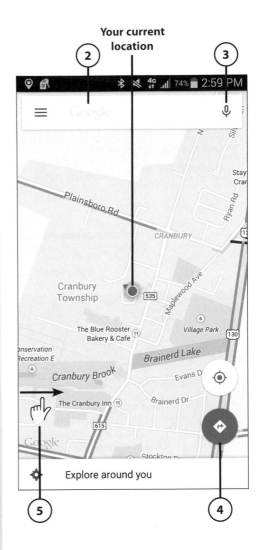

6. Tap to see your work and home addresses, plus addresses you have recently searched for. (See the "Configure Google Maps Settings" task for information on entering your home and work addresses.)

7. Tap to explore restaurants, parks, and attractions near your current location.

8. Tap to show the current traffic conditions on the map or satellite view.

9. Tap to show all public transport locations on the map view or satellite view.

10. Tap to show all bicycling routes on the map view or satellite view.

11. Tap to toggle between the map view and the satellite view.

12. Tap to see the terrain view.

13. Tap to launch the Google Earth app.

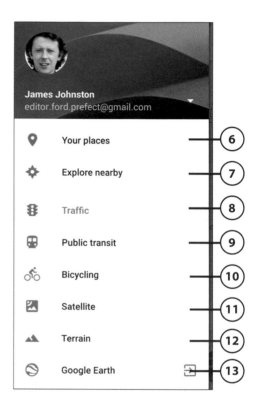

Changing Google Maps Settings

See the "Configure Google Maps Settings" task later in this chapter for more information about customizing Google Maps.

Get Directions

You can use Google Maps to get directions to where you want to go.

1. Tap the Directions icon.

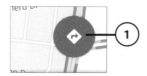

2. Tap to set the starting point or leave it as Your Location (which is your current location).

3. Tap to choose from previous destinations.

4. Type the destination address.

5. Tap to flip the start and end points.

6. Tap to use driving directions. This example uses driving directions.

7. Tap to use public transportation.

8. Tap to use bike paths (if available).

9. Tap to walk to your destination.

Public Transportation

If you choose to use public transportation to get to your destination, you have two extra options to use. You can choose the mode of public transportation to use, including bus, subway, train, or tram/light rail. You can also choose the best route (fewer transfers and less walking).

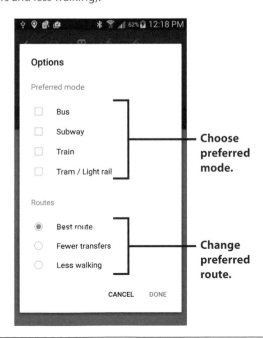

10. Tap to go back to the previous screen to change the route options (such as avoiding toll roads) or select an alternative route.

11. Tap to change what is displayed on the screen during navigation. You can show all traffic, use a satellite view, and include the terrain view.

12. Swipe up to see the list of all turns that will be taken on the trip.

13. Tap to start the audible turn-by-turn directions to your destination.

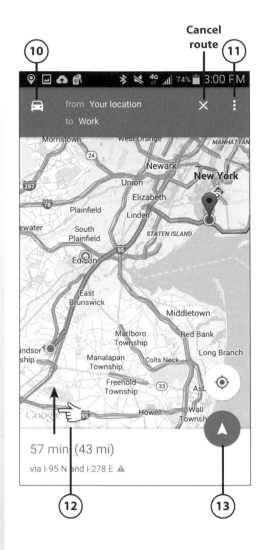

14. Drive or start walking and follow the onscreen route, or listen to the turn-by-turn directions.

15. Tap to see alternative routes.

16. Tap the Menu icon to mute the voice guidance, show traffic conditions, choose the satellite view, and show the entire route as a step-by-step list.

17. Tap to speak voice commands while en route. For example, you can ask "How is traffic ahead?" or "When will I get there?"

18. Tap to cancel the route.

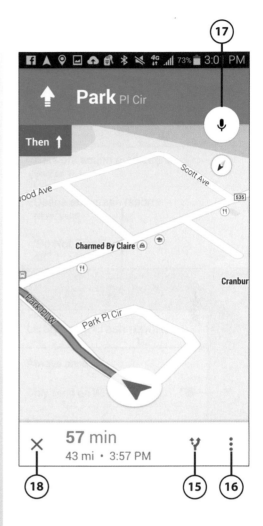

Configure Google Maps Settings

1. Swipe in from the left side of the screen.

2. Scroll down and tap Settings.

3. Tap to edit your work and home addresses.

4. Tap to enable or disable the capability for your Note 4 to report its location. You can also choose the accuracy of your location by changing the mode.

5. Tap to improve your location accuracy if you think that your Note 4 is not reporting it correctly.

6. Tap to see addresses you have looked up and received directions to. You can also delete items in this list.

7. Tap to set the distance unit of measure. You can either set it to automatic so that Google Maps adjusts it based on where you are on the planet, or you can manually set it.

8. Tap to set the volume of the turn-by-turn directions voice.

9. Check the box to enable you to simply shake your Note 4 to send feedback to Google on how Google Maps is working.

10. Tap to save your changes and return to the main Google Maps screen.

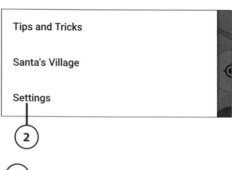

Use Offline Google Maps

Google Maps enables you to download small parts of the global map to your Note 4. This is useful if you are traveling and need an electronic map but cannot connect to a network to download it in real time.

1. Swipe in from the left of the screen.

2. Tap Your Places.

3. Scroll down to the bottom of the Your Places screen.

4. Tap Save a New Offline Map.

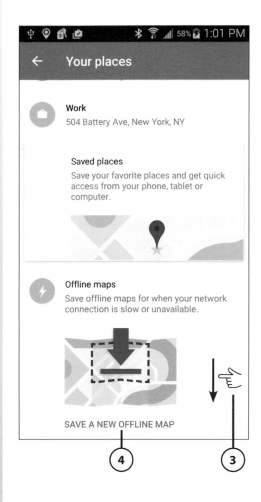

5. Pan around to find the area of the map you want to save offline.

6. Pinch to zoom out or unpinch to zoom in to the area of the map you want to save offline.

7. Tap Save when the area of the map fills the screen.

8. Type a name for the offline map and tap save.

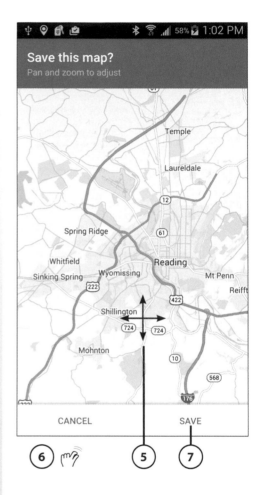

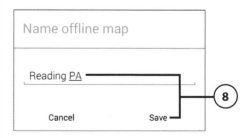

How Much Map Can I Take Offline?

When selecting the area of the map to take offline, you are limited to approximately 100MB of map data. You don't need to worry about the size of the data because if you have selected an area that is too large, Google Maps gives you a warning.

Warning that your selection area is too large

It's Not All Good

Offline Maps Have Limited Use

If you download some map data to your Note 4, you can use it to zoom in and out of the area you downloaded and also see where you are on the map in real time, even though you have no network coverage. You cannot, however, get directions within the downloaded map area or use the Navigation app to get turn-by-turn directions. You also cannot search for things in the downloaded map area or see points of interest.

So how useful is having map data already downloaded to your tablet? Because offline maps are already downloaded, they help when you have a network connection and are getting driving directions because Google Maps does not need to download the map data in real time, which could save you a lot of money in data-roaming charges.

Use the World Clock feature to track the time around the world.

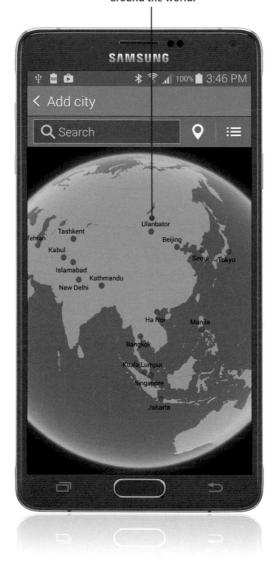

In this chapter, you find out how to set the time, use the Clock application, and use the S Planner calendaring application. Topics include the following:

→ Synchronizing to the correct time
→ Working with the Clock application
→ Setting alarms
→ Waking up with the latest weather, news, and your schedule
→ Working with S Planner

Working with Date, Time, and S Planner

Your Galaxy Note 4 has a Clock application you can use as a bedside alarm, stopwatch, timer, and world clock. The S Planner application synchronizes with your Google or Microsoft Exchange calendars and enables you to create events and meetings while on the road and to always know where your next meeting is.

Setting the Date and Time

Before you start working with the Clock and S Planner applications, make sure your Galaxy Note 4 has the correct date and time.

1. Pull down the Notifications panel.

2. Tap the Settings icon to display the Settings screen.

3. Tap the System tab to display the System screen.

4. Tap Date and Time to display the Date and Time screen.

5. Tap the Automatic Date and Time check box to enable or disable synchronizing time and date with the wireless carrier. It is best to leave this enabled because it automatically sets date and time based on where you are traveling.

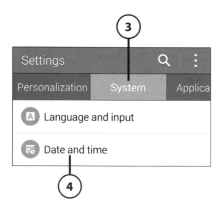

Does Network Time Sync Always Work?

In some countries, on some carriers, time synchronization does not work. This means that when you get off the plane and turn Airplane mode off (see the Prologue for information on Airplane mode), after a reasonable amount of time your time, date, and time zone will still be incorrect. In these instances, it is best to disable Automatic Date and Time and manually set the time, date, and time zone yourself. You can then try it on automatic in the next country you visit or when you are back in your home country.

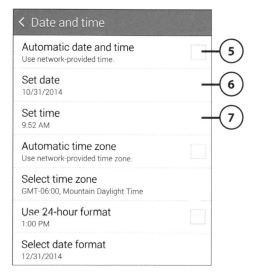

6. Tap Set Date to set the date if you choose to disable network synchronization.

7. Tap Set Time to set the time if you choose to disable network synchronization.

8. Tap the Automatic Time Zone check box to enable or disable synchronizing the time zone with the wireless carrier. It is best to leave this enabled because it automatically sets the time zone based on where you are traveling.

9. Tap Select Time Zone to set the time zone manually if you choose to disable network synchronization.

10. Tap the Use 24-Hour Format check box to enable or disable the use of 24-hour time format. This format makes your Galaxy Note 4 represent time without a.m. or p.m. For example, 1:00 p.m. becomes 13:00 in 24-hour format.

11. Tap Select Date Format to change the way in which the date is represented. For example, people in the United States normally write the date with the month first (for example, 12/31/2015). You can make your Galaxy Note 4 display the date with the day first (for example, 31/12/2015) or with the year first (for example, 2015/12/31).

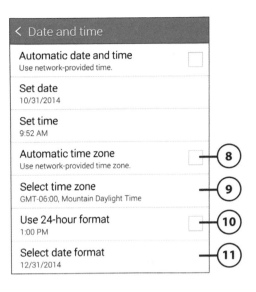

Clock Application

The Clock application is preinstalled on your Galaxy Note 4 and provides alarms, a world clock, a stopwatch, and a timer.

Navigate the Clock Application

1. Tap the Clock icon on the Apps screen.

2. Tap the Alarm tab to view and edit your alarms.

3. Tap the + icon to create an alarm.

4. Tap the World Clock tab to see the World Clock and manage the clocks on that screen.

5. Tap the Stopwatch tab to use the Stopwatch.

6. Tap the Timer tab to use the Timer.

No alarms

Manage Alarms

The Clock application enables you to set multiple alarms. These can be one-time alarms or recurring alarms. Even if you exit the Clock application, the alarms you set still trigger.

1. Tap the + icon to create a new alarm.

2. Tap the up/down arrows to set the hours and minutes.

3. Tap the AM/PM button to toggle between a.m. and p.m.

4. Tap the days of the week when you want the alarm to trigger. In this example, the alarm will sound on all days of the workweek but not on Saturday and Sunday.

5. Check the Repeat Weekly box if you want the alarm to repeat every week.

6. Tap Alarm Type to change the type of alarm. Your choices are Sound, Vibration, and Vibration and Sound.

7. Tap Alarm Tone to change the alarm tone or melody that plays.

8. Scroll down to see the remaining settings.

9. Drag the Volume slider to adjust the volume of the alarm.

10. Move the Snooze switch to enable or disable the Snooze feature. Touch the Snooze button to display the Snooze screen, where you can set how long the snooze lasts and how many times it repeats.

11. Move the Smart Alarm switch to enable or disable Smart Alarm. Smart Alarm plays a tune ahead of the alarm time to slowly start waking you up. Tap the Smart Alarm button to display the Smart Alarm screen, where you can set the build-up time and choose the alarm tone.

12. Tap the Name box and type the name for the alarm, such as Work Alarm or Weekend.

13. Tap Save to save your new alarm.

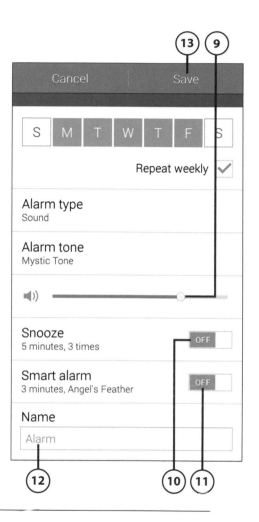

Stopping an Alarm

When the alarm goes off, tap the red circled × and drag it to either side to turn off the alarm.

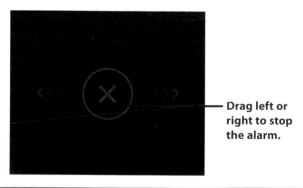

Drag left or right to stop the alarm.

Turning an Alarm On or Off

After setting up an alarm, you can turn it off so that it doesn't ring. Tap the alarm on the Alarm screen, making its alarm-clock icon (and the days for which it is set) change from green to gray.

The alarm icon indicates one or more alarms is on.

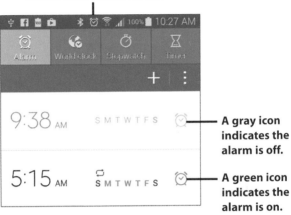

A gray icon indicates the alarm is off.

A green icon indicates the alarm is on.

Editing or Deleting an Alarm

To edit an alarm, go to the Alarm screen in the Clock app and tap the alarm you want to edit. On the alarm's screen, change the alarm as needed, and then tap Save.

To delete an alarm, tap and hold the alarm until the selection controls appear. Clock automatically checks the box for the alarm you tapped, but you can also check the boxes of any other alarms you want to delete. Then tap Delete (the trash icon) to delete the alarm or alarms.

Tap to delete the alarm.

Use the World Clock

The World Clock enables you to keep track of time in multiple cities around the world.

1. Tap World Clock to display the World Clock screen.

2. Tap Add City (+) to add a new city. The Add City screen appears.

3. Type in a partial city name to find the city you want to add.

4. Tap a city to add it to the World Clock screen.

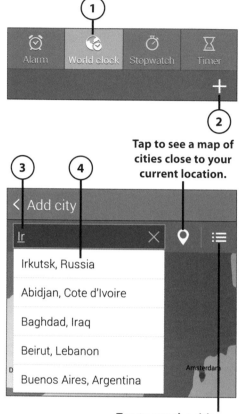

Tap to see a map of cities close to your current location.

Tap to see the cities as a list without the world map.

Managing Cities

To delete a city from your World Clock screen, or to rearrange the cities you've saved, tap the Menu button. Tap Select to select which cities to delete. Tap Change Order to display the Change Order screen; from that screen you can rearrange the cities by dragging them by the dotted handles on the left.

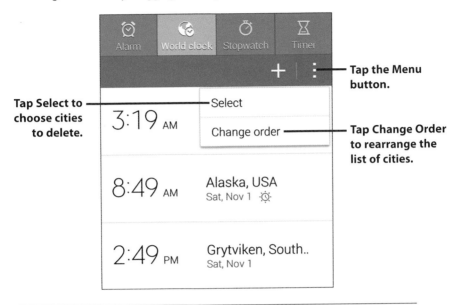

Tap the Menu button.

Tap Select to choose cities to delete.

Tap Change Order to rearrange the list of cities.

Using the S Planner Calendaring Application

The S Planner calendaring application enables you to synchronize all your Google Calendars under your primary Google account to your Galaxy Note 4. You can accept appointments and create and modify appointments right on your phone. Any changes are automatically synchronized wirelessly back to your Google Calendar.

Navigate the S Planner Main Screen

The main screen of the S Planner app shows a one-day, one-week, or one-month view of your appointments. S Planner also shows events from multiple calendars at the same time.

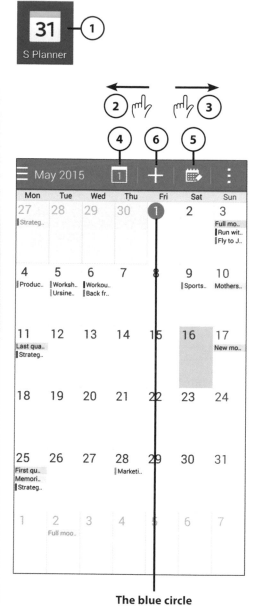

1. Tap the S Planner icon on the Apps screen.

2. Swipe left to go forward in time.

3. Swipe right to go backward in time.

4. Tap the Today icon (the square bearing the date) at the top of the screen to show today's date.

5. Tap the Writing mode icon (the calendar icon) to switch to Writing mode, where you can draw over the calendar with the S Pen. (Read more about this feature in the "Drawing All Over Your Calendar" sidebar.)

6. Tap + to create a new event.

The blue circle marks today's date.

7. Tap the button in the upper-left corner to display the navigation panel.

8. Tap the view you want to see: Year, Month, Month and Agenda, Week, Day, or Agenda.

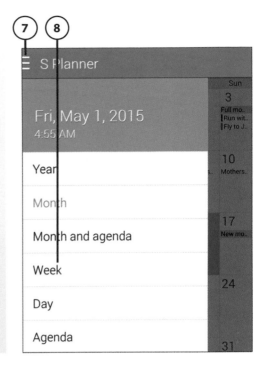

>>>Go Further

DRAWING ALL OVER YOUR CALENDAR

Instead of adding events to your calendar, you can just draw on the calendar as if it was a wall calendar or a page in a notebook. This feature only works when you are viewing the Month view and you are holding your Galaxy Note 4 in portrait orientation. When you switch into Writing mode, as described in step 5, you can draw anything anywhere on the month. This is simply free-form drawing and is not translated into real events in your calendar; however, it's an easy and creative way to mark the calendar.

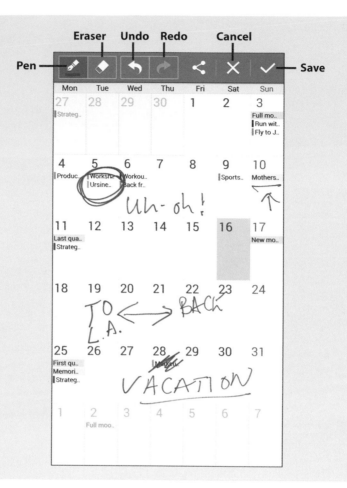

Event Colors

S Planner can display one calendar or many calendars at the same time. If you choose to display multiple calendars, events from each calendar are color coded so you can tell which events are from which calendar. In Google Calendar, you can also assign your choice of color to any event; S Planner preserves these colors.

Choose Which Calendars and Task Lists to View

If you have set up multiple accounts, which might each have multiple calendars or task lists, you can choose which calendars S Planner shows at the same time.

1. Tap the Menu button to open the menu.

2. Tap Calendars to display the Calendars screen.

3. You can check the All Calendars box to quickly display all calendars and task lists from all accounts.

4. Check a box to display the calendar or task list.

5. Uncheck a box to hide a calendar or task list.

6. Tap the Calendar Color icon to display the Calendar Color screen, where you can choose colors for the calendars.

7. Tap Calendars or the Back button to return to the main S Planner screen.

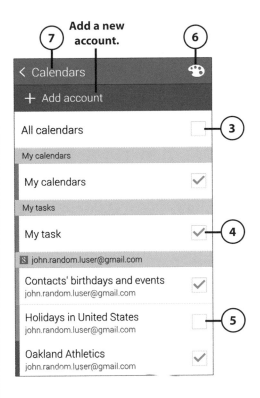

Change S Planner Settings

1. Tap the Menu button.

2. Tap Settings to display the Settings screen.

3. Check the Show Week Numbers box if you want to display week numbers. For example, March 26th is in week 13.

4. Check the Hide Declined Events box if you want to hide events you have declined.

5. Check the Hide Completed Tasks box if you want to hide tasks you have completed. Hiding what you've done may make it easier to see what you still have left to do.

6. Tap First Day of Week to display the First Day of Week dialog.

7. Tap the Locale Default radio button, the Saturday radio button, the Sunday radio button, or the Monday radio button, as needed. Locale Default means the locale determined by the time zone you are in controls what the first day of the week is.

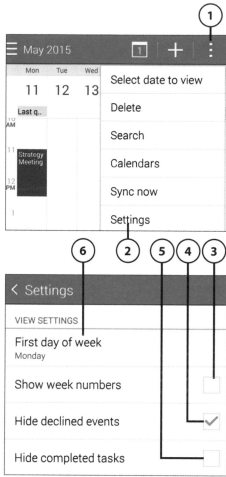

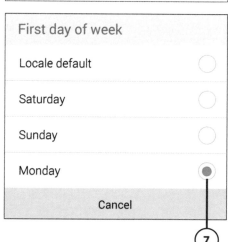

8. Check the 7-Day Weather Forecast box if you want to display the weather on your calendar.

9. Check the Lock Time Zone box when you want to force S Planner to use your home time zone or another time zone you choose when displaying the calendar and event times. You would do this when you travel but you want to keep your calendar on your home time zone (or another time zone you select) instead of letting S Planner change it to whichever time zone you find yourself in.

10. Tap Select Time Zone to set your home time zone if you enabled Lock Time Zone in step 9.

11. Tap the View Today According To button to display the View Today According To screen.

12. Tap the Fixed Time Zone radio button or the Local Time Zone radio button, as needed.

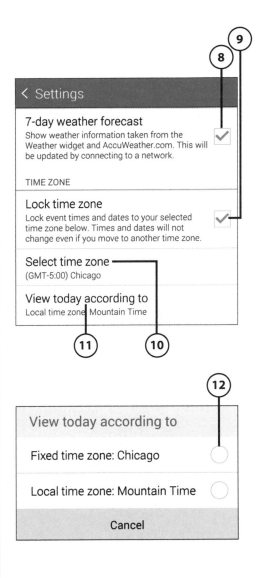

13. Tap Set Snooze Duration to display the Set Snooze Duration screen and then tap the radio button for the duration you want, such as 10 Minutes.

14. Tap Select Alert Type to display the Select Alert Type screen. You can then select the Pop-Up Notifications radio button, the Status Bar Notifications radio button, or the Off radio button, as needed.

15. Tap Notification Sound to choose the sound to play for calendar alerts.

16. Check the Vibration box if you want your Galaxy Note 4 to vibrate for alerts.

17. Tap Quick Responses to edit the four built-in Quick Responses or create custom Quick Responses. You find out how to use Quick Reponses later in this chapter.

18. Check the Online Recipient Search box if you want S Planner to search online for recipients of the address you type for shared events.

19. Tap Settings or the Back button to save your settings and return to the main S Planner screen.

Add a New Event

While you're on the road, you can add a new appointment or event—and even invite people to it. Events you add synchronize to your Google and corporate calendars in real time.

1. Tap + to add a new event.

A Quicker Way to Add an Event

You can quickly add a new event by tapping and holding on the day on which you want to create the event and the time of day you want to create it.

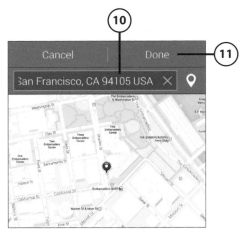

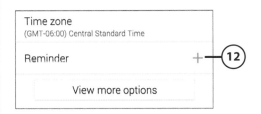

2. Tap your account name to display the Calendar screen and then tap the calendar you want to add the event to.

3. Tap the color swatch to choose the color to assign to the event. You can use colors to make important events more conspicuous.

4. Tap Title to enter a title for your event.

5. Check the All Day box to mark the event as an all-day event.

6. Tap the Start button to display the Start tab of the Start and End screen, where you set the start date and time of the event.

7. Tap the End button to display the End tab of the Start and End screen, where you set the end date and time of the event.

8. Tap Time Zone to choose the time zone for the event.

9. Tap Location to display the Location screen.

10. Type the location for the event.

11. Tap Done to return to the Add Event screen.

12. Tap the + to the right of Reminder to display the controls for configuring reminders.

13. Tap the left pop-up menu and then tap the time period, such as 15 Min Before.

14. Tap the right pop-up menu.

15. Tap the reminder type: Email or Notification.

16. Tap View More Options to display the hidden options.

17. Tap the Contacts icon to add invitees from your Contacts list. You can also add invitees by typing their names or email addresses in the text box.

18. Tap the appropriate – icon to remove an invitee.

19. Tap Show Me As to display the Show Me As screen, where you can choose Busy or Available to show your availability during this event.

20. Tap Privacy to choose the privacy of the event. You can choose Default, Public, or Private. Default uses the calendar's setting to determine who can see the details of the event. If the event is being created on your corporate calendar, setting the event to Private means that people can see you are busy, but they cannot see the event details.

21. Tap Repeat to set this as a recurring event. You can make it repeat daily, weekly, or monthly on the same date each month, but you can also set a meeting to repeat, for example, monthly but only every last Thursday regardless of the date.

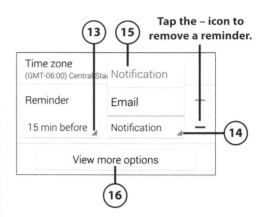

Tap the – icon to remove a reminder.

22. Tap Description and type a description for the event.

23. At the bottom of the screen, you can tap a sticker to apply it to the event. The stickers have images that might help you visually categorize events.

24. Tap Save to save the event. Any attendees you have added are automatically sent an event invitation.

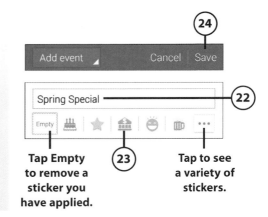

Tap Empty (23) **Tap to see**
to remove a **a variety of**
sticker you **stickers.**
have applied.

Editing and Deleting an Event

To edit an event, you must first open it for editing. How you do this depends on the view you're using, but the general approach is to tap the event or the day, depending on what you can see. If a dialog opens showing you a summary of the event or the day, tap the event's button to display the Detail View screen. When you tap an event in Agenda view or Month and Agenda view, S Planner takes you straight to the Detail View screen with no extra step.

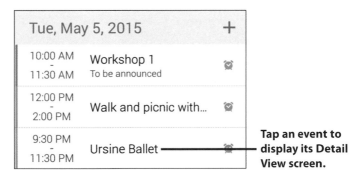

Tap an event to
display its Detail
View screen.

On the Detail View screen, tap the Edit icon to open the event for editing, or tap the Delete icon to delete the event. When you successfully delete an event to which someone has invited you, S Planner sends an event-decline notice to the event organizer. Therefore, you don't have to first decline the meeting before deleting it because this is all taken care of automatically.

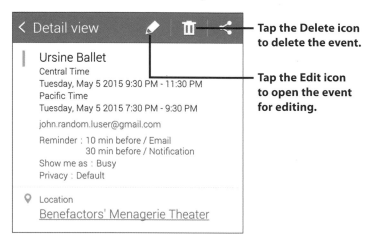

Tap the Delete icon to delete the event.

Tap the Edit icon to open the event for editing.

To delete multiple events, tap the Menu button and then tap Delete to display the Delete screen. Check the box for each event you want to delete and then tap Done.

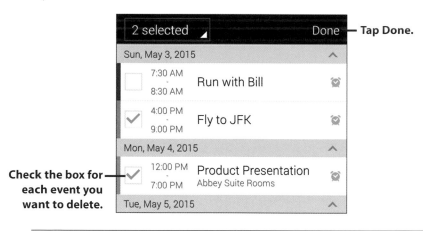

Tap Done.

Check the box for each event you want to delete.

Respond to a Google Event Invitation

When you are invited to an event, you can choose your response right in the invitation email itself.

1. Tap to open the event invitation email.

2. Tap Yes, Maybe, or No to indicate whether you will attend.

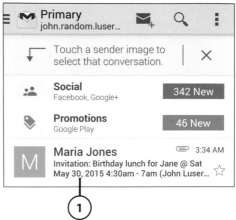

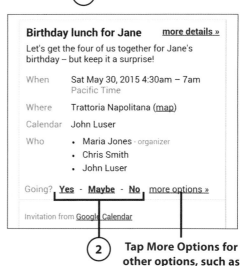

Tap More Options for other options, such as setting a reminder.

Respond to a Corporate Event Invitation

When you receive an invitation to an event, choose your response in the invitation email itself.

1. Tap to open the event invitation email.

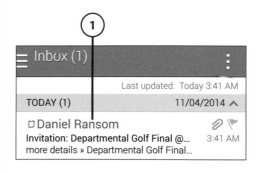

2. Tap Select Option to display the Select Option dialog.

3. Tap Accept, Tentative, or Decline to give a straightforward response.

4. If a screen opens, tap the appropriate button. For example, in the Accept screen, you can tap Edit Response Before Sending to include custom text, tap Send Response Now to send an unvarnished acceptance, or tap Do Not Send Response to accept the invitation (and add it to your schedule as accepted) but not send a response to the organizer.

Should You Send a Response to an Invitation?

Usually, it is not only good manners but also helpful to send a response to an invitation. For most events, the organizer will need to know how many people are attending and who they are, so the organizer will find even a Maybe response more useful than no response. For huge public events, however, you may choose not to send a response.

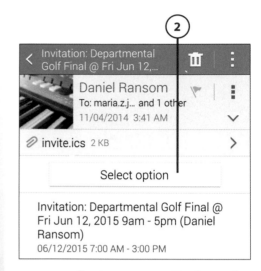

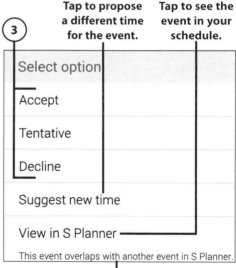

Tap to propose a different time for the event.   **Tap to see the event in your schedule.**

S Planner warns you if the event conflicts with an existing event in your schedule.

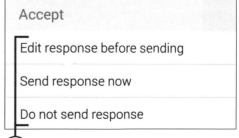

Use Quick Responses

When your Galaxy Note 4 notifies you of an upcoming event, you can choose either Snooze or Email Guests. When you choose to email guests, you can choose a Quick Response to send them.

1. Pull down the Notification bar.

2. Tap Email Guests to open the Select a Quick Response dialog.

3. Choose one of your Quick Responses or write a custom message.

4. Tap the email app you want to use to send the Quick Response.

Tap to snooze the reminder.

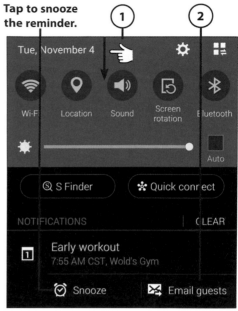

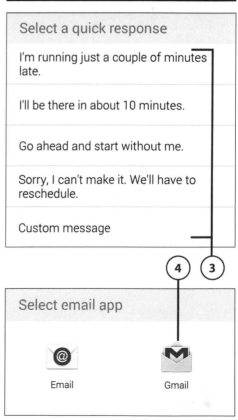

Add a Task

In addition to calendar events, you can add tasks you need to complete.

1. Tap New (+) to start adding a new item.

2. Tap the pop-up menu in the upper-left corner of the screen.

3. Tap Add Task to create a task.

4. Tap the task list that appears and use the Task screen to switch to a different task list if necessary.

5. Tap Title and type the title for the task.

6. Tap Due Date and then specify when the task is due. If the task needs no due date, check the No Due Date box instead.

7. Tap Reminder to choose when you want to be reminded of the task.

8. If you want to add a description or set a priority, tap View More Options to display the extra controls.

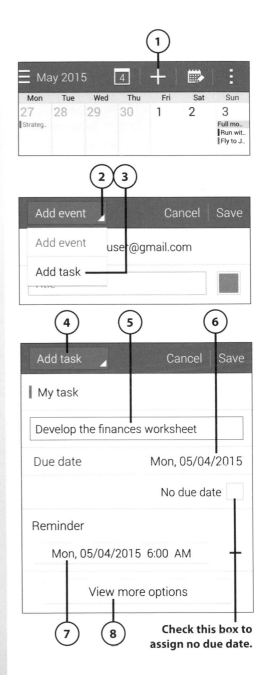

Check this box to assign no due date.

9. Tap Description and then type a description for the task.

10. Tap Priority to choose the task's priority.

11. Tap Save to save the task.

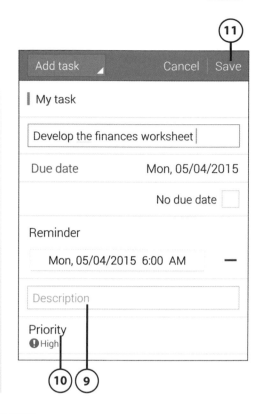

Marking a Task as Completed

To mark a task as completed, switch to Agenda view or Month and Agenda view. Check the box to the left of the task to mark it as completed.

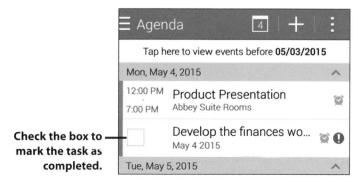

Check the box to mark the task as completed.

Add, search, and manage
your contacts.

In this chapter, you become familiar with your Galaxy Note 4's contact-management application, which is called Contacts. You find out how to add contacts, synchronize contacts, join duplicate contacts together, and even how to add a contact to your Home screen. Topics include the following:

→ Importing contacts

→ Adding contacts

→ Synchronizing contacts

→ Creating favorite contacts

Contacts

On any smartphone, the application for managing contacts is essential because it is where you keep all of your contacts' information. On the Galaxy Note 4, this application is called simply Contacts. It is the central hub for many activities, such as calling and sending text messages (SMS), multimedia messages (MMS), or email. You can also synchronize your contacts from many online sites, such as Facebook and Gmail, so as your friends change their Facebook profile pictures, their pictures on your Galaxy Note 4 change as well.

Adding Accounts

Before you look around the Contacts app, add some accounts to synchronize contacts from. You already added your Google account when you set up your Galaxy Note 4 in the Prologue.

Adding Facebook, Twitter, LinkedIn, and Other Accounts

To add accounts for your online services such as Facebook, Twitter, LinkedIn, and so on to your Galaxy Note 4, you might need to install the apps for those services from the Google Play Store. You can see how to install apps in Chapter 11, "Working with Android Apps." After the apps are installed and you have signed in to them, if you visit the Accounts settings, as shown in the following sections, you see new accounts for each online service.

Your accounts appear on the Accounts screen in the Settings app.

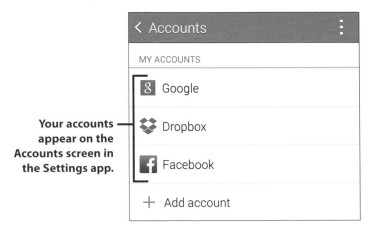

1. From the Home screen, pull down the Notification bar.

2. Tap the Settings icon.

3. Tap the Personalization tab to display the Personalization screen.

4. Tap Accounts to display the Accounts screen.

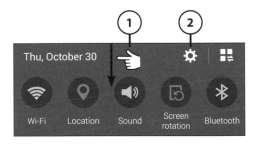

5. Tap Add Account to display the Add Account screen.

6. Tap Microsoft Exchange ActiveSync to display the Add an Exchange ActiveSync Account screen.

7. Type the email address for the account.

8. Tap Password and type the password.

9. Tap Show Password if you want to see the password rather than the dots the Galaxy Note 4 shows for security. Seeing the password can be helpful when entering complex passwords.

10. Tap Next. The Settings app tries to set up the account with the information you've provided.

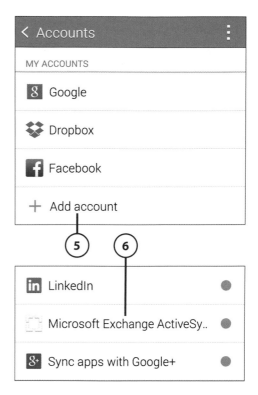

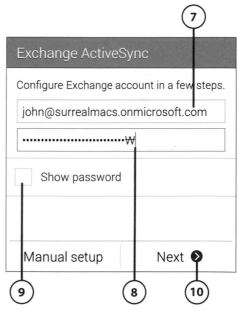

Dealing with Exchange ActiveSync Setup Problems

Your Galaxy Note 4 tries to work out some information about your company's ActiveSync setup. If it can't, it displays the Setup Could Not Finish screen to explain the problem. Often, you will see the "Authentication failed" message. Tap the OK button to dismiss the screen so that you can change the details.

> Unable to set up account
>
> Authentication failed.
>
> OK ————————— **Tap OK.**

Need Domain Name?

On the Exchange Server Settings screen that appears, type the domain name before your username, separating the two with a backslash (for example, CORP\john). Type the Exchange Server's name in the Exchange Server box. Then tap Next to try the credentials again with this extra information.

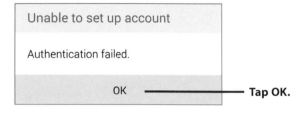

Type the domain name if the administrator says you need it. ———— CORP\john

Password

••••••••••••••••••••••••

Exchange server

Type the Exchange Server's name. ———— pod51017.outlook.com

✓ Use secure connection (SSL)

☐ Use client certificate

Client certificate

Mobile device ID

SEC1ECD881DEA43E

Next ❯ ———— **Tap Next.**

11. In the Remote Security Administration dialog, tap OK to agree
that your mail administrator may
impose security restrictions on
your Galaxy Note 4 after you connect to the Exchange Server. The
Account Options screen appears.

Remote security administration

Server outlook.office365.com must
be able to remotely control some
security features on your device.
Continue?

Cancel   OK ——— 11

What Is Remote Security Administration?

Remote Security Administration says
that when you activate your Galaxy
Note 4 against your work email servers,
your email administrator can add restrictions to your phone. These can include
forcing a device password, imposing the
need for a very strong password, and
requiring how many letters and numbers the password must contain. Your
Exchange administrator can also remotely
wipe your Galaxy Note 4, restoring it to
factory defaults. This is normally done if
you lose your phone or it is stolen.

12. Tap Period to Sync Email to choose
how many days, weeks, or months
in the past email is synchronized to
your Galaxy Note 4 or set it to All to
synchronize all email in your Inbox.

13. Tap Sync Schedule to choose how
often overall your Galaxy Note 4
syncs your Exchange email.

Push and Other Options for Getting Email

Push means that as email arrives in your
Inbox at work, it is delivered to your
phone. You can set it to Manual, which
means that your Galaxy Note 4 checks for
email only when you open the Email app.
You can also set the delivery frequency
from every 5 minutes to every 12 hours.

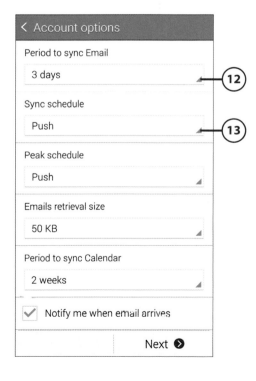

< Account options

Period to sync Email

3 days   12

Sync schedule

Push   13

Peak schedule

Push

Emails retrieval size

50 KB

Period to sync Calendar

2 weeks

✓ Notify me when email arrives

Next ❯

14. Tap Peak Schedule to choose how often your Galaxy Note 4 receives Exchange email during peak hours. You may want to check email more frequently during peak hours than off-peak hours.

15. Tap Emails Retrieval Size to choose the largest email size to retrieve. You can choose from 0.5KB to 100KB, choose All to retrieve all messages no matter how big they are, or choose Automatic to use the server's settings. 50KB or 100KB is a reasonable size unless you get vast numbers of messages.

16. Tap Period to Sync Calendar to choose how long a period of calendar appointments to synchronize. Your choices are 2 weeks, 1 month, 3 months, 6 months, and All Calendar.

17. Check the Notify Me When Email Arrives box to receive a notification when email messages arrive. This notification can be helpful, but you might find it overkill if you receive many messages.

18. Scroll down the screen to see more settings.

19. Check the Sync Email box to sync your email messages with the server. Normally, you will want to do this.

20. Check the Sync Contacts box to enable synchronizing your corporate contacts to your Galaxy Note 4.

21. Check the Sync Calendar box to enable synchronizing your corporate calendar to your Galaxy Note 4.

22. Check the Sync Task box to enable synchronizing your corporate task list to your Galaxy Note 4.

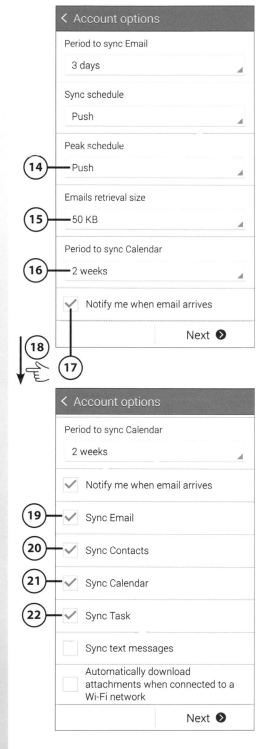

23. Check the Sync Text Messages box to enable synchronizing your SMS messages to your Galaxy Note 4.

24. Check the Automatically Download Attachments When Connected to a Wi-Fi Network box to make your Galaxy Note 4 automatically download email attachments when it's connected to a Wi-Fi network.

25. Tap Next. The Activate Device Administrator? screen appears.

What to Synchronize

You might decide that you don't want to synchronize all your work information to your Galaxy Note 4. You might decide to just synchronize email, and not the calendar, or maybe just the calendar but not the contacts and email. Unchecking these boxes enables you to choose the information you don't want to synchronize.

26. Read the details of the powers you're about to assign to the Exchange Server. Scroll down to see the full list of horrors.

27. Tap Activate.

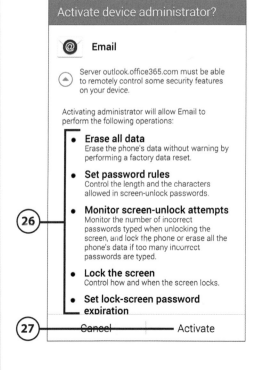

28. Enter a name for this email account. Use something meaning-ful that describes the purpose of the account, such as Exchange (Work).

29. Tap Done to complete the setup.

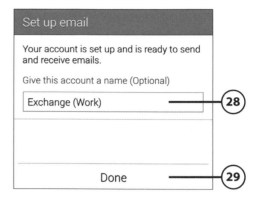

Removing an Account

To remove an account, open the Settings screen and tap the Personalization tab to display the Personalization screen. Tap Accounts to display the Accounts screen and then tap the account to be removed. On the screen for the account, tap the Menu button and then tap Remove Account.

Navigating Contacts

The Contacts app consists of four screens: Keypad, Logs, Favorites, and Con-tacts. Normally, the Contacts app displays the Contacts screen first, showing your list of contacts, but you can navigate to any of the other screens by tap-ping its tab.

1. From the Home screen, tap the Contacts icon. If the Contacts icon doesn't appear on the Home screen, tap it on the Apps screen.

2. Tap the + icon to add a new contact.

3. Tap Keypad to switch to the Phone app. From the resulting screen, you can dial a number on the keypad.

4. Tap Logs to display your call logs.

5. Tap Favorites to see your list of favorite contacts.

6. Tap Contacts to see all contacts.

7. Tap Groups to see your contact groups. See more information about creating contact groups in the later section titled "Create Contact Groups."

8. Tap the Search box to search for a contact.

9. Tap a contact to see all information about her.

10. Tap a contact picture (or picture placeholder) to see the Quick Connect bar.

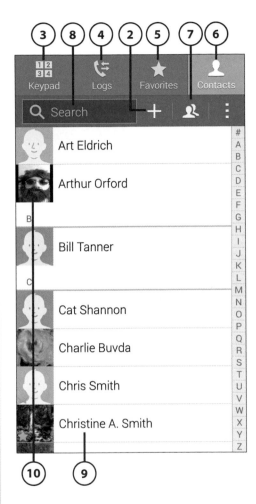

Quick Connect Bar

When you tap a contact picture, the Quick Connect bar appears. This bar enables you to quickly access different ways of communicating with the contact. If the icon list extends off the screen, swipe left to reveal further icons.

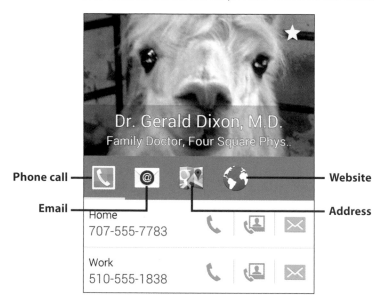

Phone call —
Email —
Website —
Address —

Home
707-555-7783

Work
510-555-1838

Check a Contact's Status

If you have added contacts that belong to social networks such as Facebook, you can check their statuses right from the Contacts app.

1. Tap a contact to display the contact record.

2. Tap the Facebook icon to view the contact's Facebook profile.

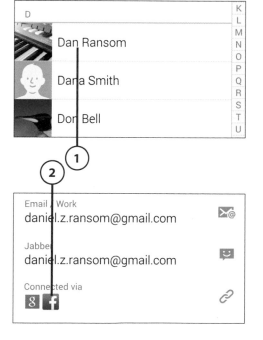

Edit a Contact

When you need to, you can easily change a contact's existing information or add further information to it.

1. Tap the contact you want to edit. The contact record appears.

2. Tap the Edit icon (the pencil) to open the contact record for editing.

3. Tap the downward caret to enter a name prefix, middle name, or name suffix.

4. Tap the – icon next to an existing field to delete it.

5. Tap a pop-up menu to change the field subcategory. For example, you can change an email address from Home to Work.

6. Tap the + icon to add a new field in a specific category. In this example, tapping + enables you to add a new phone number and choose its subcategory, such as Work.

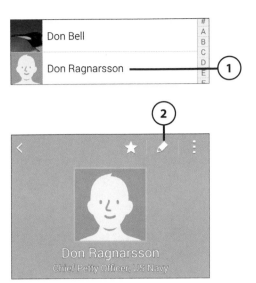

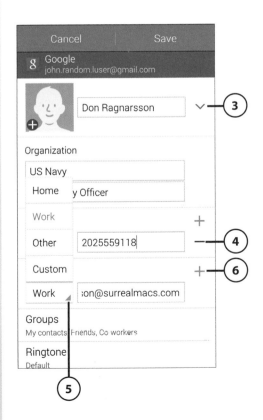

7. Tap Groups to put the contact in a contact group. The Galaxy Note 4 comes with built-in groups, including ICE – Emergency Contacts, Co-Workers, Family, and Friends, but you can also create as many other groups as you need.

8. Tap Ringtone to assign a different ringtone to calls from the contact. By giving important contacts distinctive ringtones, you can easily identify important calls.

9. Tap Message Tone to assign a distinctive noise to instant messages from the contact.

10. Tap Vibration Pattern to assign a different vibration pattern to calls from the contact. Vibration patterns help you identify important calls when you have silenced the ringer.

11. Tap Add Another Field to add a new field to the contact record. Extra fields include things such as the contact's phonetic name (to help you pronounce it correctly), IM (Instant Messaging) addresses, Notes, and Relationship, which you use to specify how someone is related to the contact—for example, an assistant or manager.

12. Tap Save to save the changes to the contact record.

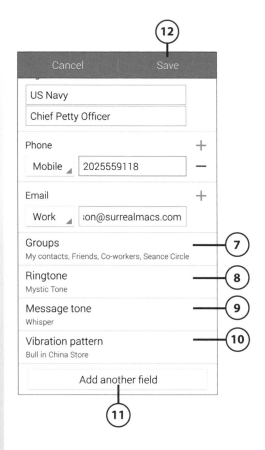

Add a Contact Photo

A contact record on your Galaxy Note 4 includes a contact photo when you link a social network account to the contact or when you import a contact record that includes a photo (for example, from a vCard file). You can manually add a picture as needed, either from an existing file or by taking a photo.

1. Tap the contact to open the contact record.

2. Tap the Edit icon (the pencil) to open the record for editing.

3. Tap the contact photo to open the Contact Photo screen.

4. Tap Image to add a photo already saved on your Galaxy Note 4.

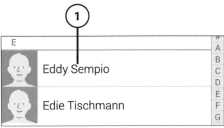

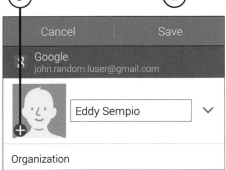

Add a photo tagged with people's names.

Take a photo with the camera.

Add an S Note to the contact record.

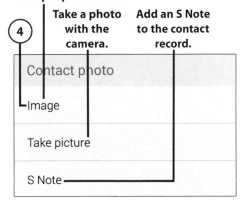

5. Tap the album that contains the photo.

6. Tap the photo you want to use.

7. Drag the cropping box to select the area of the photo you want to use for the contact photo.

8. Drag the outside of the cropping box to expand or contract it, as needed.

9. Tap Save to save the cropped photo as the contact photo.

Adding and Managing Contacts

As you add contacts to your work email account or Google account, those contacts are synchronized to your Galaxy Note 4 automatically. When you reply to or forward emails on your Galaxy Note 4 to an email address that is not in your Contacts, those email addresses are automatically added to the contact list or merged into an existing contact with the same name. You can also add contacts to your Galaxy Note 4 directly.

Add a Contact from an Email

To manually add a contact from an email, first open the email client (either Email or Gmail) and then open a message. See Chapter 4, "Email," for more on how to work with email.

1. Tap the blank contact picture to the left of the sender's name.

2. Tap Create Contact to open the Save Contact To screen.

3. Tap the Account pop-up menu.

4. Tap the account to which you want to save the contact.

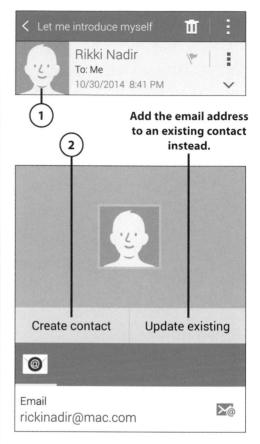

Add the email address to an existing contact instead.

Create contact   Update existing

Email
rickinadir@mac.com

5. If the Change Save Location screen opens, warning you that some contact information may be lost, tap OK.

6. Type the contact's name if Contacts has not picked it up from the email message.

7. Tap Save to save the contact.

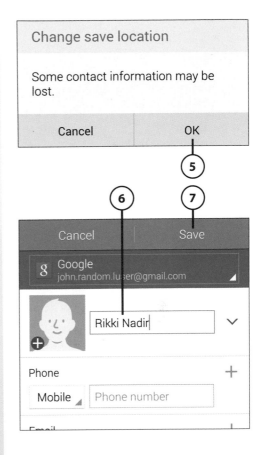

Add a Contact Manually

1. Tap the Contacts icon on the Home screen.

2. Tap New (+) to add a new contact.

3. Tap the pop-up menu to select the account you want to add the new contact to. For example, you might add the new contact to your work email account instead of to your personal account.

4. Type the person's full name, including any middle name. Your Galaxy Note 4 automatically populates the first name, middle name, and last name fields.

5. Tap the photo placeholder to choose a contact picture.

6. Tap Add Another Field to display the Add Another Field screen, where you can add other fields such as Nickname and Events.

7. Tap Save to save the new contact.

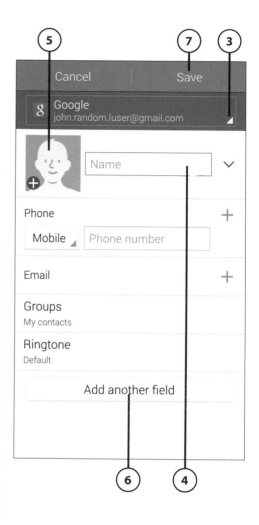

Add a Contact from a vCard

A vCard is a file that contains a virtual business card, which can include a contact's name, job title, email address, physical address, phone numbers, and so on. You can easily exchange vCards with other people by attaching them to email messages or instant messages. When you receive a vCard, you can import it into the Contacts app as a new contact by using the following steps:

1. Tap the attachment's button to display the Attachments screen.

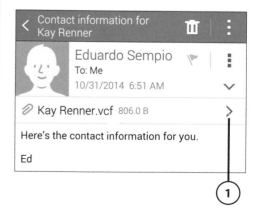

2. Tap Preview to display a preview of the vCard file.

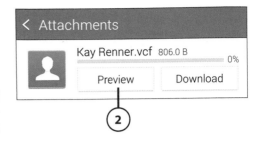

Choosing the App for vCard Files

If your Galaxy Note 4 displays the Complete Action Using dialog when you tap View to open a vCard file, tap Contacts and then tap Always.

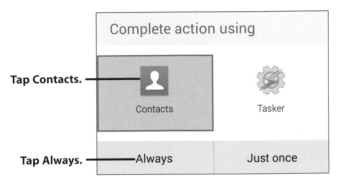

Tap Contacts.

Tap Always.

3. Tap the Save button. The Create Contact Under Account dialog opens.

4. Tap the account you want to add the new contact to. For example, you might want to add the new contact to your work email account instead of to your personal account.

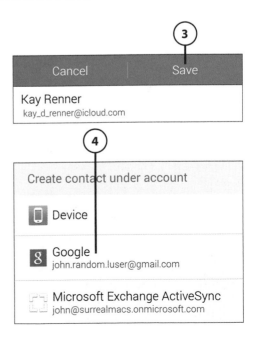

Add a Contact Using Near Field Communications

Your Galaxy Note 4 has Near Field Communications (NFC) functionality built in. NFC (discussed in Chapter 1, "Connecting to Bluetooth, Wi-Fi, and VPNs") enables you to exchange contact cards between NFC-enabled smartphones or to purchase items in a store by holding your Galaxy Note 4 near the NFC reader at the checkout counter. If you encounter someone who has an NFC-enabled smartphone, or she has an NFC tag that contains her business card, follow these steps to import that information:

1. Hold the other person's smartphone back to back with your Galaxy Note 4 and give the command for sharing via NFC, or hold the NFC tag close to the back cover of your Galaxy Note 4. Your Galaxy Note 4's screen dims and the phone plays a tone to indicate that it is reading the NFC information.

2. Tap to select which account you want to add the new contact to. For example, you might want to add the new contact to your work email account instead of to your personal account.

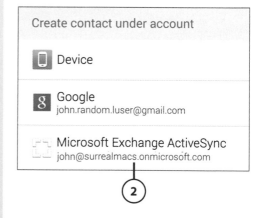

Manage Contacts Settings

To make the Contacts app display contacts the way you prefer, you can customize it. For example, you can choose the contact list display order and whether to display contacts using their first names first or last names first.

1. Tap the Contacts icon on the Home screen.

2. Tap the Menu button.

3. Tap Settings to display the Settings screen, which enables you to choose between Call settings and Contacts settings.

4. Tap Contacts to display the Settings screen for contacts.

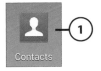

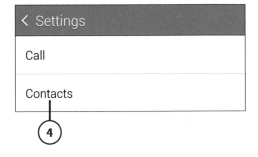

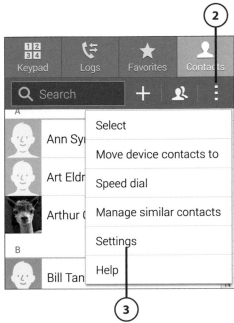

5. Check the Only Contacts with Phones box if you want the Contacts app to display only those contacts for whom you have phone numbers.

6. Tap Sort By to choose the sort order of the list of contacts in the Contacts app. You can sort the list by first name or last name.

7. Tap Display Contacts By to choose how each contact is displayed. You can display contacts with the first name first or the last name first.

8. Tap Settings or the Back button twice to save the settings and return to the Contacts app.

< Settings

Import/Export contacts

Contacts to display

Swipe to call or message ✓

Only contacts with phones
Display contacts with phone numbers and hide other contacts.

Sort by
First name

Display contacts by
First name first

Service numbers

Send multiple name cards
Send together

Online search ✓

Create Contact Groups

You can create contact groups—such as Friends, Family, Inner Circle—and then divide your contacts among them. This can be useful if you don't want to search through all your contacts. For example, to find a family member, you can simply tap the Family group and see only family members.

1. On the Contacts screen, tap the Groups icon to display the Groups screen.

2. Tap the New (+) button to display the New Group screen.

3. Tap Create Group In and then select the accounts in which to create the group.

4. Tap Group Name and type a name for your new group.

5. Optionally, tap Group Ringtone to set a specific ringtone for the group. You can use the ringtone and vibration pattern to make calls from the group easy to distinguish.

6. Optionally, tap Group Message Tone to set a distinctive message alert tone for the group.

7. Optionally, tap Group Vibration Pattern to set a specific vibration pattern for the group.

8. Tap Add Member to add members to the group.

9. Tap the check box next to each contact's name to select the members of the group.

10. Tap Done.

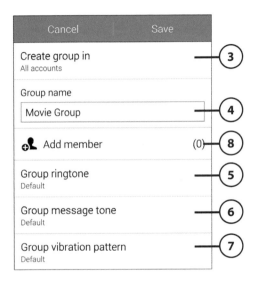

You can tap Search and type search text to find contacts quickly.

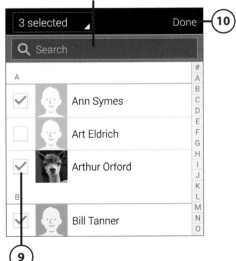

11. Tap Save to save the group.

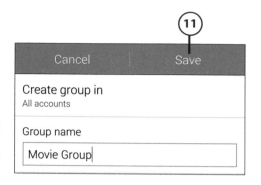

Change the Contacts in a Contacts Group

1. On the Contacts screen, tap the Groups button to display the Groups screen.

2. Tap the group to edit.

3. Tap the Add (+) button to add a contact to the group. On the resulting screen, check the box for each contact you want to add and then tap Done.

4. To remove contacts, tap and hold any contact until the screen displays selection controls.

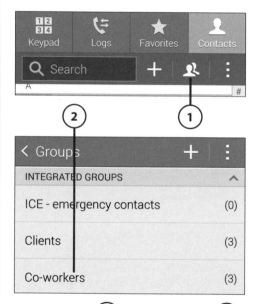

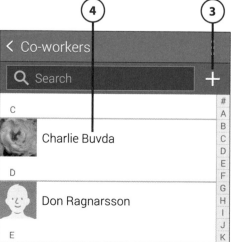

5. Check the box for each contact you want to remove.

6. Tap the Delete icon (the trash can) to remove the contacts.

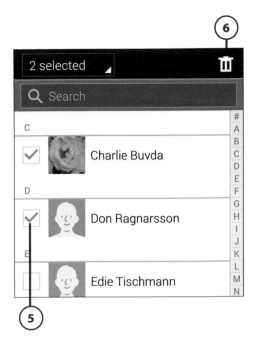

Choose Which Contacts to Display

You can choose to hide certain contact groups from the main contacts display. For example, you can choose to show only contacts from Twitter. You can also choose which contact groups in each account to include.

1. Tap the Contacts icon on the Home screen.

2. Tap the Menu button.

3. Tap Settings to display the Settings screen, which enables you to choose between Call settings and Contacts settings.

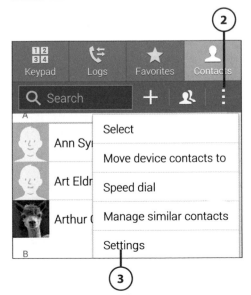

4. Tap Contacts to display the Settings screen for contacts.

5. Tap Contacts to Display to show the Contacts to Display screen.

6. Tap All Contacts to display all contacts from all accounts.

7. Tap an account to show only contacts in that account.

8. Tap Customized List to choose a customized selection.

9. Tap the Settings icon (the cog) to customize which groups in each account are displayed.

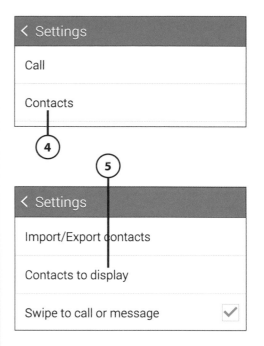

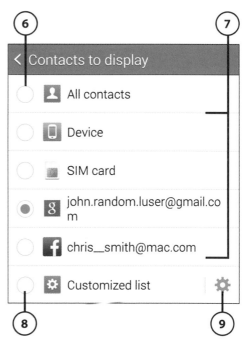

10. Tap a downward caret to expand an account to see subgroups of contacts. Tap the resulting upward caret to collapse an account again, hiding its subgroups.

11. Tap a check box to select or deselect a subgroup of contacts.

12. Tap Done to save your settings.

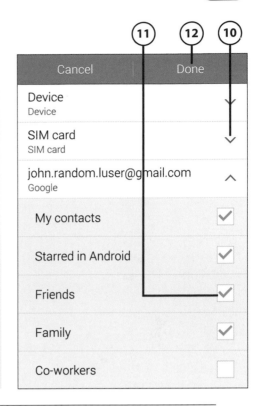

The Quick Way to the Contacts to Display Screen

After you use the Contacts to Display screen to choose a contact selection other than All Contacts, the Contacts screen displays a heading to indicate which contacts you're viewing. For example, the heading shows Contacts in Custom View when you have chosen the Customized List option; when you choose an account, the heading shows "Contacts in" and the account name. You can tap this heading to jump straight to the Contacts to Display screen, enabling you to change the contact selection easily.

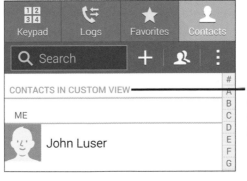

Tap the heading to go straight to the Contacts to Display screen.

Link and Unlink Contacts

As you add contacts to your Galaxy Note 4, they are automatically linked if the new contact name matches a name that's already stored. Sometimes you need to manually link contacts or unlink them if your Galaxy Note 4 has joined them in error.

Link Contacts Manually

1. In the Contacts app, tap the contact you want to link a contact to. The contact record opens.

2. Tap the Menu button.

3. Tap Link Contacts to display the Link Contact screen. The Suggestions list shows contacts in which Contacts has found apparently suitable data, but you can choose a contact from the main list if necessary.

4. Check the box for each contact you want to link with.

5. Tap Done to link the contacts.

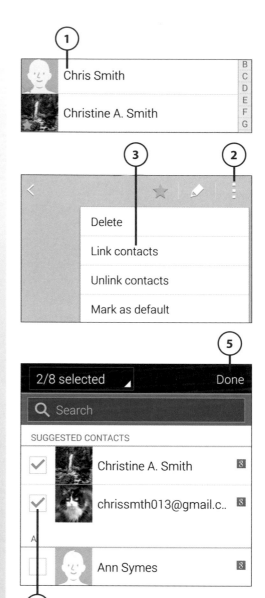

Unlink Contacts

1. In the Contacts app, tap the contact you want to unlink. The contact record opens.

2. Tap the Menu button.

3. Tap Unlink Contacts to display the Linked Contact screen.

4. Tap the red – icon to the right of each contact you want to unlink.

5. Tap Linked Contact or the Back button to return to the contact record.

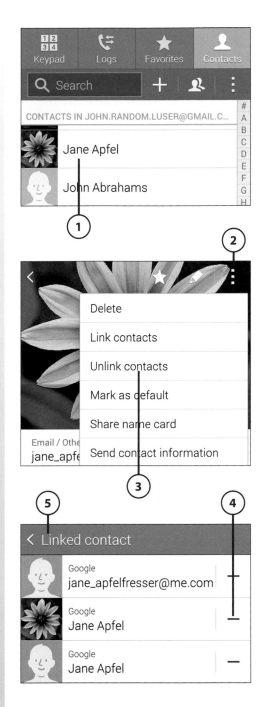

Adding a Contact to Your Home Screen

If you communicate with some contacts so much that you are constantly opening and closing the Contacts application, you can save time and effort by adding a shortcut to each of those contacts on the Home screen.

1. On the Home screen, tap and hold the Recents button until the customization controls appear.

2. Tap Widgets and then swipe left until you see the Contacts widget.

3. Tap the Contacts widget folder to display its contents.

4. Tap and hold the appropriate contact widget: Tap Contact 1 × 1 if you just want to open the contact. Tap Direct Dial 1 × 1 if you want to dial the contact directly from the Home screen, or tap Direct Message 1 × 1 if you want to message the contact from the icon. This example uses Contact 1 × 1.

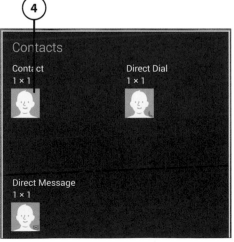

5. While still holding the widget, drag it where you want it on the Home screen, and then release your finger. The Select Contact Shortcut screen appears.

6. Tap the contact you want to add to the Home screen.

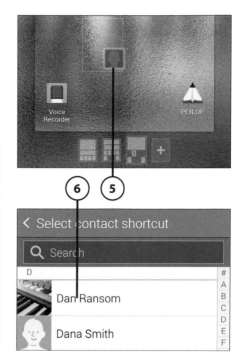

>>>Go Further

IMPORTING AND EXPORTING CONTACTS

You can import any contacts that are stored on your SIM or vCards that you have saved to your Galaxy Note 4's internal storage. You can also export your entire contact list to your Galaxy Note 4's SIM card or to a USB storage device. To access the import/export functions, open the Contacts app, tap the Menu button, and then tap Settings. On the first Settings screen, tap Contacts to display the Settings screen for contacts. You can then tap Import/Export Contacts to display the Import/Export Contacts dialog, where you choose the action to take.

Tap to import contacts from the SIM card.

Last interactions
with the caller

Turn your current call
into a conference call.

In this chapter, you find out how to make and take phone calls and send instant messages on your Galaxy Note 4. Topics include the following:

→ Making phone calls

→ Making conference calls

→ Sending and receiving text messages

→ Sending and receiving multimedia messages

Phone, SMS, and MMS

As a cellular phone, your Galaxy Note 4 includes powerful features that enable you to make phone calls swiftly and easily. Your Galaxy Note 4 can also send both text messages and multimedia messages by using the Messaging app.

Phone

With the Phone app, you can quickly make and receive calls across the cellular network. When you need to talk to more than one other person, you can turn your current call into a conference call.

Open and Navigate the Phone App

The Phone app contains four tabs that enable you to make calls in various ways and to track the calls you receive.

1. On the Home screen, tap Phone.

2. Tap the keys to dial a number.

3. If the Phone app displays a suggested contact with a matching number, you can tap the contact if it is the one you want.

4. Tap to place the call.

5. Tap Logs to see a list of the calls you have placed and received.

Making Your Logs Display the Information You Need

At first, the Phone app displays all your logs, but you can narrow the view to specific logs so you can more easily find the calls and messages you need. You find out how to do this later in this chapter.

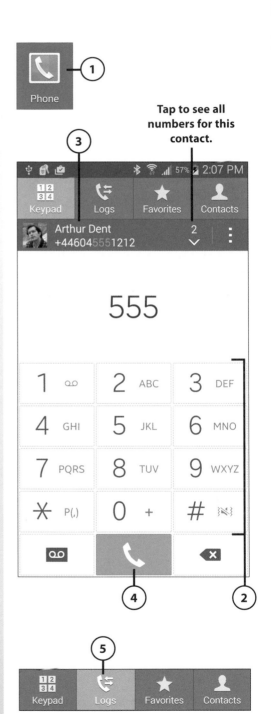

Tap to see all numbers for this contact.

6. Tap Favorites to see lists of Favorites and Frequently Contacted contacts.

7. Tap Contacts to display your full contacts list.

8. Tap Keypad to return to the keypad screen.

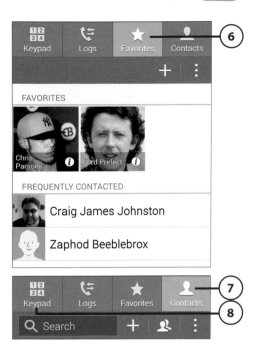

Receive a Call

When someone phones your Galaxy Note 4, you can accept the call, reject it, or reject it and send a text message.

Accept a Call

1. When the phone rings, look at the contact name (if it is available) or the phone number (if it is not) and decide whether to take the call.

2. Swipe the green phone icon to the right to accept the call.

3. Tap to switch to the speaker.

4. Tap to switch to the Bluetooth headset.

5. Tap to mute the call. Tap again to turn off muting.

6. Tap to show the keypad if you need to type extra numbers after the call is connected.

7. Tap to end the call.

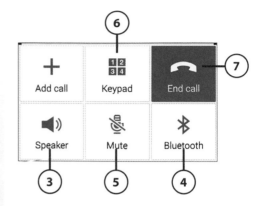

>>>Go Further
EXTRA FUNCTIONS WHILE ON A CALL

While on a call you can do a few additional things if you tap the Menu icon. You can put the call on hold; open your contacts; write an Action Memo using your S Pen and send it to the caller using MMS; send a regular text message to the caller; personalize the sound of the call; and boost the volume of the caller's voice.

Reject a Call

If you do not want to accept the call, you can reject it so that it goes to your voicemail.

1. When the phone rings, swipe the red phone icon to the left to reject the call.

The call goes to voicemail, and your Galaxy Note 4 displays the screen you were using before the call came in.

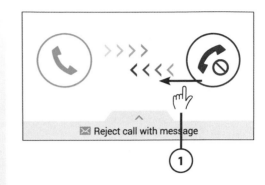

Reject a Call and Send a Message

Instead of simply declining a call and sending it to your voicemail, you can send a text message straight back to the caller. Your Galaxy Note 4 provides a selection of canned messages for general needs. You can also create your own messages or type custom messages for particular calls.

1. When the phone rings, swipe the Reject Call with Message shade up.

2. Tap to send one of the canned messages.

Creating Your Own Reject Messages

To create and save your own reject messages, open the Phone app and tap the Menu icon. On the menu, tap Call. On the Call Settings screen, tap Call Rejection and then tap Set Up Call Rejection Messages. On the Reject Messages screen, tap the plus symbol to create a new rejection message, or tap an existing message to open it for editing. You can have a maximum of six call-rejection messages.

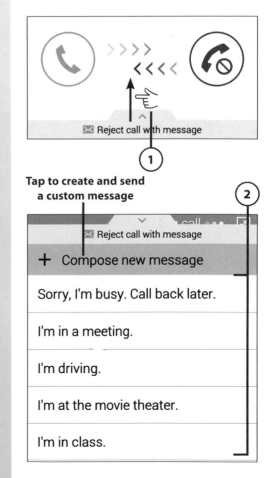

Tap to create and send a custom message

Handle Missed Calls

If you miss a phone call, you can quickly locate it in the Phone app's logs so that you can return it, but you can also take actions on missed calls from the lock screen or any other screen.

1. Tap to see the missed call from the lock screen. If you use a lock screen password or other method of locking your Note 4, you are required to use that method to unlock your Note 4 before you can continue.

2. If the Logs tab is not displayed, tap to display it.

3. If you want to change the type of log displayed, tap All Calls.

4. Choose how to filter the calls. For example, tap Missed Calls or Dialed Calls.

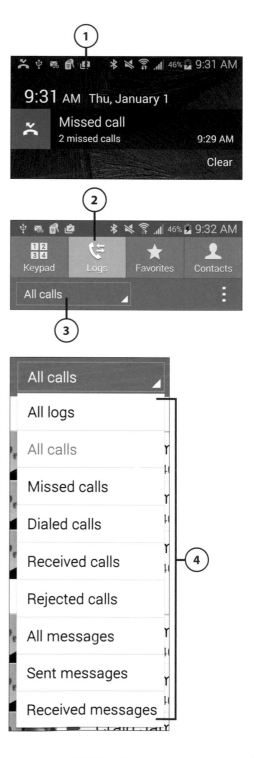

5. Tap a call to see its details.

6. Tap the Menu icon for more options.

7. Tap to view the caller's full contact information (if you already have the person in your Contacts).

8. Tap to send the caller's number to someone via text message (SMS).

9. Tap to add the caller to the reject list. This makes your Note 4 automatically reject calls from this person.

10. Tap to delete one or more call log entries for this person.

11. Tap to send the caller a text message.

12. Tap to return the call.

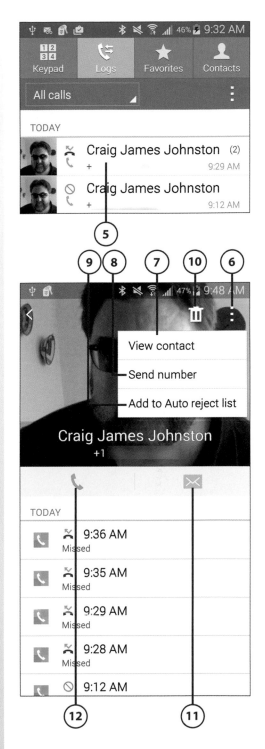

Place a Call

When you need to make a phone call, you can dial it manually using the keypad. But usually you can make a call more quickly by placing it from a contact entry or by using your voice.

Dial with the Keypad

You can use the keypad to dial a call both when you need to call a number for which you do not have a contact and when you can remember only part of the number for a contact.

1. Start typing the phone number. If you are typing to recall a number, type the part you remember.

2. If Phone suggests the correct number, tap to dial it.

3. Tap to dial the number you have typed if no matches were found.

Dial from a Contact Entry

If you know you have a contact entry for the person you want to dial, you can start from that contact entry.

1. In the Phone app, tap the Contacts tab. Your Note 4 switches from the Phone app to the Contacts app.

2. Tap the contact to display the contact's details.

Tap to see all numbers for the contact.

Use the search bar to find contacts quickly.

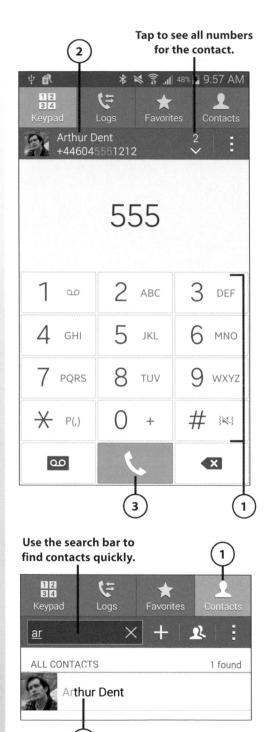

Starting a Call from the Contacts App

Instead of launching the Phone app and then tapping the Contacts tab to go to the Contacts app, you can start a call directly from the Contacts app. Tap Contacts on the Home screen or the Apps screen to launch the Contacts app, tap the contact to display his or her details, and then tap the Call button.

Arthur Dent
Earth Man

Mobile
+44 604 555-1212

Home
+44 604 555-1967

③

3. Tap the number you want to call.

Dial Using Your Voice

Your Galaxy Note 4 also enables you to dial calls using your voice.

1. Double-press the Home button to launch S Voice.

2. Say "Call," followed by the contact's name; if the contact has multiple phone numbers, say the type of number as well. For example, say "Call Dana Smith mobile" or "Call Craig at Home."

②

Call Craig at home

Tap Mic

3. Wait while S Voice dials the number. The Dialing screen appears.

>>>Go Further
SPEED DIAL

Speed dialing is a bit of a holdover from the 1980s and 1990s, where you can assign a phone number to a button on your phone. However, you may still find it useful to touch and hold one key to call a number. To add or edit your speed dial numbers, tap the Menu icon and tap Speed Dial. (Voicemail is already assigned to speed dial 1.) Tap the plus symbol to add a new speed dial. To use Speed Dial, while the keypad is visible, touch and hold a number associated with a speed dial. That number will be dialed.

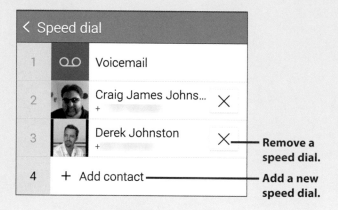

Remove a speed dial.

Add a new speed dial.

Using Other Apps During a Call

During a call, you can use most other apps freely, but you cannot play music or video. You can take photos with the Camera app, but you cannot shoot videos. To switch to another app, either use the Recent Apps list or press the Home button and use the Apps screen as usual. While you are using another app, your Galaxy Note 4 displays a green bar at the top of the screen to remind you that you are in a call. Pull down the Notifications panel to control the call or return to it. You will also see an in-call pop-up window. You can drag the in-call pop-up window anywhere on the screen, and tap it to return to the in-progress call.

In-call pop-up

Green bar indicates call is in progress.

Tap to return to your call.

>>>Go Further
DRAG AND DROP ITEMS TO CALLERS

During a call, you can drag and drop text and images to the person you are talking to. Text is sent as an SMS (text) message, and images are sent as multimedia messages (MMS). Tap the minimize icon to minimize the call window. While the call window is minimized, you can drag it around the screen if you need to. Open the app you want to drag the content from—for example, images from the Gallery app. Drag the content to the green area within the minimized call window to send it.

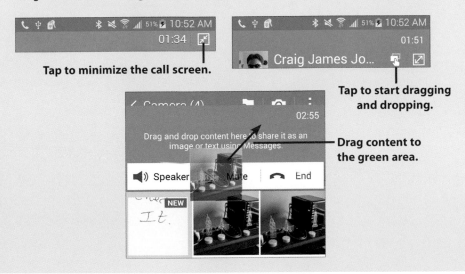

Tap to minimize the call screen.

Tap to start dragging and dropping.

Drag content to the green area.

Make Conference Calls

You can quickly turn your current call into a conference call by adding further participants.

1. With a call in progress, tap Add Call on the call screen.

2. Dial the call in the most convenient way. For example, tap the Contacts tab, tap the contact in the list, and then tap the Call button on the contact's details screen.

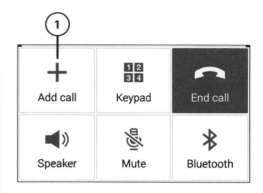

Tap to switch back to the call.

3. Tap to swap between the original call and the one you just added, if you need to.

4. Tap Merge to merge the calls and complete the conference call setup.

5. Repeat steps 1–4 to add additional callers. The exact number of callers you can have on a conference call is governed by your wireless carrier.

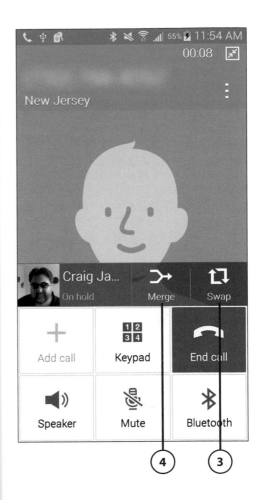

Configure the Phone App

To make the Phone app work your way, you can configure its settings.

1. Tap the Menu icon.

2. Tap Settings.

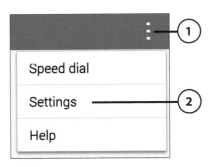

3. Tap Call (for call settings).

4. Tap to choose certain numbers for which calls will be automatically rejected. Tapping here also lets you edit your canned call rejection messages.

What Does Call Rejection Do?

Your Galaxy Note 4's call rejection mode can automatically reject either all calls or only the numbers on a list you provide. Automatically rejecting all calls can be useful when you're at meetings and social occasions when you do not want to be disturbed. Automatically rejecting specific numbers enables you to avoid calls from people you do not want to talk to. You can turn Auto Reject mode on and off by moving the Auto Reject Mode switch.

5. Tap to choose whether you want to use Voice over LTE (VoLTE) when it is available.

6. Tap to choose how you want to answer and end calls. You can choose to use your voice (saying "answer" or "reject"), press the Home button, or press the power button.

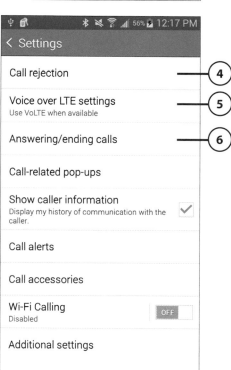

What Is VoLTE?

Firstly, LTE (or Long-Term Evolution) is the fourth generation of cellular data technology (not to be confused with the slightly faster version of 3G technology that has been incorrectly called 4G for years). VoLTE stands for Voice over LTE. Effectively, your voice call is sent as regular data over the LTE data channel as opposed to over the cellular voice channel. Voice quality is much better due to the higher rate at with the data is transmitted and received, and if the person you are calling also uses VoLTE, you can speak at the same time. Most wireless carriers treat VoLTE as regular voice minutes and don't let it count against your data plan. However, you should verify the situation with your local wireless carrier; otherwise, your data plan might take an unexpected hit.

7. Tap to control what call-related pop-up windows you see when you receive a call and when you navigate away from the Phone app while on a call.

8. Check the box to see onscreen information about your recent communication with the caller while the phone is ringing and while on the call. This information includes recent calls, text messages, and emails.

9. Tap to choose options for vibrations, cell status tones, and alerts during calls. You can choose whether your Galaxy Note 4 vibrates when someone answers your call and when they hang up. You can also choose which status tones and alerts to receive during calls and which to suppress.

10. Tap to choose how to handle accessories such as Bluetooth headsets. You can decide if you want calls automatically answered when you have the headset plugged in or connected via Bluetooth (this includes your car's built-in Bluetooth), and if you want to be able to make outgoing calls even if your Note 4's screen is locked while you are using a Bluetooth headset.

11. Tap to enable or disable Wi-Fi Calling.

12. Scroll down for more settings.

What Is Wi-Fi Calling?

The technical name for Wi-Fi Calling is Universal Media Access (UMA). This technology is provided by some carriers around the world and enables your Galaxy Note 4 to roam between the cellular network and Wi-Fi networks. Typically when you are connected to a Wi-Fi network, any calls you make are free and of higher audio quality because of the faster speeds. As you move out of Wi-Fi coverage, your Note 4 hands the call off to the cellular network—and vice versa—allowing your call to continue without interruption. If you want to read more about UMA or Wi-Fi Calling, read this online article: http://crackberry.com/saving-call-charges-recession-your-blackberry. The article is on a BlackBerry blog, but the descriptions of the technology still apply.

13. Tap to see additional settings, including how Caller ID is handled, call forwarding, call waiting, and Fixed Dialing Numbers (FDN). When you tap, the settings are loaded over the wireless network, so you might need to wait a few seconds before they appear.

14. Tap to choose the ringtone and vibration pattern for incoming calls, whether to play the ringtone and vibrate at the same time, and whether to play the keypad tones.

15. Choose to customize how the audio on phone calls sounds. You can choose from among Soft Sound, Clear Sound, and Adapt Sound, or choose Off to use standard audio. If you choose Adapt Sound, you're asked to go through steps to set it up while wearing a headset.

16. Tap to enable or disable noise reduction by default while on a call. Noise reduction uses the additional microphones on your Note 4 to reduce background noise.

17. Tap to choose which voicemail service to use (if you have more than one option). If you use Google Voice, it is common to use the Google Voice voicemail system as opposed to the one provided by your wireless carrier.

18. Tap to adjust voicemail settings (if options are available).

19. Tap to choose your ringtone for announcing voicemail.

20. Tap to choose vibration settings for voicemail.

21. Tap to save your changes and return to the main phone screen.

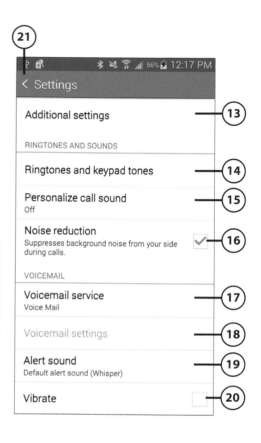

SMS and MMS

Short Message Service (SMS), also known as text messaging, has been around for a long time. Multimedia Message Service (MMS) is a newer form of text messaging that can contain pictures, audio, and video as well as text. Your Galaxy Note 4 can send and receive both SMS and MMS messages.

Get to Know the Messages App

The Messages app is what you use to send and receive text messages. This app has all the features you need to compose, send, receive, and manage these messages.

1. Tap the Messages icon.

2. Tap to compose a new text message.

3. Tap the picture of someone who has sent you a message to show the Quick Connect bar that allows you to contact the person using email, phone, and other methods.

4. Tap a message thread to open it.

5. Tap the Menu icon to see more options.

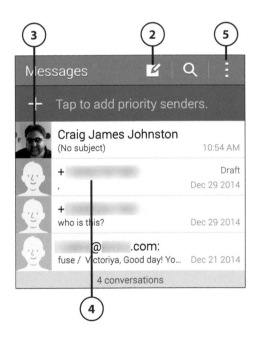

6. Tap to select one or more message threads and delete them or mark them as spam.

7. Tap to open the Locked Messages folder. Locked messages are messages that you have chosen to lock so they are not accidentally deleted. See the "How Do I Lock Messages?" margin note for more information.

8. Tap to open the Spam Messages folder.

9. Tap to select from a list of Quick Responses to send and manage the current Quick Responses. When you select a Quick Response, a new message opens with that Quick Response added to the text field.

10. Tap to choose to use your Note 4's built-in font size, or select a smaller or larger size while you have the Messages app open.

11. Tap to open the Settings screen. See the next section for more on Settings.

How Do I Lock a Message?

You might want to lock a message so that it does not get accidentally deleted when you delete the message thread. To lock a message, touch and hold on the message and choose Lock when the menu pops up. The lock symbol displays just below the locked message. To unlock the message, touch and hold on the message and choose Unlock.

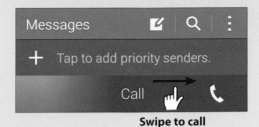
Manage Settings for the Messages App

You use the settings of the Messages app to manage how the app handles your SMS and MMS messages. Before you actually start working with SMS and MMS, let's take a look at the settings.

1. Tap the Menu icon.

2. Tap Settings.

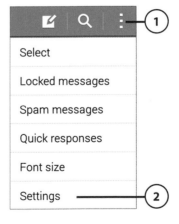

3. Tap to change the default messaging app from Messages to Google Hangouts. If you use Google Hangouts a lot for text and video chatting, you may decide that using it for text and multimedia messages makes sense. Read more about using Google Hangouts in the "Using Google Hangouts for SMS and MMS" sidebar at the end of this chapter.

4. Tap to manage how the Messages app looks. You can choose what kind of bubble style is used for text message display, choose which background the app uses for messages, choose to use a split view when you turn your Galaxy Note 4 to landscape orientation, and enable changing text size by pressing the volume buttons.

5. Tap to control and manage text messages. This includes choosing to receive a delivery report for text messages you send, choosing the input mode (leaving it set to Automatic is recommended), and managing text messages that may still be on your old SIM card.

6. Tap to control how the Messages app handles multimedia messages. Settings include the ability to request delivery and read reports and as well as to control whether to automatically retrieve multimedia messages while roaming outside your wireless carrier's home area.

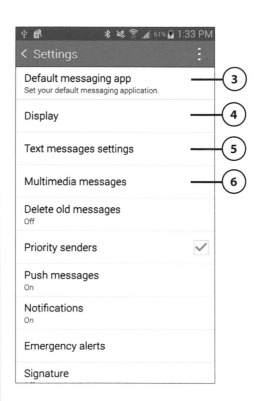

What Does the Manage SIM Card Messages Option Do?

Many old cell phones store text messages on the SIM card and not in the phone's memory. If you have just upgraded from an older phone, you might still have text messages on the SIM card that you would like to retrieve. If you choose the option to manage text messages on your SIM card, as mentioned in step 5, you can then copy the messages to your Galaxy Note 4's memory and copy the senders to your contacts in the Contacts app.

Don't Auto-Retrieve MMS While Roaming

Disable the automatic retrieval of multimedia messages when you travel to other countries because automatically retrieving these messages when you're roaming can result in a big bill from your provider. International carriers love to charge large amounts of money for people traveling to their countries and using their networks. The only time it is a good idea to leave this enabled is if your carrier offers an international SMS or MMS bundle, where you pay a flat rate up front before leaving. When you have the auto-retrieve feature disabled, you see a Download button next to a multimedia message. You have to tap it to manually download the message.

7. Tap to enable or disable automatically deleting old text or multimedia messages when the limit you set is reached. When the limit is reached, messages within the thread or conversation are deleted using the FIFO method.

8. Tap to enable or disable seeing the Priority Senders bar in the main Messages app screen.

9. Tap to enable or disable receiving messages "pushed" from the server. Push messages arrive at your Galaxy Note 4 shortly after they arrive at the server, which is usually faster than waiting until the Galaxy Note 4 checks for messages. You can also choose how to handle remote requests to load services. Your choices are Always, Prompt, and Never.

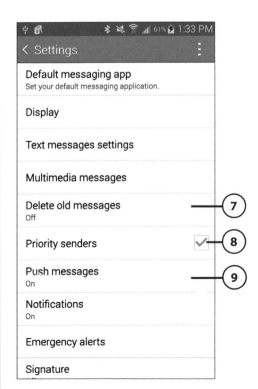

What Are Priority Senders?

If you choose to add priority senders, their names appear in the Priority Sender bar in the Messages app. This allows you to quickly tap their names to send them messages.

What Setting Should I Choose for Service Loading?

Samsung's Service Loading feature has been used for attacks that remotely wipe smartphones without the owner's consent. Because of this danger, never choose Always as the Service Loading setting. Choose Prompt if you want your Galaxy Note 4 to let you decide about service-loading requests. Choose Never if you prefer to suppress service-loading requests.

10. Tap to manage notifications for text and multimedia messages. You can also control the ringtone, whether your Note 4 vibrates, whether the alert repeats, and whether a preview of the message is displayed in the Notification bar or on the lock screen.

11. Tap to manage which emergency alerts you want to receive. These alerts are sent out by your government or law enforcement (for example, AMBER alerts).

12. Tap to turn on or off adding a signature to each message you send. Remember that the text in the signature counts against the text message size.

13. Scroll down for more settings.

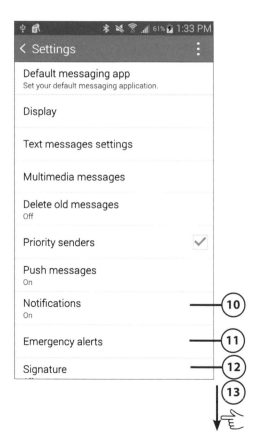

14. Tap to manage the settings for detecting spam messages. Spam messages are unwanted commercial messages. You can also choose what mobile numbers and text phrases are treated as spam.

15. Check the box to enable access to all links included in text or multimedia messages. When this is checked, you can tap a link to open it in the web browser.

16. Tap to save your changes and return to the previous screen.

Compose Messages

When you compose a new message, you do not need to make a conscious decision whether it is an SMS message or an MMS message. As soon as you add a subject line or attach a file to your message, your Galaxy Note 4 automatically treats the message as an MMS message.

Here is how to compose and send messages:

1. Tap the pencil compose icon to compose a new message.

2. Start typing the recipient's phone number, or if the person is in your contacts, type the name. If a match is found, tap the mobile number.

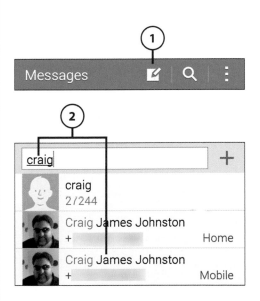

3. Tap and start typing your message.

4. Tap to send your message.

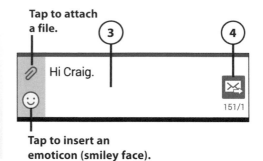

Tap to attach a file. ③

④

Hi Craig.

151/1

Tap to insert an emoticon (smiley face).

It's Not All Good

Inserting Smiley Icons

By tapping the smiling face icon, you can insert emoticons (also known as smiley faces). Just be aware that the very first emoticon you insert into a new text message counts as 92 characters. Each additional emoticon counts only one character each. Each text message is limited to 160 characters, so after inserting your first emoticon, you'll only have 68 characters left.

Delay Sending the Message

You might decide that you want a text message to be sent automatically at a later time. To do this, before sending the message, tap the Menu icon and choose Schedule Message. Choose the date and time you want your message to be sent and tap Done. Then tap the Send button, and your message will only send when you set it to.

What's the Difference Between a Delivery Report and a Read Report?

A delivery report indicates that the message has reached the destination device. A read report indicates that the message has been opened for viewing. There is still no guarantee that whoever opened the message has actually read it, let alone understood it.

>>>*Go Further*

MESSAGE LIMITS AND MESSAGES

Text messages can only be 160 characters long. To get around this limit, most modern phones simply break up text messages you type into 160-character chunks. Your Galaxy Note 4 displays a readout showing the number of characters remaining and the number of messages it will send: The readout starts at 160/1 when you begin a new message and runs down to 1/1; then it starts at 145/2 (fewer characters because there is some overhead in linking the messages). The phone receiving the message simply combines them into one message. This is important to know if your wireless plan has a text message limit. When you create one text message, your Galaxy Note 4 might actually break the message into two or more.

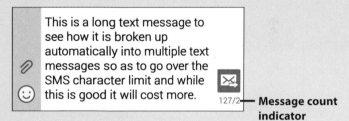

This is a long text message to see how it is broken up automatically into multiple text messages so as to go over the SMS character limit and while this is good it will cost more.

127/2 —— **Message count indicator**

Attach Files to Messages

If you want to send a picture, audio file, or video along with your text message, all you need to do is attach the file. Be aware that attaching a file turns your SMS text message into an MMS multimedia message and may be subject to additional charges.

1. Tap the paperclip icon to attach a file.

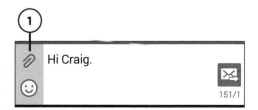

Hi Craig.

151/1

2. Tap to attach a picture already stored in your Gallery or Photos app.

3. Tap to take a picture using your Note 4's camera and attach it.

4. Tap to attach a video already stored in your Video app.

5. Tap to capture a video and attach it.

6. Tap to attach an audio file that is already stored on your Galaxy Note 4.

7. Tap to record audio and attach it.

8. Tap to attach an S Note document.

9. Tap to attach a calendar item.

10. Tap to attach your location.

11. Tap to attach a contact record from the Contacts app.

12. Tap to send your MMS.

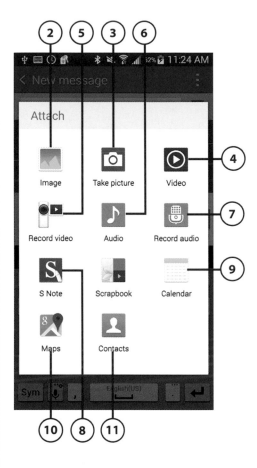

It's Not All Good

Is It Worth Attaching Files?

Attaching files to text messages is not as useful as you might desire. Most carriers limit the attachment size to around 300KB. This means that you can only really attach about 60 seconds of very low-quality video; pictures with low resolution, high compression, or both; and very short audio files. The Messaging app automatically compresses larger picture files to make them small enough to send, but you will often find that it simply refuses to send video files because they are too large. Choosing the option of capturing pictures, capturing video, or recording audio when you choose to attach is the only way you can guarantee that the files are small enough. This is because when you do this, the camera and audio recorder apps are set to a mode that makes them record low-quality audio and take low-quality pictures.

Receive Messages

When you receive a new SMS or MMS message, you can read it, view its attachments, and even save those attachments to your Galaxy Note 4.

1. When a new SMS or MMS message arrives, your Galaxy Note 4 plays a ringtone and displays a notification in the status bar.

2. Pull down the notification shade to see newly arrived messages.

3. Tap a message alert to display the message and reply to it.

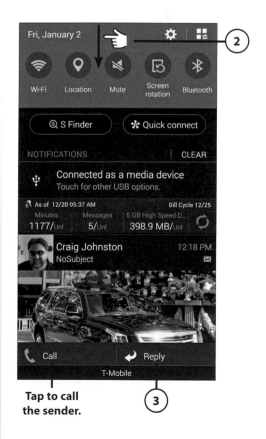

Tap to call
the sender.

4. Tap an attachment to open it for viewing.

5. Touch and hold a message to display the Message Options dialog. Skip to step 7 for more about the additional options.

6. Tap to write a reply to the message.

7. Tap to delete the message. This deletes just the message and not the entire thread.

8. Tap to view a slideshow of attached images.

9. Tap to copy the message text so you can paste it elsewhere.

10. Tap to forward the message and attachment to someone else.

11. Tap to lock the message against deletion if you later decide to delete the message thread.

12. Tap to save the attachment to your Galaxy Note 4.

13. Tap to share the message via social media or other methods.

14. Tap to view the message details, such as its size and the date and time it was sent.

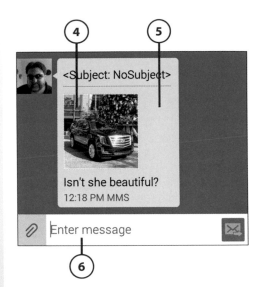

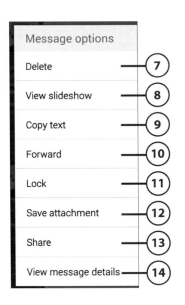

Usable Content

If a text message contains links to websites, phone numbers, or email addresses, tapping those links makes the Galaxy Note 4 take the appropriate action. For example, when you tap a phone number, your Galaxy Note 4 calls the number; when you tap a web link, the Galaxy Note 4 opens the page in Chrome or your other default browser.

>>>Go Further

USING GOOGLE HANGOUTS FOR SMS AND MMS

You may decide that because you already use Google Hangouts to instant message your friends and family, as well as to video chat with them, it makes sense to set the Google Hangouts app to handle text messages (SMS) and multimedia messages (MMS) so that all communications with your friends and family are in one place. To set this, from the Messages app, tap the Menu icon and tap Settings. Tap Default Messaging App and then choose Hangouts. The way in which you interact with SMS and MMS while using the Hangouts app is very similar to the way it works in the Messages app, so the steps in this chapter should help you. Even the settings for handling SMS and MMS are similar. When one of your contacts has signed up for a Google account and has started using Google Hangouts, you can switch from sending and receiving SMS and MMS messages with them and start using Hangouts messages instead. Doing this saves you from costly SMS and MMS charges and just uses your data plan.

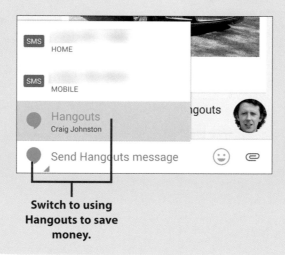

Switch to using Hangouts to save money.

Browse through and purchase music.

Search for music.

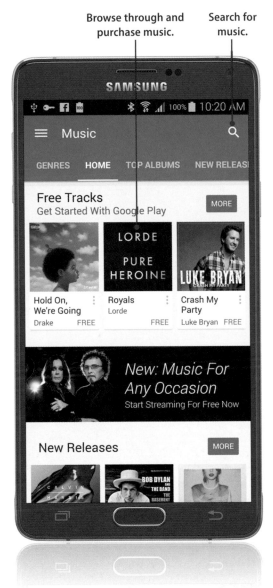

In this chapter, you discover your Galaxy Note 4's audio and video capabilities, including how your Galaxy Note 4 plays video and music as well as how you can synchronize audio and video from your desktop or laptop computer or Google Music. This chapter also covers how to take pictures and videos. Topics include the following:

9

→ Using Google Music for music
→ Using the Gallery app for pictures and video
→ Shooting still photos and videos
→ Enjoying videos with the YouTube app

Audio, Video, Photos, and Movies

Your Galaxy Note 4 is a powerful multimedia smartphone with the ability to play back many different audio and video formats. The large screen enables you to turn your Galaxy Note 4 sideways to enjoy a video in its original 16:9 ratio. You can also use your Galaxy Note 4 to take photos and videos, watch videos, and even upload videos to YouTube right from your phone. Android fully embraces the cloud, which enables you to store your music collection on Google's servers so you can access it anywhere.

Enjoying Music with the Music Application

To get the most out of music on your Galaxy Note 4, you probably want to use the Play Music app, which enables you to listen to music stored on your phone as well as from your collection in the Google Music cloud.

>>>Go Further

INSTALL THE PLAY MUSIC APP IF NECESSARY

If your Galaxy Note 4 does not include the Play Music app, you need to install it. Tap Apps on the Home screen and look through the list of apps. The Play Music app may appear either directly on the Apps screen or in a Google folder that gathers apps such as Chrome, Gmail, and Google+ together with Play Newsstand, Play Movies & TV, and Play Music.

If you don't find the Play Music app, tap the Apps icon on the Home screen and then tap the Play Store icon to open the Play Store app. Tap Apps, tap the search icon, and type **play music**. Tap the Google Play Music search result, tap Install, and then tap Accept & Download. Your Galaxy Note 4 downloads the Play Music app and installs it.

Find Music

When you're certain the Play Music app is installed on your Galaxy Note 4, you can add some music. One way to add music is to purchase it from Google.

1. Tap the Play Music icon on the Apps screen or in the Google folder.

2. Tap the Menu button in the upper-left corner to display the menu panel.

3. Tap Shop to display the Play Store screen.

4. Tap to see new releases.

5. Swipe right to see a list of music genres.

6. Swipe left or tap to see the Top Albums list. Swipe right again from the Top Albums list to see the Top Songs list.

7. Tap to search for music.

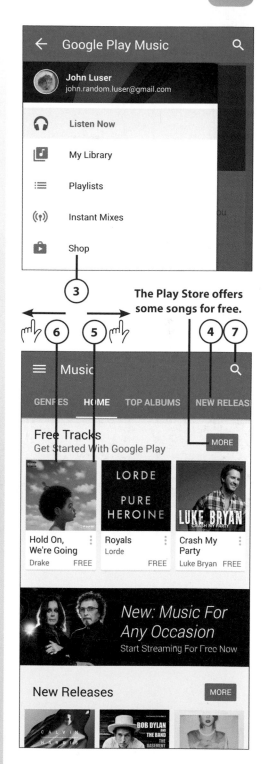

The Play Store offers some songs for free.

Purchase Music

After you find a song or album you want to purchase, use the following steps to make the purchase.

Free Music

Sometimes songs are offered for free. If a song is offered for free, you see the word "Free" instead of a price for the song. Even though the song is free, you still need to follow the steps outlined in this section; however, the price appears as 0.

1. Tap the price to the right of the song title or album.

2. Tap Buy. Google Play processes your payment, and Play Music downloads the song. You can then play it.

Tap to play a preview of the song before purchasing it.

Tap to change your payment method.

It's Not All Good

Cloud and Data Usage

Although cloud storage (where your music is stored on Google computers as opposed to on your Galaxy Note 4) can be very beneficial, it does mean that any time you listen to your music collection it is streamed over the network.

If you are connected to Wi-Fi, this data streaming is free; however, if you are not connected to Wi-Fi, the data is streamed over the cellular network and counts against your data package. If you don't have a large or unlimited data package, you could incur large overage fees, so please be careful. Be extra careful about this when traveling abroad because international data-roaming charges are very expensive.

Another disadvantage of streaming from the cloud is that when you have no cellular or Wi-Fi coverage, or you have very slow or spotty coverage, you are unable to access and listen to your music collection, or the songs stutter because of the poor connection.

Add Your Existing Music to Google Music

You can upload up to 20,000 songs from Apple iTunes, Microsoft Windows Media Player, or music stored in folders on your computer to your Google Music cloud account by using the Google Music Manager app on your desktop computer. If you haven't already installed Google Music Manager, follow the steps in the "Install Google Music Manager" section in the Prologue.

1. Click (right-click for Windows) the Google Music Manager icon. On the Mac, this icon appears in the menu bar at the top of the screen. On Windows, the icon appears in the taskbar at the bottom of the screen.

2. Choose Preferences on the Mac; choose Options on Windows.

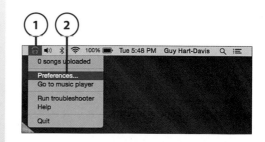

3.   Click Add Folder to add a folder of music to upload.

4.   Click Remove Folder to remove the folder you have selected in the list box from your Google Play account.

5.   Click Upload after you have made your selections.

6.   Select the Automatically Upload Songs Added to My Selected Folders check box to allow Google Music Manager to automatically upload new songs added to the folders you have specified.

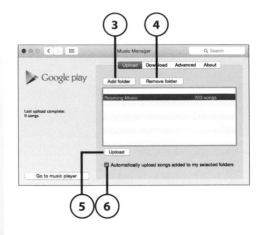

Automatic Upload

If you choose to have your music uploaded automatically in step 6, Google Music Manager continually monitors the folders you specified to see if music has been added. If Google Music Manager finds new music, it automatically uploads it. After you install Google Music Manager, the app runs continuously, enabling it to detect music you add to iTunes, Windows Media Player, or your Music folders.

Can I Download Music to My Computer?

You can download your entire music collection from Google Music to your computer, or just download music you have purchased on your Galaxy Note 4. While in Google Music Manager Preferences, click Download.

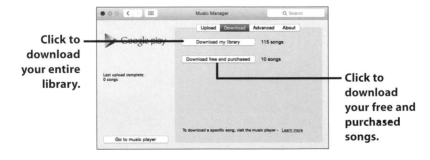

Click to download your entire library.

Click to download your free and purchased songs.

Use the Music Application

Now that you have synced some music to Google Music, and maybe bought some music online, it's time to take a look at how to use the Google Music app on your Galaxy Note 4.

Open and Navigate in the Music App

1. Tap the Play Music icon on the Apps screen or in the Google folder.

2. Tap the Menu button in the upper-left corner to display the This panel enables you to switch among your different sources of music. You can also open the menu panel by swiping right from the left edge of the screen.

3. Tap Listen Now on the menu panel to display the Listen Now screen, which contains music you have added recently. Listen Now also recommends music to you based on the music you have and your recent listening habits.

4. Tap My Library to display your music library. Your library contains both the music on your Galaxy Note 4 and the music in your Google account.

5. Tap Playlists to display the Playlists screen. The Play Music app automatically creates some playlists for you, and you can manually create as many other playlists as you want. Read more about playlists later in this chapter.

6. Tap Instant Mixes to display the Instant Mixes screen, which contains both instant mixes you create yourself and ones that Google Play recommends to you. An *instant mix* is a selection of songs based on—and supposedly related to—a particular starting song. For example, you can create an instant mix based on "Berzerk" or "Blurred Lines."

7. Tap Shop to switch to the Play Store app and go to the Music section of Google Play, where you can browse and buy music as explained earlier in this chapter.

Listen to Music in Your Library

1. Tap the Menu button in the upper-left corner to display the menu panel.

2. Tap My Library to display your music library.

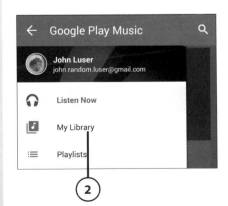

3. Tap to search for music using search terms.

4. Tap Genres to display the list of genres. You can then tap the genre by which you want to browse your library.

5. Tap Artists to display the list of artists so you can browse by artists.

6. Tap Albums to display the list of albums so you can browse by albums.

7. Tap Songs to display the list of songs. You can then easily locate a song by name in the alphabetical list.

8. Tap the Menu button on an item to display a pop-up menu of commands you can perform for that item. In this example, you can start an instant mix for this artist, shop the artist's music at the Play Store, or shuffle the artist's songs.

9. Tap the Play button or Pause button to control playback on the current song or most recent song played.

10. Tap an artist to display the albums and songs your library contains by that artist.

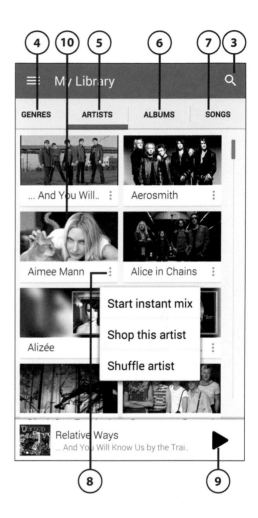

11. Tap the album you want to open. The album's songs appear.

The My Library section shows the items in your music library.

Tap Instant Mix to create an instant mix from this artist's songs.

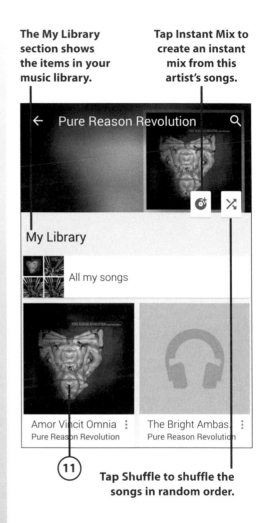

Tap Shuffle to shuffle the songs in random order.

12. Tap the song you want to start playing.

13. Tap Pause to pause playback. Tap the resulting Play button to start the music playing again.

14. Tap the album picture to display the Now Playing screen, which gives you full control of your music, as explained in the next section.

Indicates the song that is now playing (12)

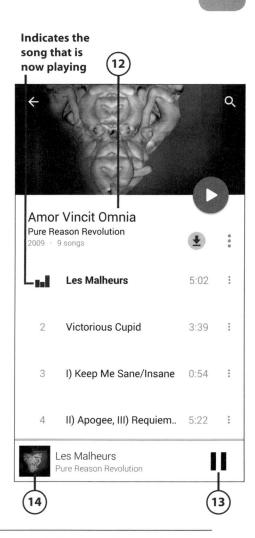

Switching Between Your Songs Online and Your Songs on the Galaxy Note 4

The Play Music app enables you to play both the songs you have stored on your Galaxy Note 4 and the songs you have uploaded to Google Music. By default, Play Music presents both the songs on your Galaxy Note 4 and songs on Google Music as being available: When you go to play a song that is stored on Google Music, the Play Music app streams it automatically for you.

When you don't want to stream songs across the Internet—for example, when you are using a cellular connection—you can set Play Music to show you only the songs on your Galaxy Note 4. To do so, tap the Menu button and then set the Downloaded Only switch to the On position (so it appears orange instead of gray).

Control Playback

While playing music, you can control both how the music plays and the selection of music that plays.

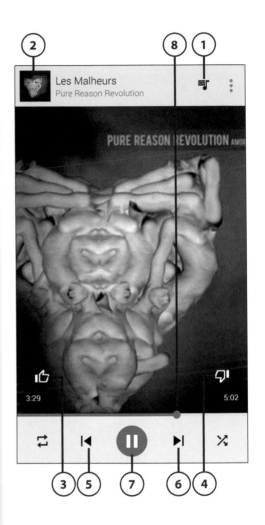

1. Tap the Queue icon to display the queue, which shows the songs that are lined up to play. You can then tap a song to start it playing.

2. Tap the album art to return from the Now Playing screen to the previous screen.

3. Tap the Like (thumbs-up) icon to indicate you like the song. The Like icon turns solid to indicate you have applied the rating. Tap again to remove the rating. The Google Music app also adds the song to the "Thumbs Up" playlist.

4. Tap the Dislike (thumbs-down) icon to indicate you do not like the song. The Dislike icon turns solid to indicate you have applied the rating, and Play Music starts playing the next song.

5. Tap Previous once to go back to the start of the current song. Tap again to skip back to the previous song in the album, playlist, or shuffle.

6. Tap Next to skip ahead to the next song in the album, playlist, or shuffle.

7. Tap Pause to pause the song. The button turns into the Play button when a song is paused. Tap Play to resume playing a paused song.

8. Tap and drag the Playhead to change the position in the song.

9. Tap Shuffle to enable or disable song shuffling. When Shuffle is enabled, songs in the current playlist, album, or song list play in a random order.

10. Tap Repeat to control repeating. Tap once to repeat all songs, tap again to repeat the current song only, and tap a third time to disable repeating.

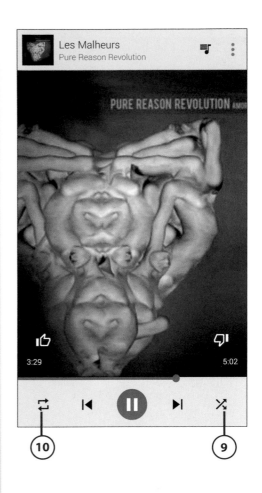

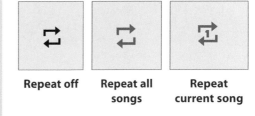

Repeat off   **Repeat all songs**   **Repeat current song**

11. Tap the Menu button to display the menu of actions you can take with the song.

12. Tap Start Instant Mix to create an instant mix based on the song.

13. Tap Add to Playlist to add the song to a playlist. In the Add to Playlist dialog that opens, you can either tap New Playlist to start creating a new playlist or tap the name of an existing playlist to use that playlist.

14. Tap Go to Artist to display the artist the song is by.

15. Tap Go to Album to display the album that contains the song.

16. Tap Share to share the song via a post on Hangouts. Depending on how you have configured your Galaxy Note 4, other means of sharing might be available.

17. Tap Clear Queue to clear the playback queue.

18. Tap Save Queue to save the playback queue. In the Add to Playlist dialog that opens, you can either tap New Playlist to create a new playlist containing the songs in the queue or tap the name of an existing playlist to add the songs to that playlist.

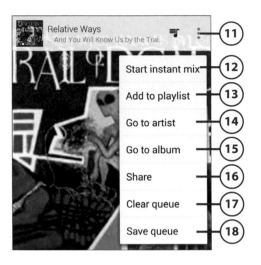

What Is an Instant Mix?

If you are playing a song and choose to create an instant mix as mentioned in step 12, the Google Music app creates a new playlist and adds songs to it that are supposedly similar to the one you are currently playing. The name of the playlist is the name of the current song plus the word "Mix." For example, if you are playing the song "Piquant" and choose to create an instant mix, the playlist is called "Piquant Mix."

Work and Listen to Music

You don't have to keep the Play Music app displayed while you are playing music. Instead, you can switch back to the Home screen and run any other app but still have the ability to control the music.

1. Pull down the Notification bar.

2. Tap Pause to pause the song.

3. Tap Next to skip ahead to the next song in the list, album, or playlist.

4. Tap the song title or the album art to open the Google Music app for more control.

5. Tap × to stop playing the song and remove the playback control from the Notification screen.

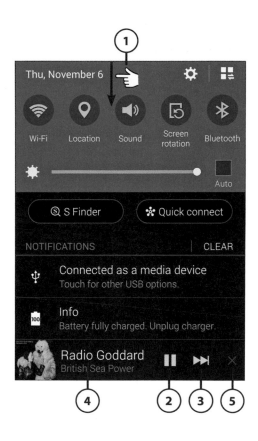

What If I Get a Call?

If someone calls you while you are listening to music, your Galaxy Note 4 pauses the music and displays the regular incoming call screen. After you hang up, the music resumes playing.

Work with Playlists

Playlists can be a great way of listening to music, enabling you to group together related songs or simply those you want to hear in a particular sequence. On your Galaxy Note 4, you can create new playlists, add songs to existing playlists, rename playlists, and change the order of the songs they contain.

Create a New Playlist on Your Galaxy Note 4

1. Using the techniques described earlier in this chapter, navigate to a song you want to add to the new playlist.

2. Tap the song's Menu button to display the menu of actions you can take with the song.

3. Tap Add to Playlist. The Add to Playlist dialog opens.

4. Tap New Playlist. The Playlist Name dialog opens.

5. Type the name for the new playlist.

6. Optionally, type a description for the playlist to make it easier to identify.

7. Set the Public switch to On if you want to make the playlist publicly accessible on Google Play.

8. Tap Create Playlist. You can now add songs to the playlist as explained in the next section.

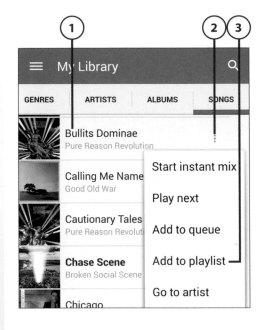

Add a Song to an Existing Playlist

1. Using the techniques described earlier in this chapter, navigate to a song you want to add to the new playlist. You can also use the song on the Now Playing screen, as in this example.

2. Tap the song's Menu button to open the menu of actions you can take with the song.

3. Tap Add to Playlist. The Add to Playlist dialog opens.

4. Tap the playlist you want to add the song to.

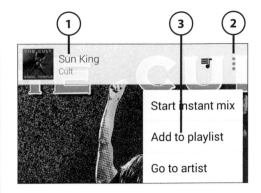

Delete a Playlist

When you no longer need a playlist, you can delete it in moments. Deleting the playlist doesn't delete its songs—only the list is deleted.

1. Tap the icon in the upper-left corner of the screen to display the navigation panel, and then tap Playlists to display the Playlists screen.

2. Tap the Menu button for the playlist you want to delete.

3. Tap Delete. A confirmation dialog opens.

4. Tap OK.

Renaming a Playlist

To rename a playlist, go to the Playlists screen, tap the Menu button for the playlist, and then tap Edit Playlist on the menu. In the Edit Playlist dialog that opens, change the name and description as needed; you can also set the Public switch to On or Off, depending on whether you want to make the playlist public. Tap Save when you finish.

Change the playlist's description if you want.

Change the playlist's name as needed.

You can also make the playlist public or private.

Rearrange the Songs in a Playlist

You can keep a playlist fresh by adding songs to it, as explained earlier in this chapter, but you can also delete songs from the playlist and rearrange the songs it contains.

1. On the Playlists screen, tap the playlist to display its songs.

2. Tap the song you want to move, drag it up or down until it is in the right place, and then release it. You can tap anywhere except for the Menu button on the right side of the song.

3. To remove a song, swipe it to the left or to the right. You can also tap its Menu button and then tap Remove from Playlist.

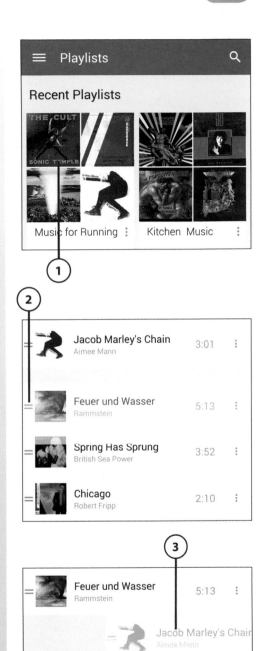

Listen to Music with No Wireless Coverage

If you use Google Music and store your music online, your Galaxy Note 4 streams the music over the cellular or Wi-Fi network when you play the music. If you know you are going to be without a signal but still want to listen to your music, you need to store it on your Galaxy Note 4.

1. Using the techniques discussed earlier in this chapter, go to the music you want to store on your Galaxy Note 4.

2. Tap the gray arrow, which indicates that the music is not stored on your Galaxy Note 4.

3. The Play Music app downloads and stores the music. As it does so, the arrow displays a progress indicator. When the music is available, the arrow appears on an orange background.

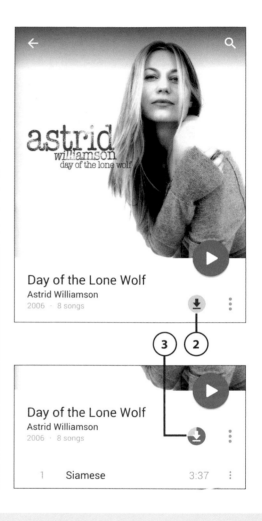

>>>Go Further

SYNCHRONIZE MUSIC AND OTHER MEDIA USING A USB CABLE

If you don't use Google Music, or Google Music is not available in your country, you can synchronize music and other media using a USB cable or Wi-Fi. You can use Kies, the program that Samsung provides for managing its phones and tablets, or another app such as doubleTwist (www.doubletwist.com). Alternatively, you can connect your Galaxy Note 4 via USB and access its file system using Windows Explorer or Android File Transfer (www.android.com/filetransfer/) on the Mac.

>>>*Go Further*

ENJOY MUSIC ON YOUR GALAXY NOTE 4 USING OTHER APPS

As you have seen so far in this chapter, Google's Play Music app is easy to use and enables you to access the music you store in your Google account. However, you will probably also want to explore the Music app that most Galaxy Note 4 models include.

Music is an easy-to-use app for playing back music. Music includes features such as the SoundAlive equalizer, which provides both basic and advanced features for making the audio sound the way you like it. To configure SoundAlive, tap the Menu button, tap Settings, and then tap SoundAlive on the Settings screen.

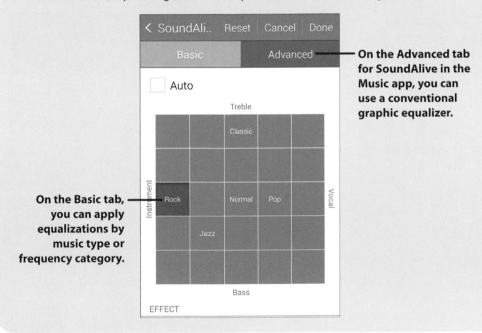

On the Advanced tab for SoundAlive in the Music app, you can use a conventional graphic equalizer.

On the Basic tab, you can apply equalizations by music type or frequency category.

Playing and Sharing Videos

The Gallery app enables you to view pictures and video; you can also share pictures and video with people on Facebook, or via MMS, Bluetooth, You-Tube, and email. This section explains how you can view and share videos.

Understanding the Two Ways to Access Videos

Your Galaxy Note 4 enables you to access videos in two main ways: through the Gallery app and through the Videos app. This section shows you how to use the Gallery app, which enables you to review your photos and videos at the same time and choose which to use or view. From the Gallery app, you can open the video for viewing in either the Photos app, as explained here, or in the Videos app.

This section explains how to view and share videos. Later in this chapter, you learn how to take pictures and share them.

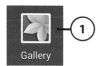

1. Tap the Gallery icon on the Apps screen to launch the Gallery app.

2. Tap the navigation pop-up menu in the upper-left corner.

3. In the View By section, tap Time to see the items listed by time or tap Album to see the items listed by albums. This example uses Album.

4. Tap an album to open it, revealing the pictures and videos it contains.

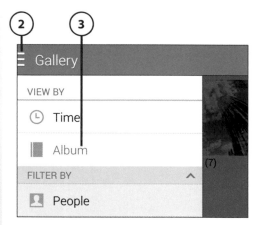

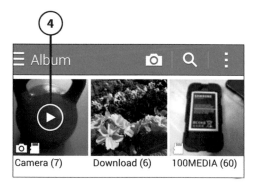

5. Tap a video to open it for playback. Videos have a little Play icon on them.

6. Tap the Play icon to start the video playing.

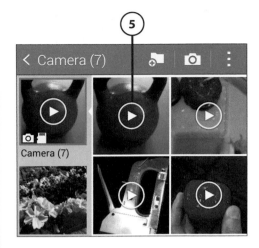

Choosing the App to Use for Playing Videos

The first time you tap the Play icon for a video in the Gallery app, your Galaxy Note 4 displays the Complete Action Using dialog to let you choose between the available video players. Normally, these are the Photos app and the Video Player app, but you might have installed other video-capable apps on your Galaxy Note 4.

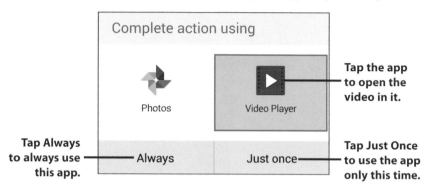

Complete action using

Photos   Video Player

Tap the app to open the video in it.

Tap Always to always use this app. ——— Always

Just once ——— **Tap Just Once to use the app only this time.**

Tap the app you want to use. Then tap Always if you want to always use that app. Tap Just Once if you want your Galaxy Note 4 to prompt you again in the future.

7. Tap the screen while the video is playing to reveal the video controls. If you do not use the controls, they disappear after a few seconds.

8. Tap Pause to pause the video. Tap the Play button (which replaces the Pause button) to resume playback.

9. Drag the slider to scrub quickly forward and backward.

10. Tap Next to skip to the end of the video.

11. Tap Previous to return to the beginning of the video.

12. Tap to switch between viewing the video full screen and viewing it as best fits the Galaxy Note 4's screen.

13. Tap to display the video in a popup window. You can then switch to another screen and continue to watch the video as you work or play.

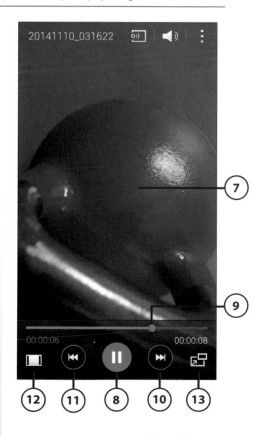

Changing the Orientation for a Video

When watching a video shot in landscape orientation, rotate your Galaxy Note 4 from portrait orientation to landscape orientation so you can enjoy the video full screen.

14. Tap the pop-up window to display the playback controls at the bottom and the × button in the upper-right corner.

15. Use the playback controls to control playback.

16. Tap the × button to close the pop-up video window.

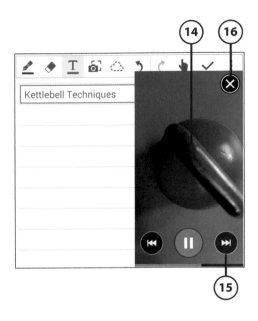

Share Videos

From the Gallery app, you can share small videos with other people.

1. Tap and hold the video you want to share. After a moment, a green check mark appears on the video.

2. Tap the Share icon to open the Share Via dialog.

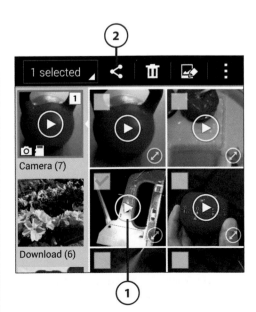

3. Scroll if necessary to display other methods of sharing.

4. Tap a method for sharing the video. Refer to the following sections for specific directions for sharing via YouTube or Facebook.

Sharing Only Small Videos

It is best to share only small videos from your Galaxy Note 4. Even when using email, try to share videos no larger than 10MB, which is only two or three minutes of high-quality video. Otherwise, your videos will be too large to transfer successfully.

Bluetooth Sharing Might Fail

Many phones do not accept incoming Bluetooth files, but devices such as computers do. Even on computers, the recipient must configure her Bluetooth configuration to accept incoming files.

Share a Video on YouTube

YouTube gives you a quick, easy, and effective way to share your videos with the whole wired world.

If you have not previously set up your YouTube account on your Galaxy Note 4, you are prompted to do so before you can upload your video. You can read more about YouTube later in the chapter in the "Enjoying Videos with the YouTube App" section.

1. Enter the title of your video.

2. Enter a description of your video.

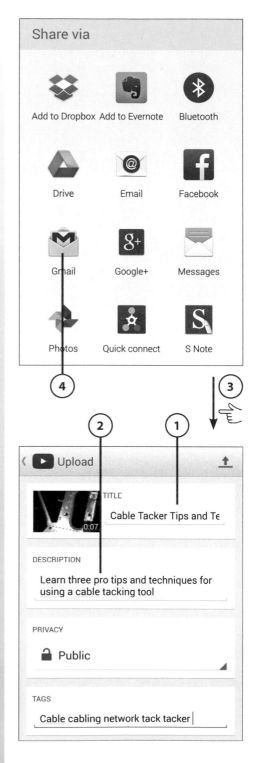

3. Select whether to make your video public for everyone to see or to keep it private.

4. Enter any tags for your video. Tags are keywords that help people find videos by searching.

5. Tap Upload.

Sharing a YouTube Video Only with Specific People

As well as the Public setting and the Private setting, the Privacy pop-up list provides an Unlisted setting. Choose Unlisted when you need to share the video with some people but not with everyone. The video then does not appear in the public view of your YouTube account, but you can send the URL for the video to anyone you want to view it.

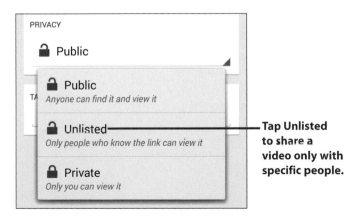

Tap Unlisted to share a video only with specific people.

>>>*Go Further*

LIMITING YOUR YOUTUBE UPLOADS TO WI-FI NETWORKS

When you go to upload a video to YouTube, your Galaxy Note 4 may display the Upload dialog, prompting you to choose between uploading only when on Wi-Fi networks and uploading on any network. Normally, it is best to tap Only When on Wi-Fi and then tap OK, because uploading even relatively small video files over the cellular network can quickly become expensive.

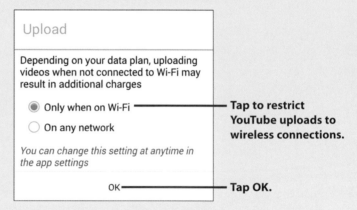

Upload

Depending on your data plan, uploading videos when not connected to Wi-Fi may result in additional charges

◉ Only when on Wi-Fi ——————— **Tap to restrict YouTube uploads to wireless connections.**

○ On any network

You can change this setting at anytime in the app settings

OK ——————— **Tap OK.**

If you need to change this setting later, open the YouTube app, tap the Menu button, and then tap Settings. Tap General to display the General screen, tap Uploads to display the Uploads dialog, and then tap Only When on Wi-Fi.

Share Video on Facebook

After you have set up a Facebook account on your Galaxy Note 4, you can upload videos to your account.

1. Tap the To line and then tap the group with which you want to share the video, such as Friends or Public.

2. Enter a description of your video.

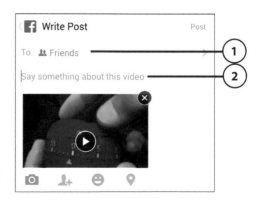

Write Post   Post

To: 👥 Friends ——————— ①

Say something about this video ——————— ②

3. Tap the Location icon if you want to add the location to the video.

4. Tap Post to post the video.

Delete Videos

1. In the Gallery app, tap and hold the video you want to delete. After a moment, a green check mark appears on the video.

2. Tap the Delete icon to delete the video.

3. Tap Delete in the Delete confirmation dialog.

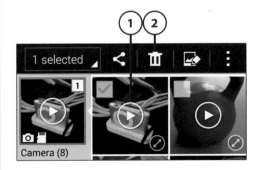

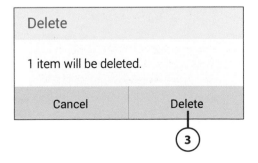

Taking Photos and Videos with the Camera App

The Camera app enables you to take still photos and record videos. You can either shoot photos and videos with the default settings or choose among the many options the Galaxy Note 4 offers.

Take Photos

1. Tap the Camera icon on the Home screen or the Apps screen to launch the Camera app. The Camera app opens and displays the input from the rear camera (the main camera) at first.

2. Tap the Switch Cameras icon to switch from the rear camera to the front camera so you can take photos of yourself. The front camera is lower resolution than the rear camera, but it works well for capturing candid self-portraits. When you switch to the front camera, the Camera app changes to the Selfie mode automatically on the assumption that you want to take a photo of yourself.

3. Tap the HDR readout to turn the HDR feature on or off. HDR stands for High Dynamic Range and tries to improve the color balance and lighting by taking multiple shots and combining them into a single shot.

4. Tap the Settings icon to access other settings. You can read about these settings later in this chapter.

5. Tap the Shutter icon to take a photo.

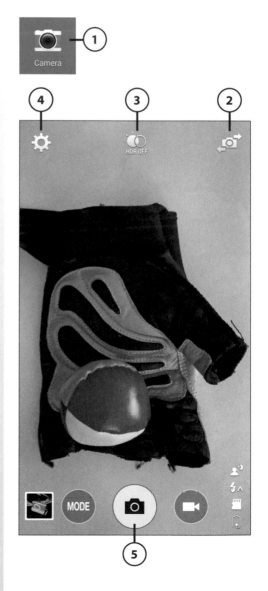

Taking a Burst of Photos

Instead of taking a single shot, the Camera app can take a burst of photos. This feature is great when you do not have time to compose your photo perfectly or your subject is moving. To take a burst of photos, tap and hold the shutter release.

Zoom In and Out

Your Galaxy Note 4's Camera app includes a powerful digital zoom that enables you to close in on the objects you want to photograph.

1. Open the Camera app and point the lens so that your subject occupies the center of the screen.

2. Place two fingers (or a finger and a thumb) on the screen. A zoom indicator appears in the middle of the screen, with a readout showing the zoom factor. A factor of ×1.0 represents no zoom.

3. Move your fingers apart to zoom in. The readout shows the zoom factor you've reached.

4. Tap the Shutter icon to take the photo.

The readout shows the zoom factor.

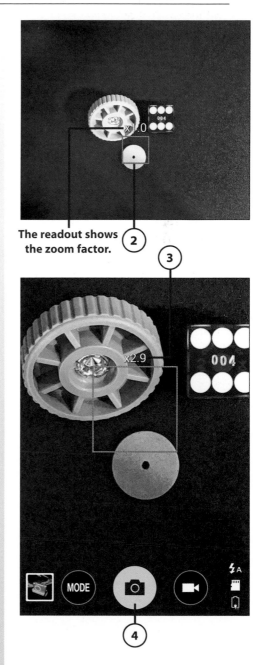

Zooming Out

When you need to zoom back out, place two fingers (or a finger and a thumb) on the screen and pinch them together.

It's Not All Good

Digital Zoom Can Make Photos Grainy

In digital cameras, there are two main types of zoom: optical zoom and digital zoom. Optical zoom implements the zoom by moving the lens (or sometimes changing the lens used), which retains full quality even if you zoom in as far as the camera can. By contrast, digital zoom works by enlarging the pixels (the dots that make up the picture) of the part of the picture that you want to zoom in on.

Larger pixels can make the photos grainy, especially if you zoom in to extremes. So if you have the choice between moving your Galaxy Note 4 closer to your subject and using digital zoom, it's best to move closer because your photos will be higher quality. However, when moving closer isn't an option, digital zoom is still pretty good as long as you don't push it too far.

>>>Go Further

CHOOSE WHERE TO FOCUS

When you take a photo, the Camera app focuses on the center of the screen by default, because that's where the subject is most likely to be. Much of the time this works well, but at other times you may need to focus manually.

To focus manually, tap the point on the screen where you want the focus to be. The Camera app displays a white circle where you tap, and then it plays a chirping noise and displays a green rectangle momentarily to indicate it has refocused.

If the focus is correct, tap the Shutter button to take the photo. If the focus still isn't right, tap again to refocus.

Tap where you
want to focus.

The focus symbol
appears while
Camera focuses.

MODE

Tap to take the photo.

You can also lock the focus and exposure for a couple of seconds by tapping and holding the point on which you want to lock them. A dashed blue circle appears around where you tap and hold, and the Focus/Exposure readout appears. Tap the Shutter icon to take the photo as usual.

Focus/Exposure

**Tap and hold to lock the
focus and exposure.**

Apply Effects to Photos

To make your photos more glamorous, more artistic, or simply more fun, you can apply effects to them. The Camera app includes effects such as Cartoon, Faded Color, Fisheye, Grayscale, Moody, Oil Pastel, Rugged, Sepia, Tint, Turquoise, Vignette, and Vintage.

1. Tap the Settings icon to display the Settings bar. This bar contains a handful of icons for settings you're likely to want to change often.

2. Tap the Effect icon to display the Effects panel.

3. Scroll left or right to see further effect options, and then tap the effect you want to apply.

4. Tap outside the Effects panel to close the panel. You can then see how the effect looks full screen.

Tap No Effect to remove the existing effect.

5. Tap the Shutter icon to take the photo.

Change Key Camera Settings

You can get good photos by using your Galaxy Note 4 as a point-and-shoot camera, as described in the previous section. However, you can get better photos by changing settings to harness the full power of the Camera app.

1. Tap the Settings icon to display the Settings bar.

2. Tap the Flash icon to cycle the flash setting among Off, On, and Auto Flash.

3. Tap the Timer icon to display the Timer dialog, where you can set the timer by tapping the 2 Sec radio button, the 5 Sec radio button, or the 10 Sec radio button. Tap the Off radio button to turn the timer off.

4. Tap the Effects icon to display the Effects bar, as explained in the previous section.

5. Tap the Picture Size icon to display the Picture Size dialog.

6. Tap the radio button for the picture size you want. Normally, it's best to use the 5312×2988 (16:9) resolution—because it gives you the highest quality—unless you need a different aspect ratio, such as 4:3 or 1:1 (square). You can crop your photos afterward if needed.

7. Tap the More (…) button to display the Settings panel, which is covered in the next section.

Making the Most of the Flash

Choose the Off setting for the flash when you need to take photos where the flash would be disruptive. Choose the On setting when you need to light the foreground of a shot, even though the rest of the scene is amply lit—for example, to light your subject's face in front of a bright background. Choose the Auto setting for general use.

Choose Advanced Camera Settings

The Settings bar in the Camera app enables you to change key settings easily. However, when you need to take complete control of the Camera app, you can open the Settings panel and work with the full range of settings it offers.

1. Tap the Settings icon to display the Settings bar.

2. Tap the More (…) button to display the Settings panel.

3. Tap Exposure Value to increase or decrease the exposure—for example, increase the exposure when filming against a bright background.

4. Tap ISO to set the ISO rating, which specifies the digital equivalent of film sensitivity. The default setting is Auto, but you can set ISO 100, ISO 200, ISO 400, or ISO 800 manually.

5. Tap White Balance to display the White Balance dialog.

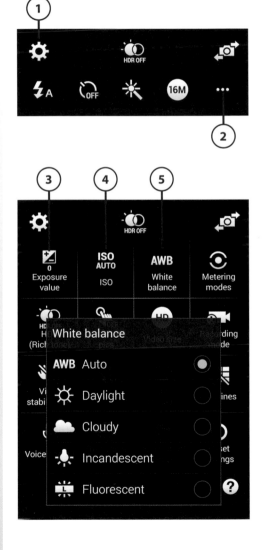

6. Tap the radio button for the lighting conditions you're using: Daylight, Cloudy, Incandescent, or Fluorescent. Tap the Auto radio button when you want the Camera app to choose the setting that appears most suitable.

7. Tap Metering Modes to display the Metering Modes dialog, where you can choose which light-metering method to use. See the nearby note for details.

Adjusting the Light Metering for Your Photos

By default, your Galaxy Note 4 uses center-weighted light metering, giving most importance to the light conditions in the center of the photo. Open the Metering dialog and choose Spot to base the light metering on the spot you tap in the frame. Choose Matrix to base the metering from samples across the entire frame.

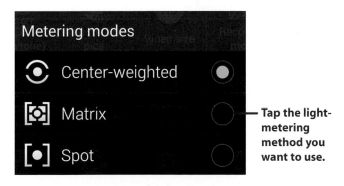

Tap the light-metering method you want to use.

8. Tap HDR to toggle HDR on or off.
    Usually, it's easier to use the HDR
    control at the top of the screen.
    Turning on HDR disables the Expo-
    sure Value, ISO, Metering Modes,
    and Video Stabilization controls.

9. Use Tap to Take Pics to enable or
    disable the Tap to Take Pics feature.
    When this is on, you can take a
    photo by tapping the screen instead
    of tapping the Shutter button.

10. Tap Video Size to display the Video
    Size dialog, and then tap the radio
    button for the video size you want.
    See the "Choosing the Video Size
    and Recording Mode" sidebar for
    recommendations.

11. Tap Recording Mode to display the
    Recording Mode dialog, and then
    tap the recording mode you want.
    See the "Choosing the Video Size
    and Recording Mode" sidebar for a
    discussion of the options.

>>>Go Further

CHOOSING THE VIDEO SIZE AND RECORDING MODE

To shoot suitable video, you must choose the appropriate video size and recording mode.

In the Video Size dialog, tap the radio button for the video size you want:
3840×2160 (16:9), 2560×1440 (16:9), 1920×1080 (16:9), 1280×720 (16:9), or
640×480 (4:3). Unless you need to shoot at super-high resolution, 1920×1080 (16:9)
is a good choice, because it offers high quality and a widely used resolution.

If you use the 3840×2160 resolution, make sure you have plenty of free space,
because this format takes up four times as much space as 1920×1080—around
1GB for three minutes of shooting.

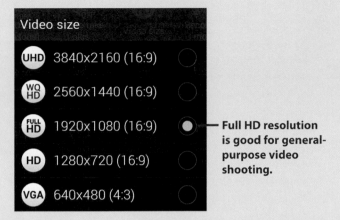

Full HD resolution is good for general-purpose video shooting.

In the Recording Mode dialog, tap the radio button for the recording mode you need. Use Normal mode all the time unless you need one of the other kinds of videos. Choose Limit for MMS to shoot low-resolution video suitable for sending via instant messaging (which cannot transmit large files).

Choose Slow Motion to shoot at a high frame rate that will play back in slow motion. In the Slow Motion dialog that opens, tap the ×1/2 radio button, the ×1/4 radio button, or the ×1/8 radio button to set the speed. You would normally use slow motion as a special effect—for example, to create a dreamlike effect.

Choose Fast Motion to shoot a video clip that will play back at higher speed. In the Fast Motion dialog that opens, tap the ×2 radio button, the ×4 radio button, or the ×8 radio button to set the speed.

Choose Smooth Motion to shoot at a high frame rate that will play back at normal speed. You would normally use smooth motion for shooting sports, animals, and moving objects.

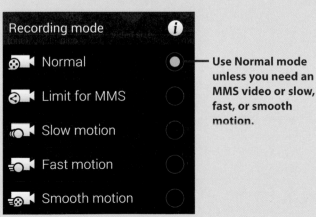

Use Normal mode unless you need an MMS video or slow, fast, or smooth motion.

12. Tap Video Stabilization to enable or disable video stabilization. Normally, using stabilization is a good idea, unless you are using a tripod or another device to hold your Galaxy Note 4 still.

13. Tap Location Tags to enable or disable adding the GPS location to the photos and videos you take. Adding the location enables you to sort the photos and videos by location but may raise privacy issues.

14. Tap Storage Location to choose between storing the photos on your Galaxy Note 4 (tap the Device radio button) and on an SD card you've inserted (tap the Memory Card radio button).

15. Tap Grid Lines to show or hide a grid of lines that help you compose your shots and orient the camera.

16. Tap Voice Control to enable or disable the Voice Control feature. As mentioned earlier, you can say words such as "Cheese!" to take a photo using your voice.

17. Tap The Volume Key to display the dialog called Set the Volume Key To.

18. Tap the Take Pictures radio button, the Record Video radio button, or the Zoom radio button, depending on the action you want pressing the Volume button to take.

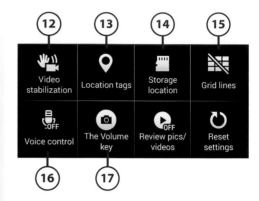

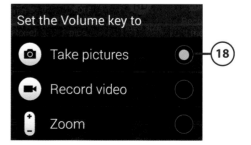

19. Tap Review Pics/Videos to enable or disable displaying each photo or video for review immediately after you take it. Reviewing is helpful for studio work. When you're shooting in the wild, turn off Review so that you can shoot photos freely, especially if your subjects are live and restless and the moments are unrepeatable. You can then review the photos later at your leisure.

20. Tap Reset Settings if you want to reset the Camera app's settings to their defaults.

21. Tap the ? icon to get help with the Camera app.

22. Tap outside the Settings dialog to close the dialog.

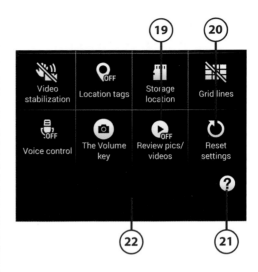

>>>Go Further
USING THE SHOOTING MODE SETTINGS

Your Galaxy Note 4's Camera app gives you a wide choice of shooting modes. By choosing the right mode for the type of photos you are taking, you improve your chances of getting high-quality pictures that look the way you want them to.

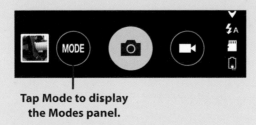

Tap Mode to display
the Modes panel.

To choose the shooting mode, tap Mode on the main Camera screen. You can then scroll through the modes in the Modes panel and tap the one you want to apply. Scroll down if the list goes off the bottom of the screen.

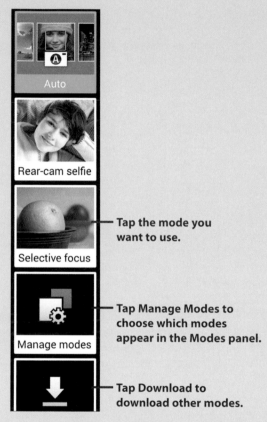

Auto

Rear-cam selfie

Selective focus

— Tap the mode you want to use.

Manage modes

— Tap Manage Modes to choose which modes appear in the Modes panel.

— Tap Download to download other modes.

Tap Manage Modes in the Modes panel to display the Manage Modes screen. On this screen, check or uncheck the boxes to control which modes appear. You can tap and hold a mode and then drag it to a different position on the screen to control where it appears in the Modes panel. Tap Done when you've finished customizing the selection of modes.

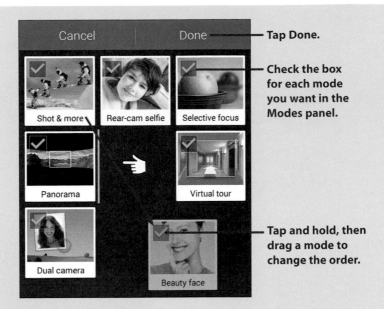

Tap Done.

Check the box for each mode you want in the Modes panel.

Tap and hold, then drag a mode to change the order.

Some of the shooting modes are straightforward. For example, tap Auto to have the Camera app handle as many decisions as possible, leaving you free to shoot, or tap Panorama when you need to stitch together a sequence of photos into a panorama photo. Beauty Face helps you capture portraits and improve their complexion and features at the expense of reality. Dual Camera mode enables you to superimpose yourself (via the front camera) on the scene the back camera is shooting. On the front camera, use Selfie mode for self-portraits of just yourself, or Wide Selfie for self-portraits of you and others.

Other modes might need more explanation.

Shot & More mode is a group of modes that enables you to take a burst of photos and then pick among them afterward. The submodes are Best Photo, Best Face, Drama Shot, Eraser, and Panning Shot. When you tap the Shutter button in Shot & More mode, the Camera app takes a burst of photos and displays a list of available submodes based on what you shoot. Best Photo enables you to select which photos to keep from the burst; Best Face submode enables you to select the best version of each person's face in a group shot and merge them into a single photo; Drama Shot enables you to capture the same moving object (say, a runner) in multiple shots that you combine into a single shot featuring multiple instances of that object (such as the runner passing you). Eraser enables you to remove unwanted objects, such as a lovable pet that's photo-bombing a group portrait. Panning Shot blurs the background to make the subject appear to be moving faster.

Rear-Cam Selfie enables you to take self-portraits using the rear camera (which gives higher resolution than the front camera). You can't see what's on the screen, but in Rear-Cam Selfie mode, you can wave the Galaxy Note 4 in approximately the right direction and have Camera shoot when your face is in the frame you have sized and positioned. This feature gets top marks for ingenuity and is pretty effective if you can compose your features while positioning the Galaxy Note 4.

Selective Focus helps you to make your subject stand out from the background. The subject must be positioned close to the lens (Samsung recommends within 18 inches) and at least three times as far from the background (say, five feet for that 18 inches). As you take the photo, you move the Galaxy Note 4 up to help Camera establish the relative distance of the objects.

Virtual Tour enables you to make a walkthrough of a location. This mode works surprisingly well but benefits from a device to steady the Galaxy Note 4, such as a monopod or a Steadicam rig.

View the Photos You Take

After taking photos, you can quickly view the ones you have taken, mark them as favorites, share them with other people, or simply delete them.

1. In the Camera app, tap the thumbnail to view the last photo you took.

Zooming In and Out on Your Photos

When viewing a photo, you can zoom in by placing two fingers on the screen and pinching outward or by double-tapping on the area you want to expand. Pinch inward or double-tap again to zoom back out.

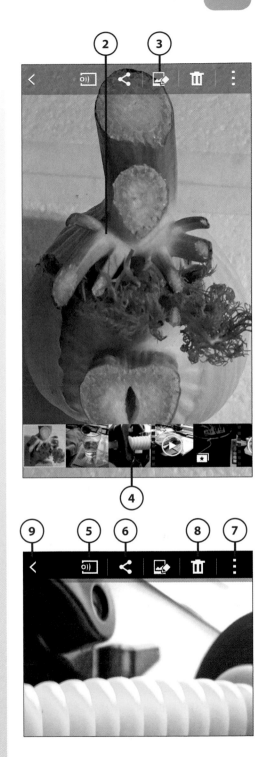

2. Tap to display the onscreen controls and the row of thumbnails. They disappear after a few seconds of not being used.

3. Tap the Edit icon to edit the photo. You can rotate it, crop it, apply a color filter, apply an effect, or take other actions.

4. Tap a thumbnail to display its photo; scroll the thumbnails first if necessary. You can also swipe left from the photo displayed; after that, you can swipe either left or right.

5. Tap to open the Select Device dialog, where you can tap the device to which you want to send the photo.

6. Tap the Share icon to share the photo. In the Share Via dialog, tap the means of sharing and then provide any information needed—for example, the recipient for a photo you share via email.

7. Tap the Menu button to access other commands, such as Screen Write (which lets you write on a photo) and the Rotate Left and Rotate Right commands.

8. Tap the Delete icon (the Trash icon) to delete the photo. Tap Delete in the Delete confirmation dialog that opens.

9. Tap < or the Back button to return to the previous screen. You can then tap the Camera icon to return to the Camera app.

Record Videos with the Camera App

Recording videos with the Camera app is even easier than taking still photos because there are fewer options to choose.

1. Tap Camera on the Home screen or the Apps screen to launch the Camera app.

2. Tap Video to switch to the video camera and start recording video.

3. If necessary, place two fingers (or a finger and a thumb) on the screen and pinch apart to zoom in. Pinch together to zoom back out.

4. Tap the Shutter icon to take a still photo.

5. Tap Pause to pause recording.

6. Tap Stop to stop recording.

Using Automatic and Manual Focusing

While the Camera app is recording video, it automatically adjusts the focus for the object in the center of the screen. If you need to focus on another part of the screen, tap it.

Using Other Features When Recording Video

When recording video, you can use other features such as Dual Camera mode and Effects. Just tap the appropriate icons and choose settings, as described earlier in this chapter. Some features aren't available when you're shooting video at the Galaxy Note 4's highest resolutions.

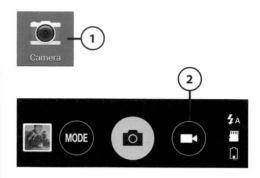

The time readout shows the time elapsed.

The REC indicator shows that video is recording.

REC
00:09
17M / 14266M

The size readout shows the file size of the video and the amount of free space.

Enjoying Videos with the YouTube App

Your Galaxy Note 4 comes with a YouTube app that enables you to find and watch videos, rate them, add them to your favorites, and share links with other people. The app even enables you to upload your own videos to YouTube.

Meet the YouTube Main Screen

1. Tap the YouTube icon on the Apps screen to launch the YouTube app.

2. Tap the navigation button or the current heading to display the navigation panel.

3. Tap the Search icon to search YouTube using keywords.

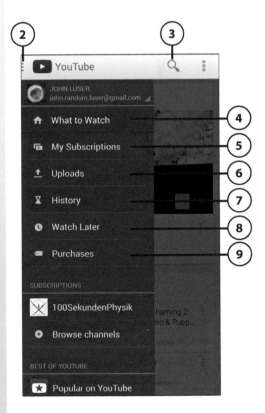

4. Tap What to Watch to display the What to Watch screen, which contains recommendations for you.

5. Tap My Subscriptions to display the My Subscriptions screen, which shows updates from the channels you have added.

6. Tap Uploads to see the list of videos you've uploaded.

7. Tap History to display the History screen, which enables you to return to videos you watched earlier.

8. Tap Watch Later to display the Watch Later screen, which contains any videos you have marked for watching later.

9. Tap Purchases to display the My Purchases screen, which contains items you have purchased.

10. Tap Browse Channels to display the Browse Channels screen, which contains channels such as Recommended for You, Most Subscribed, Most Viewed, and Local.

11. Swipe left if you want to close the Account pane without navigating to another screen from it.

12. Tap a channel to display its screen. You can then tap a video to display more information about it and play it. You can also tap Subscribe to subscribe to a channel.

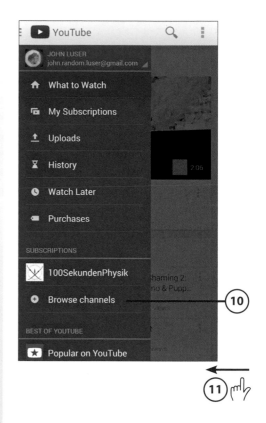

Play a Video

While playing a YouTube video, you can rate the video, read comments about it, or share it with other people.

1. Tap the video to display the on-screen controls for a few seconds.

2. Tap Play to start the video or tap Pause to pause it.

3. Tap Full Screen to switch the video to full screen in Landscape mode.

4. Drag the Playhead to scrub forward or backward through the video.

5. Tap + to display the Add Video To dialog, where you can add the video to your Watch Later list, your Favorites list, or a playlist.

6. Tap the Share icon to share the video's link (its URL) via apps such as Gmail, Facebook, or Twitter.

7. Tap the down-arrow icon to see information about the video, including who uploaded it, the video title, a description, and how many times it has been viewed.

8. Tap the channel icon to see the YouTube channel of the person who uploaded the video.

9. Tap the Like (thumbs-up) icon to like the video.

10. Tap the Dislike (thumbs-down) icon to dislike the video.

11. Tap Subscribe to subscribe to this channel.

12. Tap the Menu button to display the Captions icon, Quality icon, and Report icon.

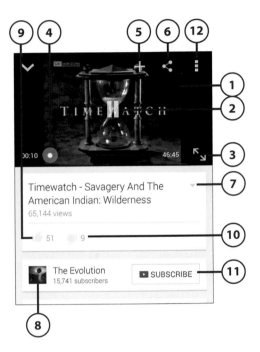

13. Tap to report the video as inappropriate—for example, for hateful or abusive content, or because it infringes upon your rights.

Tap to watch with closed captioning.

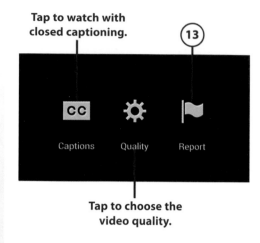

Tap to choose the video quality.

Change YouTube Settings

To get more out of YouTube, you might want to change your settings. Your options include choosing whether to watch high-quality videos on cellular connections, clearing your YouTube search history, and enabling the preloading of items on your subscriptions list or your Watch Later list.

1. From within the YouTube app, tap the Menu button.

2. Tap Settings to display the Settings screen.

3. Tap General to display the General screen.

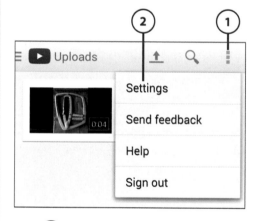

4. Check the Limit Mobile Data Usage box to prevent the YouTube app from streaming high-definition (HD) video across cellular connections. This is normally a good idea. When your Galaxy Note 4 is connected to a Wi-Fi network, the YouTube app streams HD video.

5. Tap Uploads to choose when your Galaxy Note 4 uploads videos to YouTube. Your choices are Only When on Wi-Fi or On Any Network.

6. Tap Content Localization to choose a specific country or region that you want to prioritize—for example, the country you live in.

7. Check the Notifications box to receive notifications of new videos that YouTube claims may match your interests.

8. Tap General or the Back button to return to the main Settings screen.

9. Tap Connected TVs to display the Connected TVs screen.

10. Tap Add a TV to pair your Galaxy Note 4 with a TV so you can broadcast to the TV.

11. Tap Edit TVs to edit your list of paired TVs. You can rename a TV for clarity or remove a TV you no longer want to use.

12. Tap Connected TVs or the Back button to return to the main Settings screen.

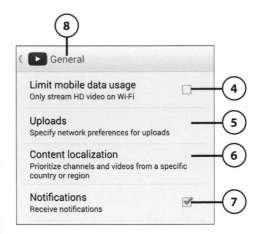

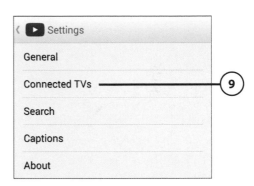

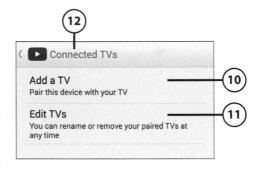

13. Tap Search to display the Search screen.

14. Tap Clear Search History to clear your YouTube search history. Tap OK in the Clear Search History? dialog that opens.

15. Check the Pause Search History box to temporarily stop YouTube from storing the history of what you search on your Galaxy Note 4.

16. Tap SafeSearch Filtering to set the types of videos that are displayed when you search. Your choices are Don't Filter and Strict. If you set SafeSearch Filtering to Don't Filter, no videos are filtered out based on content.

17. Tap Search or the Back button to return to the main Settings screen.

18. Tap Captions to display the Captions screen.

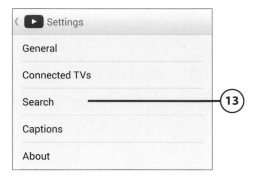

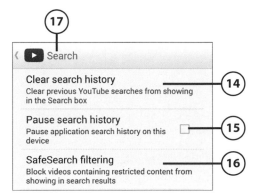

19. Tap Text Size to display the Text Size dialog, and then tap the radio button for the text size you want for captions: Very Small, Small, Normal, Large, or Very Large.

20. Tap Subtitles Style to display the Subtitles Style dialog, and then tap the radio button for the caption style you want, such as White on Black or Yellow on Blue.

21. Tap Captions or the Back button to return to the main Settings screen.

22. Tap Settings or the Back button to return to the YouTube app.

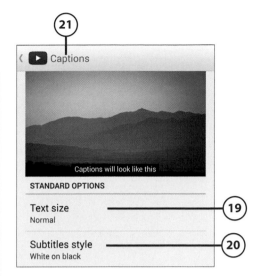

Uploading a Video from the YouTube App

After you create your own channel, you can easily upload your videos to YouTube straight from the YouTube app. Open the navigation panel, and then tap Uploads to display your Uploads screen. You can then tap the Upload icon (an arrow pointing upward), select the video, add the appropriate information to it, and upload it.

Browse quickly by news categories.

Where to Get Books

Depending on where you bought your Galaxy Note 4, your library might include several public-domain books as samples—plus any books you have already added to your library on your Note 4 or another Android device. If your library is empty, you can get books from the Play Store.

Downloading a Book to Your Galaxy Note 4

A white pushpin on a blue circle indicates the book is stored on your Galaxy Note 4, so you can read it offline. To download a book to your Galaxy Note 4, tap the book's Menu button (the button showing three vertical dots) and then tap Keep on Device on the pop-up menu.

Tap the book's menu button.

A pushpin indicates the book is stored on your Galaxy Note 4.

Tap Keep on Device.

6. Tap the Menu button.

7. Tap Sort to display the Sort By screen.

8. Tap the way you want to sort: Recently Read, Title, or Author. The Play Books app displays the books in that sort order.

9. Tap a book to open it. If the book is not stored on your Galaxy Note 4, Play Books downloads the book and then opens it.

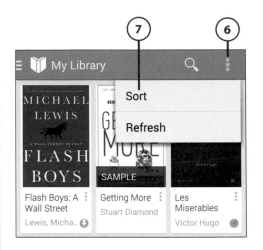

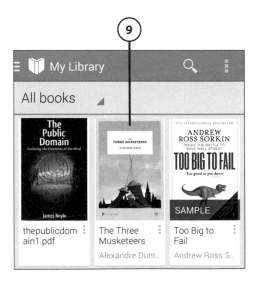

Get Books from the Play Store

The Books area of the Play Store offers a fair number of e-books for free and a much larger number of e-books for sale. You can access the Books area of the Play Store easily from the Play Books app.

1. Tap the button in the upper-left corner of the Play Books app to display the navigation panel.

2. Tap Shop to display the Books area of the Play Store. The Play Books Home screen appears first.

3. Tap the Search icon to search for books.

4. Tap Top Selling to see the list of top-selling books.

5. Tap New Releases to see books that have been newly added to the Play Store.

6. Tap a featured book or a recommended book to see its details.

7. Tap a featured category to see the list of books it contains.

8. Tap Categories to display the list of categories. You can also swipe right once from the Home screen to display the list of categories.

Navigate Quickly Among Tabs by Swiping

The Books area of the Play Store contains various tabs, including Categories, Home, Top Selling, New Releases in Fiction, New Releases in Nonfiction, and Top Free. You can navigate among these tabs by tapping their names on the tab bar, but it is usually quicker to swipe left or right one or more times to change tabs.

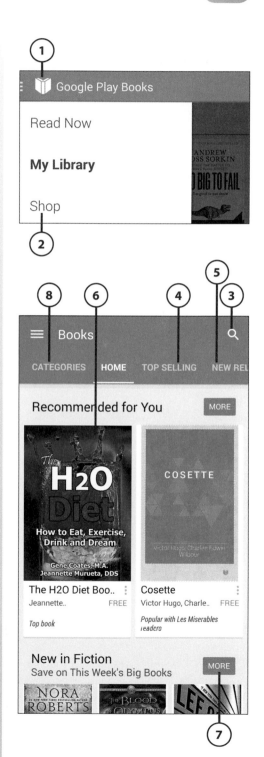

9. Tap the category you want to display. The Top Selling list for the category appears first.

10. Swipe up to see more of the list.

11. Tap the New Releases tab or swipe left to see the New Releases list for the category.

12. Tap a book to display its details.

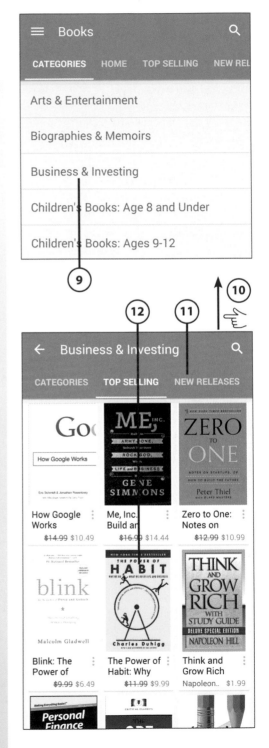

13. Tap the blue bookmark symbol bearing a + sign to add the book to your wishlist.

14. Tap Read More to expand the description.

15. Swipe up to read the reviews or to rate the book yourself (even if you haven't yet read it), to read the About the Author blurb, and to see lists of other books by the same author and similar books.

16. Tap Free Sample to download a free sample of the book. Reading the sample can be a great way to decide whether to spend the money on the book. Android downloads the book and displays its first page in the Google Books app.

Buying Books from the Play Store

To buy a book from the Play Store, you must either add a credit card to your Google account or redeem a voucher. When you begin to buy a book, the Play Store app prompts you to add a credit card and walks you through the steps for adding it.

17. Tap the price button to buy the book, and then follow through the payment process on the next screen. If the book is free, tap the Open button. Android downloads the book and displays its first page in the Play Books app.

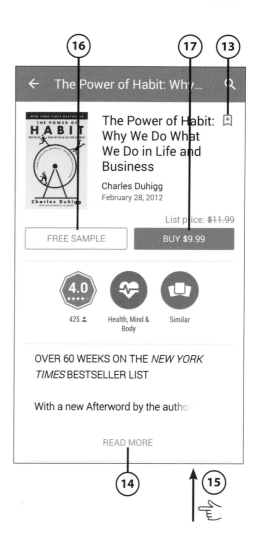

Share a Book with Other People

When you find a book you simply must tell someone about, you can do so easily from the Play Store app. Tap the Share button in the upper-left corner of the screen to display the Share screen, tap the means of sharing you want to use, and then complete the sharing in the app that Android opens.

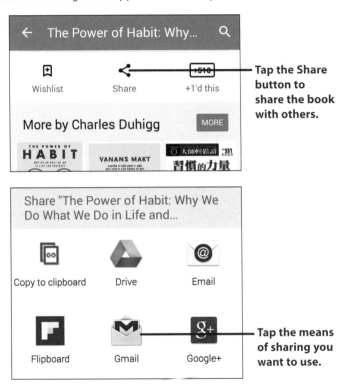

Tap the Share button to share the book with others.

Tap the means of sharing you want to use.

Finding Free E-Books Online

Apart from buying e-books online at Google's Play Store or other stores such as Amazon (www.amazon.com) and Barnes & Noble (www.barnesandnoble.com), you can find many books for free. Most online stores offer some free e-books, especially out-of-copyright classics, so it is worth browsing the Free lists. Other good sources of free e-books include ManyBooks.net (www.manybooks.net) and Project Gutenberg (www.gutenberg.org).

Read Books with the Play Books App

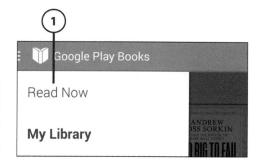

1. In the navigation panel of the Play Books app, tap Read Now to display your Read Now screen. This screen shows the books you have been reading recently plus books you have recently bought (or downloaded for free) or uploaded to your Google account. Further down the screen is a Recommended for You section that suggests books you might be interested in based on the books you have.

2. Tap the book you want to open. The cover or default page appears if this is the first time you have opened the book. Otherwise, the page at which you last left the book appears.

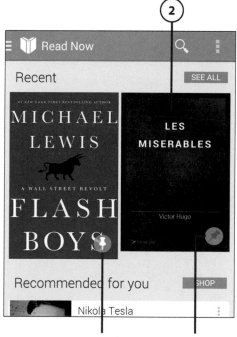

A white pin means your Galaxy Note 4 has downloaded the book.

A gray pin means the book has not been downloaded yet.

3. Tap the middle of the screen to display the navigation controls at the top and bottom of the screen. The controls remain onscreen for a few seconds and then disappear if you do not use them. You can make them disappear more quickly by tapping the screen again.

4. Tap the Search icon to search within the book for specific text.

5. Tap the Contents icon to display the Contents screen. From here, you can tap Chapters to display a list of the book's chapters and major headings, and then tap the place you want to display; tap Bookmarks to display a list of the bookmarks you have created in the book, and then tap the bookmark you want to go to; or tap Notes and then tap the note you want to view.

6. Drag the slider to move quickly through the book.

7. Tap the right side of the screen or drag left to turn the page forward. Dragging lets you turn the page partway to peek ahead.

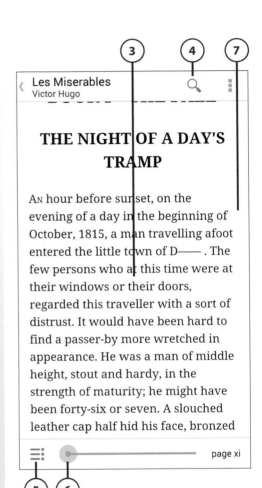

8. Tap the left side of the screen or drag right to turn the page back.

Choose Options for the Play Books App

You can configure the Play Books app to make it work your way. Options include switching between flowing text and the original pages of the book, adding bookmarks, and having your Galaxy Note 4 read aloud to you.

1. With the Play Books app open and active, tap the Menu button.

2. Tap Original Pages to display the book's pages as they are laid out in the physical book. This option is available only for some books. Tap the Menu button again and then tap Flowing Text when you want to change the display back to flowing text.

3. Tap About This Book to display the book's page in the Play Store. If the book is a sample, you can tap Buy on the menu to start the process of buying the book.

4. Tap Share to share the book's URL on the Play Store via Facebook, Gmail, Twitter, or another means of sharing.

5. Tap Add Bookmark to add a bookmark to the current page. To remove the bookmark, go to the page, tap the Menu button, and then tap Remove Bookmark.

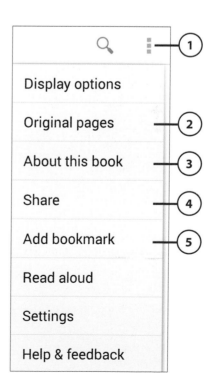

6. Tap Read Aloud to start Android reading the text out loud. To stop it, tap the Menu button and then tap Stop Reading Aloud.

7. Tap Help & Feedback to display the Help screen, from which you can access various help resources, such as Help Center, Contact Us, and Report a Problem.

8. Tap Display Options to open the Display Options panel.

9. Tap the Theme pop-up menu to choose among the Day theme, the Night theme, and the Sepia theme. The Day theme uses black text on a white background, the Night theme uses white text on a black background, and the Sepia theme uses black text on a sepia background.

10. Tap the Typeface pop-up menu to change the typeface used.

11. Tap the Text Alignment pop-up menu to change the text alignment. The choices are Default, Left, and Justify.

12. Tap the Auto box to enable or disable automatic brightness.

13. Drag the Brightness slider to adjust the brightness manually.

14. Tap T– to decrease the font size.

15. Tap T+ to increase the font size.

16. Tap the – button under Line Height to decrease the spacing between lines.

17. Tap the + button under Line Height to increase the spacing between lines.

18. Tap the book page to close the Display Options panel.

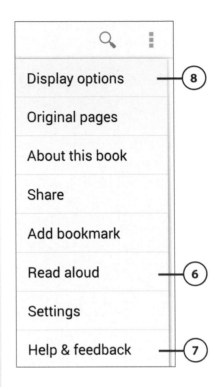

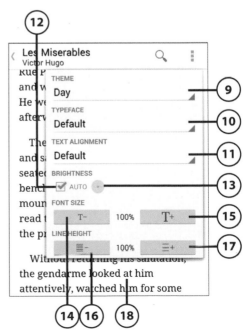

19. Tap the Menu button.

20. Tap Settings to display the Settings screen.

21. Tap Account if you need to change the Google account you are using for the Play Books app.

22. Tap Auto-Rotate Screen to display the Auto-Rotate Screen dialog.

23. Tap the means of rotation you want to use. Your options are Use System Setting, Lock in Portrait, and Lock in Landscape.

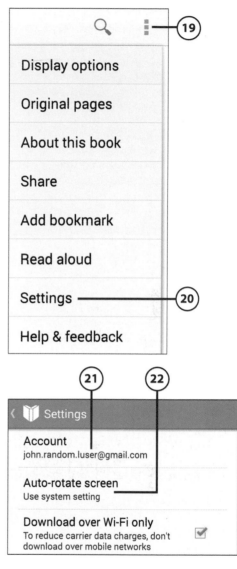

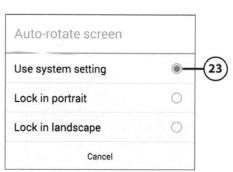

24. Check the Download over Wi-Fi Only box if you want to prevent Play Books from downloading over a cellular network. This is a good move if your cellular plan gives you only a miserly data allowance.

25. Check the Use Volume Key to Turn Pages box if you want to use the physical volume key to turn the pages in the Play Books app. This setting can be helpful if you normally hold your Note 4 with your fingers over the volume key.

26. Check the Use 3D Effect for Page Turning box if you want Play Books to use the 3D animation for turning pages.

27. Check the Enable PDF Uploading box if you want to be able to upload PDFs to Play Books from sources such as email and your Downloads folder.

28. Check the Automatically Read Aloud box if you want Android to start reading aloud automatically when you open a book in Play Books.

29. Check the High-Quality Voice box if you want Play Books to use a more natural voice when reading aloud to you. This setting can make a substantial improvement to Android's reading, but it requires a network connection, so you will need to be careful not to rack up charges by using it across a cellular connection.

30. Tap Settings or the Back button to leave the Settings screen and return to the screen you were previously using in the Play Books app.

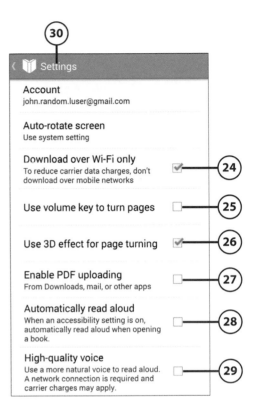

Delete a Book from Your Play Books Library

When you no longer want a particular book in your library, you can delete it directly using the Play Books app. Note that deleting the book removes it from your Google Play library entirely, not just from your Galaxy Note 4 (or whichever other device you're using).

1. In the My Library view in Play Books, tap the Menu button that appears on the book's listing.

2. Tap Delete from Library. The Delete from Library confirmation screen opens.

3. Tap Delete.

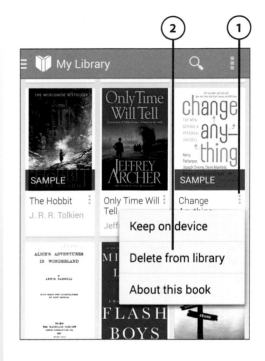

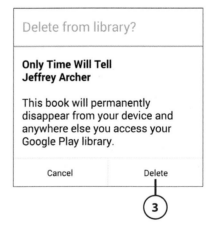

>>>Go Further

UPLOAD YOUR DOCUMENTS TO GOOGLE PLAY BOOKS

The Play Books app is great for reading books you buy or get for free from the Play Store, but you can also use it to read your own PDF files and e-books in formats such as the widely used ePub format. To do so, you use your computer to upload the files to your Google account, from which the Play Books app can then access them.

To upload the files, open your computer's web browser and go to play.google.com. Click the Sign In button, and then sign in with your Google account. Click Books in the navigation panel on the left, and then click My Books to display the screen containing your books. Now click the Upload Files button in the upper-right corner of the window, and then follow the instructions onscreen to select the file or files.

Tap the pop-up button and then tap Uploads to display only your uploaded files.

Tap Menu and Refresh to get the latest list of books.

Tap a file to open it for reading in Play Books.

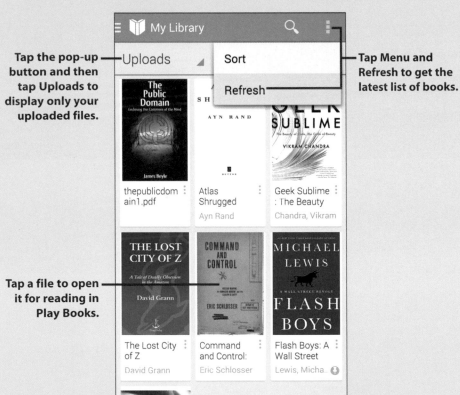

After you upload a file, Google processes it to make it compatible with the Play Books app. The books appear in your library, but you might find it easier to access them on the Uploads screen; to display this screen, tap the pop-up menu in the upper-left corner of the My Library screen, and then tap Uploads. If the books do not appear, tap the Menu button and then tap Refresh to force Play Books to refresh the list. You can then tap a book to download it and read it.

Install the Kindle App

Google's Play Store has a good selection of books, but if you want to buy or download books from Amazon's vast bookstore, you need to use the Kindle app instead. If you already own any Kindle books, installing the Kindle app gives you most of the benefits of owning a Kindle reader without having to buy or haul around an extra device.

Installing the Kindle App

If the Kindle app is not already installed on your Galaxy Note 4, you need to install it from the Play Store. Tap Play Store on the Apps screen, tap Apps on the Google Play screen, tap the Search icon, and type **kindle**. Tap the Kindle result and then tap Install.

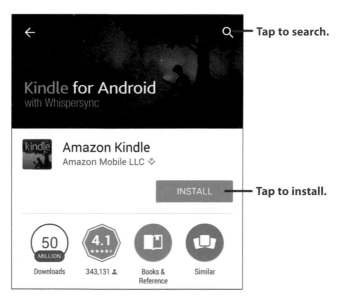

Tap to search.

Tap to install.

Sign In and Navigate the Kindle App

1. On the Apps screen, tap the Amazon Kindle icon. The first time you run the Kindle app, it displays the Start Reading screen.

2. Tap the Start Reading button to display the Sign In screen.

3. Type your email address.

Creating an Amazon Account

To buy books or download free books from Amazon, you must have an Amazon account. If you do not have one, tap the Create an Account button on the Sign In screen and then follow through the screens to create an account.

4. Type your Amazon password.

5. Tap Sign In. The Kindle app signs you in to your account and then displays its Home screen with the menu panel open.

Tap to start creating a new Amazon account.

6. Tap Search to search your Kindle library for the terms you type.

7. Tap Sync to refresh the display of books. You would do this if you have just bought a book using your computer or a different device and the book hasn't yet appeared on the Kindle app on your Galaxy Note 4.

8. Tap Store to go to the Kindle Store, where you can browse and buy books.

9. Tap All Items to display the All Items screen. This screen shows all the items in your Kindle library, whether they are on your Galaxy Note 4 or not.

10. Tap On Device to see the list of books and other items stored on your Galaxy Note 4.

11. Tap Collections to display the Collections screen, which contains the collections you have created to organize your library.

12. Tap Books to see the list of books, rather than documents, newspapers, and magazines.

13. Tap Docs to display the documents stored in your Kindle account. These are documents you have sent via email to your Send to Kindle email address, a Kindle-only address that Amazon provides with Kindle accounts.

14. Tap Newsstand to display your Newsstand items.

15. Tap Home to close the menu panel. The Home screen appears, showing the books in your Kindle library on a carousel.

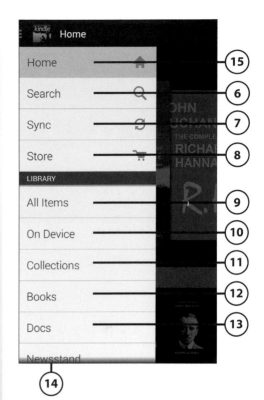

16. Scroll left or right to find the book you want.

17. Tap the Store icon to go to the Kindle Store to browse or buy books.

Books in your (16) Kindle library (17)

Books that Amazon recommends for you

Tap to display the books as a list instead of covers.

Read a Book with the Kindle App

1. In the Kindle app, tap the book you want to open. This example uses the On Device screen, but you can also start from another screen, such as the Home screen or the All Items screen.

Reaching the On Device Screen from a Book

If you currently have a book open in the Kindle app, tap the Back button to go back to the main screen, tap the Menu button, and then tap On Device. Alternatively, tap the Menu button, tap Home to display the Kindle Home screen, and then tap On Device.

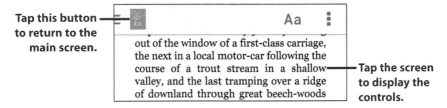

Tap this button to return to the main screen.

out of the window of a first-class carriage, the next in a local motor-car following the course of a trout stream in a shallow valley, and the last tramping over a ridge of downland through great beech-woods

Tap the screen to display the controls.

2. Tap the middle of the screen to display the title and location bar. Tap again to hide these items.

3. Drag the slider to change the location in the book.

4. Tap the right side of the screen to display the next page. You can also display the next page by dragging or swiping left.

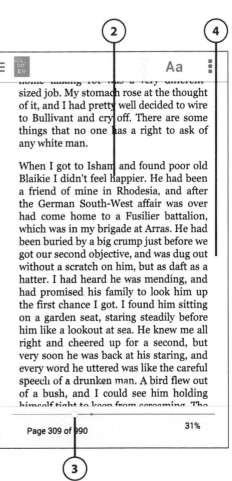

② ④

sized job. My stomach rose at the thought of it, and I had pretty well decided to wire to Bullivant and cry off. There are some things that no one has a right to ask of any white man.

When I got to Isham and found poor old Blaikie I didn't feel happier. He had been a friend of mine in Rhodesia, and after the German South-West affair was over had come home to a Fusilier battalion, which was in my brigade at Arras. He had been buried by a big crump just before we got our second objective, and was dug out without a scratch on him, but as daft as a hatter. I had heard he was mending, and had promised his family to look him up the first chance I got. I found him sitting on a garden seat, staring steadily before him like a lookout at sea. He knew me all right and cheered up for a second, but very soon he was back at his staring, and every word he uttered was like the careful speech of a drunken man. A bird flew out of a bush, and I could see him holding himself tight to keep from screaming. The

Page 309 of 990   31%

③

5. Tap the left side of the screen, or drag or swipe right, to move back a page.

6. Tap the Menu button to display the menu.

7. Tap Shop in Kindle Store to go shopping for Kindle books.

8. Tap My Notes & Marks to view the list of notes and bookmarks you have added to the current book. From there, you can tap one of your bookmarks or notes to go to its page.

9. Tap Add a Bookmark to bookmark the current page. Adding a bookmark gives you an easy way to return to a particular page by using the My Notes & Marks command on the menu.

10. Tap Share Progress to display the Share Progress dialog, in which you can pick a way to share your reading progress. For example, you can post a link to Facebook or send an email message saying you're 50% through the book.

11. Tap the book cover thumbnail or the menu-panel button to display the menu panel.

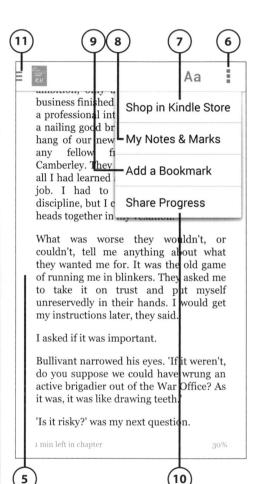

12. Tap Cover to display the cover.

13. Tap a section in the Table of Contents list to go straight to that section. Scroll down as needed to find the section you want.

14. Tap Search to search in the book. For example, you can search for a distinctive word on a page.

15. Tap Sync to Furthest Page to go to the furthest page you've read in this book on any of your Kindle devices. Normally, you'll want to do this after reading on another device.

16. Tap the Go To button to go to a page by number or to go to a location. The locations are numbered divisions of the text. You can see the number of the current location by tapping the middle of the screen and looking at the Location slider. However, unless you know the number of the location to which you want to go, this command is of little use.

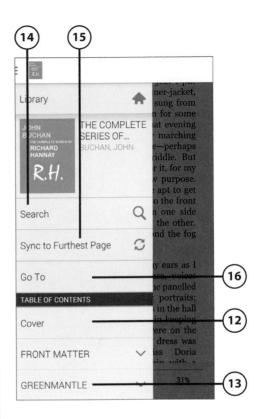

>>>Go Further

ADDING MARKS TO A BOOK

You can easily add a bookmark to the current page by tapping the Menu button and then tapping Add a Bookmark, but the Kindle app also enables you to add highlights, add notes, and copy text to the clipboard so that you can paste it elsewhere.

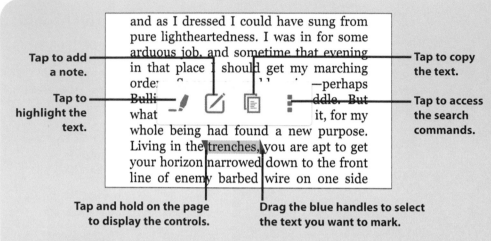

Tap to add a note.

Tap to highlight the text.

Tap to copy the text.

Tap to access the search commands.

Tap and hold on the page to display the controls.

Drag the blue handles to select the text you want to mark.

Tap and hold the relevant part of the text until the Kindle app selects it. Drag the blue selection handles to encompass the text you want to mark, and then tap the appropriate button on the pop-up toolbar.

Choose View Options for the Kindle App

To make your books easy to read, you can choose view options for them.

1. With a book open in the Kindle app, tap the screen to display the controls.

2. Tap the Aa icon to display the View Options panel.

3. Drag the Brightness slider to adjust the screen brightness.

4. Check the Use System Brightness box to make the Kindle app use the same brightness as the Galaxy Note 4 as a whole.

5. Tap the – icon to decrease the font size.

6. Tap the + icon to increase the font size.

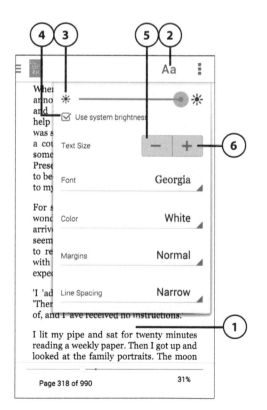

7. Tap the Font pop-up menu to change the font.

8. Tap the Color pop-up menu to choose the color scheme. Your choices are White, Black, Sepia, and Green.

9. Tap the Margins pop-up menu to adjust the margin width.

10. Tap the Line Spacing pop-up menu to change the line spacing. Your choices are Narrow, Normal, and Wide.

11. Tap the document to close the View Options panel.

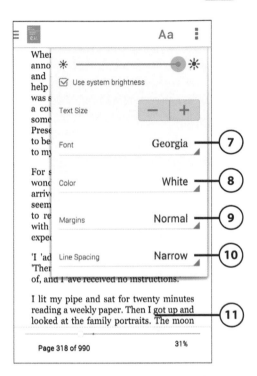

>>>Go Further

EXPLORE OTHER BOOK READERS

Between them, the Play Books app and the Kindle app give you access to a phe-
nomenal range of books. However, there are many other book readers you might
want to explore to give yourself access to other bookstores and other books. In
particular, the Aldiko app, the Kobo app, and the Nook app are worth trying. You
can get each of these apps from the Play Store for free. The Nook app ties into
Barnes & Noble's online bookstore.

Reading Newspapers and Magazines with Play Newsstand

Your Galaxy Note 4 includes Google's Play Newsstand app, which gives you access to a wide range of newspapers and magazines.

Exploring Other News and Magazine Apps

If the Play Newsstand app does not deliver the content you need, or does not otherwise suit you, explore other news and magazine apps such as PressReader and Zinio. You can download both these apps for free from the Apps section of the Play Store.

Open the Play Newsstand App and Choose Your Topics

The first time you open Play Newsstand, the app prompts you to select the topics you like, so that it can show you relevant stories.

1. On the Apps screen or in the Google folder, tap Play Newsstand. The first time you open it, the app displays the Select the Topics You Like screen.

2. Tap an unchecked topic that you want to add. A check mark appears on the topic.

3. Tap any checked topic that you want to remove. The topic's check mark disappears.

4. Tap Done when you finish making your choices. The news screens appear.

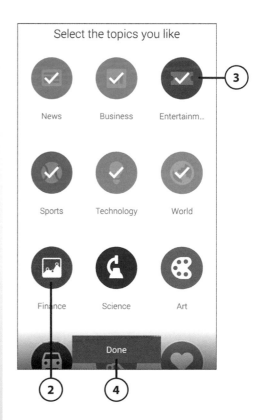

Read News with the Read Now Feature

1. Tap the category of news you want to view, such as News, World, or Sports. You can also swipe left or right to move from one category to another.

2. Tap an icon to display that publication's stories.

3. Tap the story you want to display.

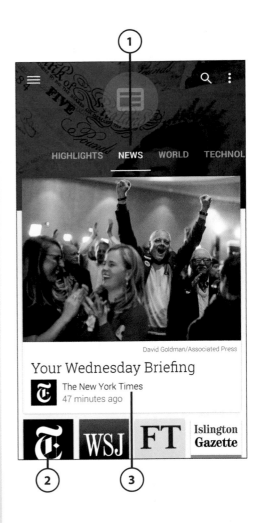

4. Tap the screen to display the controls at the top. Tap the text rather than a picture, because tapping a picture displays that picture and its caption.

5. Tap the Share icon to share the story using the means you select in the Choose an Action screen that opens. For example, you can share the story on Facebook, add it to Dropbox, or share it via email.

6. Tap Bookmark to create a bookmark for the story so that you can access it again easily.

7. Tap the arrow or the Back button to return to the previous screen so that you can browse and read other stories.

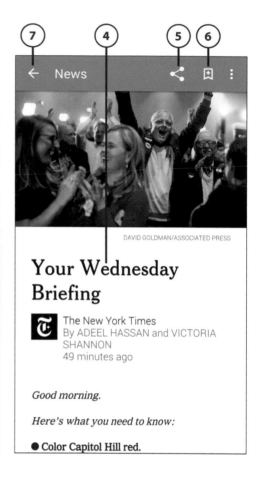

Build Your Newsstand Library

The Play Newsstand app enables you to build a library containing the publications you prefer to read.

1. Tap the navigation button to display the navigation panel.

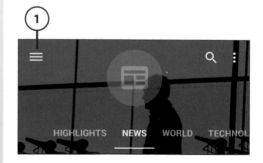

2. Tap My Library to display the My Library screen.

3. Tap News, Magazines, or Topics to display the content type you want to customize.

4. Tap the menu button on one of the items.

5. Tap Download to download the item.

6. Tap Translate to translate the item.

7. Tap Move to Top to move the item to the top of the list.

8. Tap Share to share the item via any of the means available, such as Twitter or Email.

9. Tap Remove Source to remove this news source from your library.

10. Tap Add More to start adding another news source.

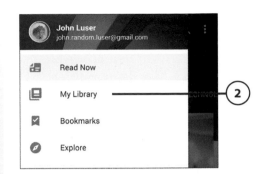

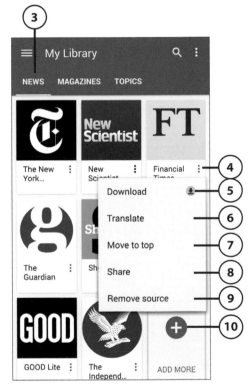

Choose Options for the Play Newsstand App

The Play Newsstand app has several settings you can choose to control when it downloads magazines and when it notifies you about new issues. You can also change the account you use to pay for Play Newsstand.

1. Tap the navigation button to display the navigation panel.

2. Tap Settings to display the Settings screen.

3. Tap Article Text Size to display the Article Text Size screen, where you can tap the Small radio button, the Normal radio button, or the Large radio button, as needed.

4. Check the Show Notifications box if you want to receive notifications when a new issue is available for a magazine that you have added to your library.

5. Check the Download via Wi-Fi Only box if you want to restrict Play Newsstand to downloading content to when your Galaxy Note 4 has a Wi-Fi connection. Because newspaper and magazine files can be relatively large, checking this box is a good idea if your cellular data plan is limited.

6. Check the Download While Charging Only box if you want Play Newsstand to download content only when your Galaxy Note 4 is charging. You may want to do this if your Galaxy Note 4 tends to run out of battery power.

7. In the About section, you can tap the buttons to display information about open source licenses, the terms of service, and the privacy policy and usage policy. You can also see the build number of the Play Newsstand app, which you may sometimes need to know for troubleshooting purposes.

8. Tap the arrow or the Back button when you finish choosing settings.

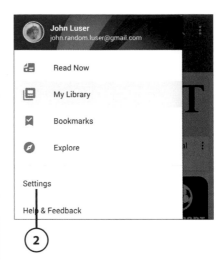

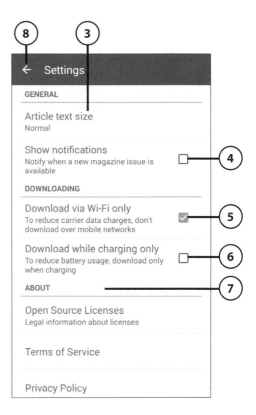

Browse for apps.

Search for apps.

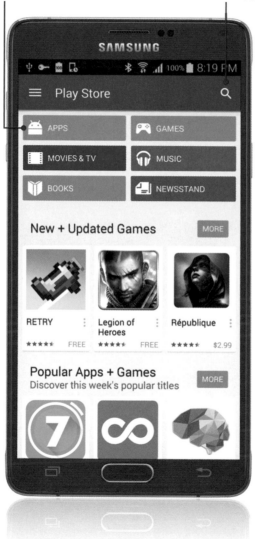

In this chapter, you find out how to purchase and use Android apps on your Galaxy Note 4. Topics include the following:

→ Finding apps with Google Play
→ Purchasing apps
→ Keeping apps up to date

Working with Android Apps

Your Galaxy Note 4 comes with enough apps to make it a worthy smartphone. However, wouldn't it be great to play games, work on business or school documents, or keep a grocery list? Well, finding these types of apps is what the Google Play Store is for. Read on to learn about finding, purchasing, and maintaining apps.

Configuring Google Wallet

Before you start buying apps in the Play Store app, you should sign up for a Google Wallet account. If you plan to only download free apps, you do not need a Google Wallet account.

1. From a desktop computer or your Galaxy Note 4, open the web browser and go to http://wallet.google.com.

2. Sign in using the Google account that you will be using to synchronize email to your Galaxy Note 4. See Chapter 4, "Email," or Chapter 7, "Contacts," for information about adding a Google account to your Galaxy Note 4.

3. Choose your location. If your country is not listed, you have to use free apps until it's added to the list.

4. Enter your name.

5. Enter your ZIP Code.

6. Enter your credit card number. This can also be a debit card that includes a Visa or MasterCard logo, also known as a check card, so that the funds actually are withdrawn from your checking account.

7. Select the month and year of the card's expiration date.

8. Enter the card's CVC number, which is also known as the security code. This is a three- or four-digit number that's printed on the back of your card.

9. Check this box if your billing address is the same as your name and home location. Otherwise, uncheck this box and enter your billing address and phone number when prompted.

10. Uncheck this box unless you want to receive Google Wallet special offers, invitations, and other marketing messages.

11. Click Accept and Create when you finish filling in the form.

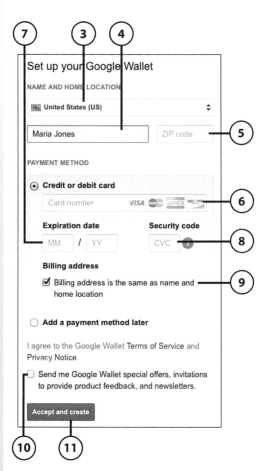

Navigating Google Play

Android is the operating system that runs your Galaxy Note 4, so any apps that are made for your Note 4 need to run on Android. The Google Play Store is a place where you can search for and buy Android apps.

1. On the Apps screen, tap the Play Store app icon to launch the Play Store app.

2. Tap Apps to browse all Android apps.

3. Tap Games to browse all Android games.

4. Tap the Search icon to search Google Play.

5. Tap the Menu button to display the menu panel.

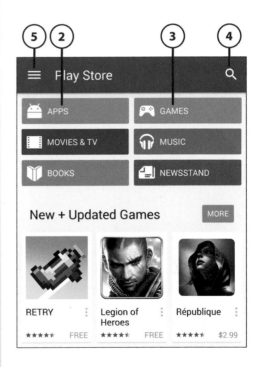

6. Tap Store Home to display the Home page of the Play Store.

7. Tap My Apps to display the list of apps you have already purchased or acquired for free.

8. Tap My Wishlist to display your wishlist. This is a list to which you can add items you want to buy or you want others to buy for you.

9. Tap People to see the People feed, which shows what apps people you know are downloading.

10. Tap Redeem to redeem a gift card or promotional code.

Download Free Apps

You don't have to spend money to get quality apps. Some of the best apps are actually free. Other free apps are feature-light versions that give you a chance to test-drive the app without paying and decide whether you want to upgrade to the full version.

1. Tap the app you want to download. The screen for the app appears.

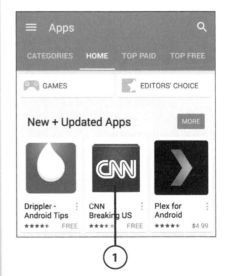

2. Scroll down to read the app features, reviews by other people who installed it, and information on the person or company who wrote the app.

3. Scroll left and right to see the app screenshots.

4. Tap Install to download and install the app.

5. Tap Accept to accept the app permissions and proceed with the download.

Beware of Permissions

Each time you download a free app or purchase an app from Google Play, you are prompted to accept the app permissions. App permissions are permissions the app wants to have to use features and functions on your Galaxy Note 4, such as access to the wireless network or access to your phone log.

Pay close attention to the kinds of permissions each app is requesting and make sure they are appropriate for the type of functionality the app provides. For example, an app that tests network speed will likely ask for permission to access your wireless network, but if it also asks to access your list of contacts, it might mean that the app is malware and just wants to steal your contacts.

Review the permissions to your phone the app is requesting.   **Tap a downward caret to expand a section.**   **Tap an upward caret to collapse a section.**

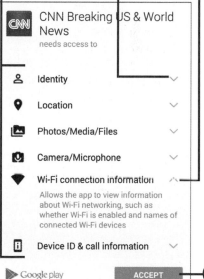

6. After your Galaxy Note 4 downloads and installs the app, the Open button appears in the Play Store app. Tap Open to open the app.

> >>>*Go Further*
> # OPEN A NEWLY INSTALLED APP IN OTHER WAYS
>
> If you keep the Play Store app open while downloading an app, the Open button on the app's screen provides a handy way to open the app and put it through its paces. However, if the app is large or your Internet connection is slow, you probably won't want to hang about in the Play Store app until the download completes.
>
>
>
> **Tap the Successfully Installed notification to open a freshly installed app.**
>
> When the installation finishes, a notification briefly appears telling you that the app has been installed successfully. You can then launch the app by opening the Notifications panel and tapping the Successfully Installed notification for the app. Alternatively, go to the Apps screen, tap the Downloaded button to the right of the Widgets button, and then tap the app's icon on the Downloaded Applications screen.

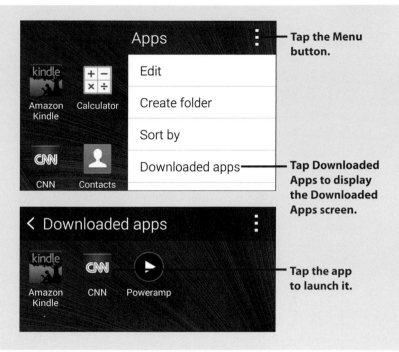

Tap the Menu button.

Tap Downloaded Apps to display the Downloaded Apps screen.

Tap the app to launch it.

Buy Apps

If an app is not free, the price appears next to the app icon. If you want to buy the app, remember that you need to already have a Google Wallet account. See the "Configuring Google Wallet" section, earlier in the chapter, for more information.

1. Tap the app you want to buy.

What If the Currency Is Different?

When you browse apps in Google Play, you might see apps that have prices in foreign currencies, such as in euros. When you purchase an app, the currency is simply converted into your local currency using the exchange rate at the time of purchase.

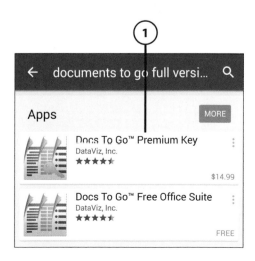

2. Scroll down to read the app's features, reviews by other people who have used it, and information on the person or company who created the app.

3. Scroll left and right to see the app screenshots.

4. Tap the price button to download and install the app.

5. Review the app permissions and make sure you can accept them. Some apps, such as the one shown here, do not require any permissions, but most require at least some. Tap Accept to proceed with the purchase.

6. Tap Buy to purchase the app. You will receive an email from Google Play after you purchase an app. The email serves as your invoice.

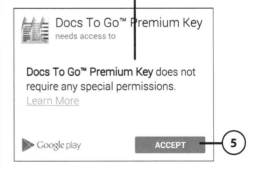

Review the permissions the app requires, if any.

Getting a Refund on an App

If you realize you've bought the wrong app, or otherwise regret a purchase, you can return it within two hours and get a full refund. To do this, open the Play Store app, go to the My Apps screen, tap the app to display its screen, and then tap Refund. If the Refund button doesn't appear, you're too late.

Tap Refund to get a refund on an app you've just bought.

Manage Apps

You can use the My Apps section of Google Play to update apps, delete them, or install apps that you have previously purchased.

1. In the Play Store app, touch the Menu button to display the menu panel.

2. Tap My Apps.

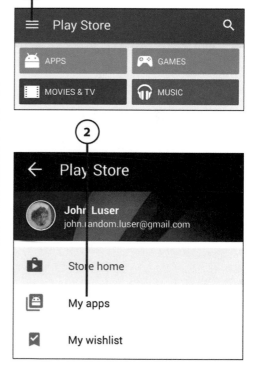

3. Tap All to see all apps that you have purchased on this Google account.

4. Look for the Installed indicator to see whether the app is currently installed.

5. Tap the Update indicator to update an installed app with the latest version.

6. Tap an unmarked app to install it. The lack of marking indicates a free app. This might be either an app you installed but then removed or an app you "purchased" (for free) on another device.

7. Tap the × button to remove an app from the list of apps.

8. Tap an app marked as Purchased to reinstall an app that you previously purchased and installed, but that is no longer installed, or an app that you purchased on another device. Because you have already purchased the app, you do not need to pay for it again.

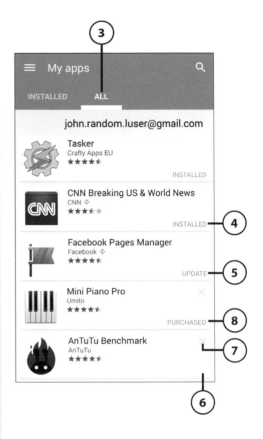

Allowing an App to Be Automatically Updated

When the developer of an app you have installed updates it to fix bugs or add new functionality, you are normally notified in the Notification bar and Notifications panel so that you can manually update the app.

Google Play enables you to choose to have the app automatically updated without your intervention. To do this, open the My Apps screen, tap the Installed tab, and then tap the app you want to update automatically. On the app's screen, tap the Menu button and then check the Auto-Update box. Be aware that if these updates occur while you are on a cellular data connection, your data usage for the month will be affected.

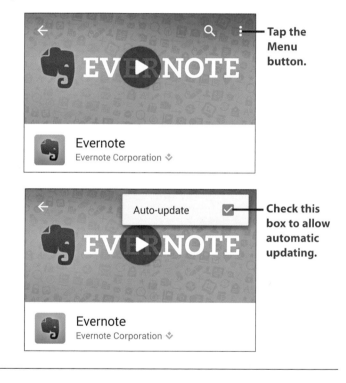

Tap the Menu button.

Check this box to allow automatic updating.

Uninstalling an App

To uninstall an app, tap the app's button on the My Apps screen, and then tap Uninstall on the app's screen. Uninstalling the app removes both the app itself and its data from your Galaxy Note 4. Although the app no longer resides on your Note 4, you can reinstall it as described in step 8 because the app remains tied to your Google account.

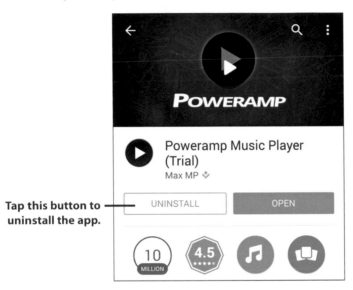

Tap this button to uninstall the app.

Manage Google Play Settings

1. In the Play Store app, tap the Menu button.

2. Tap Settings.

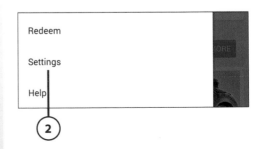

3. Tap the Notifications box to enable or disable notifications of app or game updates.

4. Tap Auto-Update Apps to display the Auto-Update Apps dialog.

5. Tap the appropriate radio button: Do Not Auto-Update Apps, Auto-Update Apps at Any Time, and Auto-Update Apps over Wi-Fi Only. Because apps can be large, choosing Auto-Update Apps over Wi-Fi Only is usually the best choice unless you want to disable automatic updating.

6. Tap the Add Icon to Home Screen box to control whether each app you install can add its app icon to the Home screen.

7. Tap Clear Search History to clear the Google Play search history. There's no double-check or confirmation beyond a quick blink of the button.

8. Tap Require Authentication for Purchases to display the Require Authentication dialog.

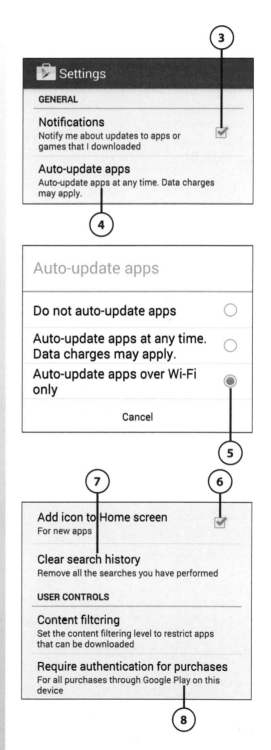

9. Tap the radio button for the authentication you want: For All Purchases Through Google Play on This Device (the most secure option), Every 30 Minutes (which gives moderate security), or Never (which gives none). The Confirm Password dialog opens.

10. Type your Google account password.

11. Tap OK.

12. Tap Content Filtering to display the Allow Apps Rated For dialog, where you can adjust or set your content filtering for apps.

Require authentication

For all purchases through Google Play on this device ⦿

Every 30 minutes ○ ──9

Never ○

Cancel

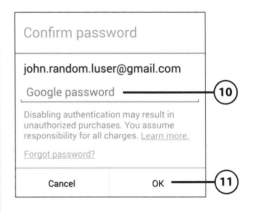

Confirm password

john.random.luser@gmail.com

Google password ──10

Disabling authentication may result in unauthorized purchases. You assume responsibility for all charges. Learn more.

Forgot password?

Cancel | OK ──11

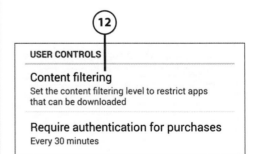

12

USER CONTROLS

Content filtering
Set the content filtering level to restrict apps that can be downloaded

Require authentication for purchases
Every 30 minutes

13. Tap the radio button for the highest level of maturity you want to allow: Everyone, Low Maturity, Medium Maturity, High Maturity, or Show All Apps.

14. Tap OK to close the Allow Apps Rated For dialog. The Content PIN dialog opens.

15. Tap the keypad to set a four-digit PIN that must be typed in before changing the Google Play User Control.

16. Tap OK. The Content PIN dialog closes, and the Enter Content PIN dialog opens.

17. Type the PIN again and then tap OK again. Android returns you to the Play Store app (not to the Settings screen).

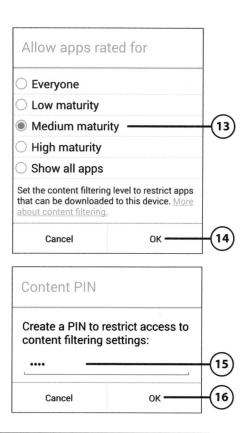

Why Lock the User Settings?

Imagine if you buy a Galaxy Note 4 for your child but want to make sure that he doesn't get to any undesirable content. First, you set the content filtering to restrict the content visible in Google Play. Next, you set the PIN so he can't change that setting. A similar idea goes for limiting purchases.

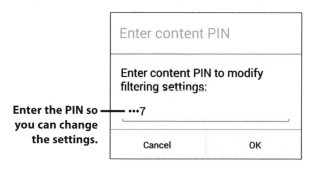

Enter the PIN so you can change the settings.

Accidentally Uninstall an App?

What if you accidentally uninstall an app or you uninstalled an app in the past but now decide you'd like to use it again? To get the app back, go to the My Apps screen in Google Play. Scroll to that app and tap it to display the app's screen. Tap Install to reinstall the app.

Keeping Apps Up to Date

Developers who write Android apps often update their apps to fix bugs or to add new features. With a few quick taps, you can easily update the apps you have installed.

1. On the Apps screen, touch the Play Store icon to launch the Play Store app.

2. Tap the Menu button to display the menu panel.

3. Tap My Apps to display the My Apps screen.

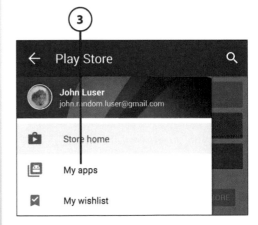

4. Tap Installed to display the Installed screen.

5. Tap Update to update an app.

Tap Update All to apply all available updates in one move.

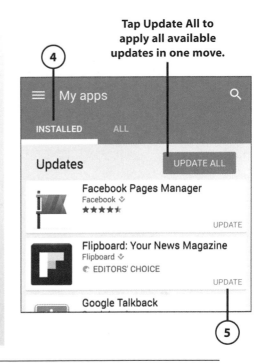

Starting an Update from the Notifications Panel

When your Galaxy Note 4 detects an update available for one of the apps you have installed, it displays the update notification in the Notification bar. You can open the My Apps screen in Google Play quickly by pulling down the Notifications panel and tapping the notification.

Tap an update notification to go straight to the My Apps screen.

Swipe up to read.

In this chapter, you discover how to set up your Android Wear smartwatch and use it with your Samsung Galaxy Note 4. Topics include the following:

→ Setting up your Android Wear watch
→ Choosing settings and installing apps
→ Navigating the Android Wear watch's interface
→ Using the Android Wear watch's apps

12

Using Your Samsung Galaxy Note 4 with an Android Wear Smartwatch

To get the most out of your Galaxy Note 4, you can link it to an Android Wear smartwatch. Android Wear watches are sold by vendors such as Samsung, LG, and Motorola and act as a companion for any Android smartphone, including your Note 4. The Android Wear watch enables you to display essential information, make phone calls, and allow simple interactions with apps without taking your Galaxy Note 4 out of your pocket.

Setting Up Your Android Wear Watch

To set up the Android Wear watch, you need to use your Galaxy Note 4.

1. Unpack the Android Wear watch and identify its components: the Android Wear watch itself, a charging dock/clip, and the charger.

2. Fully charge your Android Wear watch.

3. Turn the Android Wear watch on by pressing and holding its button for a moment. The button is on the right side of the Android Wear watch.

4. Tap to choose your preferred language on the watch screen.

5. When you see a screen on your watch telling you to install the Android Wear app on your phone, switch to your Note 4 for steps 6–14.

6. Search the Google Play Store for the Android Wear app. When you find it, tap Install.

7. Tap Accept to accept the permissions that the Android Wear app needs to run correctly. After the app installs, run it to start setting up your watch.

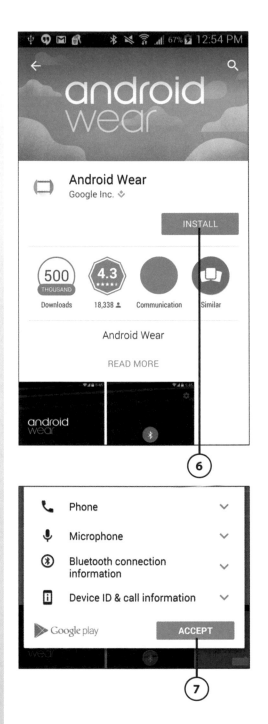

8. Tap the right arrow to start setting up your watch.

9. Tap Accept to accept that the Android Wear app will synchronize data between your watch and your Note 4.

10. Tap the name of the watch you want to use. In this example, it is a Samsung Gear Live, listed as "Gear Live 10C9."

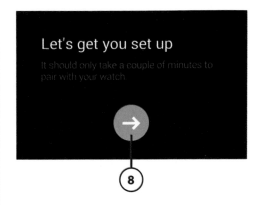

11. When prompted, accept the Bluetooth Pairing PIN on both your Note 4 and your watch. The PIN should be the same on both devices.

12. When your watch and Note 4 are paired over Bluetooth, you see a screen preparing you to configure Android to allow the Android Wear app to have access to notifications. Tap Notification Settings.

13. Check the box to allow the Android Wear app to receive access to Android notifications.

14. Tap OK to verify that you want the Android Wear app to have access to all Android notifications.

Android Wear Smartwatches Explained

Android Wear is a framework that Google created to support smartwatches connecting to Android devices. This enabled different vendors to create and sell smartwatches that have their own unique look and build quality but can all be compatible with any Android device as long as the owner installs the Android Wear app. Smartwatches that use the Android Wear framework can have square or round faces. Examples of Android Wear watches that have a round face are the Motorola Moto 360 and the LG G Watch R. Examples of Android Wear watches that have a square face are the Asus ZenWatch, Sony SmartWatch 3, Samsung Gear Live, and the LG G Watch. No matter whom you buy your Android Wear–based smartwatch from, and regardless of whether it has a square or round face, the instructions and guidance in this chapter are relevant.

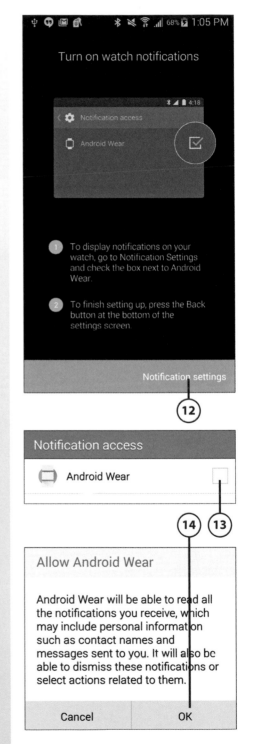

Choosing Settings for Your Android Wear Watch

After pairing your Android Wear watch with your Galaxy Note 4, you'll probably want to spend some time customizing the Android Wear watch. You can use the Android Wear app on your Galaxy Note 4 to configure overall settings for the Android Wear watch, as explained in this section. To configure other settings, you use the Settings app on the Android Wear watch itself, as discussed in the following section.

Navigate the Android Wear App

The Android Wear app gives you access to features and settings for configuring and managing your Android Wear watch.

1. Tap to launch the Android Wear app.

2. Tap a watch face to change it on your watch.

3. Tap to see all watch faces you have installed and find more.

4. Scroll down to see all voice actions and what apps are launched when the voice action triggers.

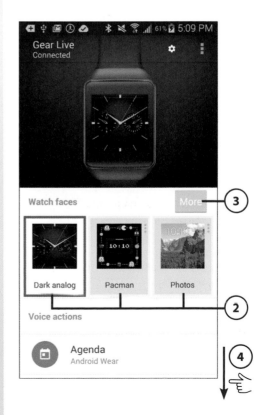

Set Voice Actions

Voice actions are voice commands you speak to your watch. Based on what you say, your watch either launches an app or takes an action, or it tells your Note 4 to launch an app. Some voice actions can be customized to make use of third-party watch apps that you install. Voice actions that are gray are voice actions that cannot use third-party watch apps, or you have not installed a third-party watch app to make use of them.

1. Your watch shows your agenda.

2. Your watch launches the Google Maps Micro watch app and allows you to get a list of turn-by-turn directions. The Google Maps Micro watch app also launches the Google Maps app on your Note 4, which actually provides the navigation to your watch.

3. Opens the Google Play Music app on your Note 4 and plays music.

4. Sets a timer on your watch.

5. Sets an alarm on your watch.

6. Shows the alarms set on your watch.

7. Shows your heart rate. Tap to choose which watch app launches to show your heart rate.

8. Scroll down for more voice actions.

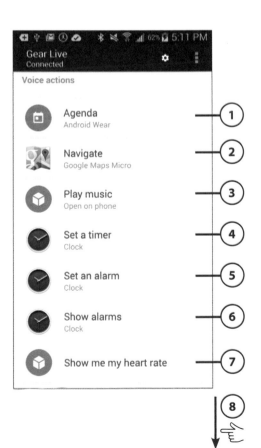

9. Shows how many steps you have walked with your watch on.

10. Starts a stopwatch on your watch. Tap to select which watch app launches to start the stopwatch.

Why Is the Icon Gray?

In the following steps, each of the voice actions shown in the figure have a gray Google Play icon next to them. That icon indicates that there is currently no app installed to handle the function provided by the voice action. After you install an appropriate app on your Note 4, these actions will be available.

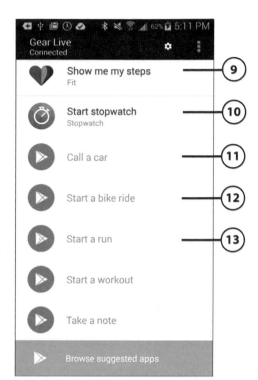

11. Call a car to pick you up. Install an app such as Lyft to make this voice action available. If you have two apps installed that both handle this function, tap Call a Car to choose the app you prefer to use.

12. Allows you to launch an app to start a bike ride. Install an app such as RunKeeper to make this voice action available. If you have two apps installed that both handle this function, tap Start a Bike Ride to choose the app you prefer to use.

13. Allows you to launch an app to start a run. Install an app such as RunKeeper to make this voice action available. If you have two apps installed that both handle this function, tap Start a Run to choose the app you prefer to use.

14. Allows you to launch an app to start a workout. Install an app such as RunKeeper to make this voice action available. If you have two apps installed that both handle this function, tap Start a Workout to choose the app you prefer to use.

How to Handle Riding, Running, and Workouts

Start a Bike Ride, Start a Run, and Start a Workout are functions that do not work until you install an app on your Note 4 to handle them. It is your choice which apps you want to install to handle these functions. The one used for writing this chapter was RunKeeper. It just so happens that RunKeeper handles all three functions, however that does not mean that you need to use only one app for all three functions. You can install three different apps to handle each of the three functions separately. Your favorite apps that you already use for tracking bike rides, for example, may already support Android Wear. If that is the case, you will select that app to support the bike ride function. If you have two apps installed that handle one or more of the functions, tap the function to choose which app you want to use. For example, to change what app handles Start a Bike Ride, tap Start a Bike Ride and choose your preferred app.

15. Allows you to launch an app to take a note. If you do not install an app to handle this voice action, when you use this feature, the note you dictate will be emailed to your Gmail address. Installing an app such as Chaos Control allows this voice action to launch your favorite note-taking app.

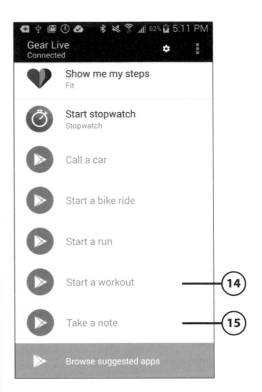

16. Tap to browse the Google Play store for watch apps to handle voice actions and standalone watch apps that provide additional functionality.

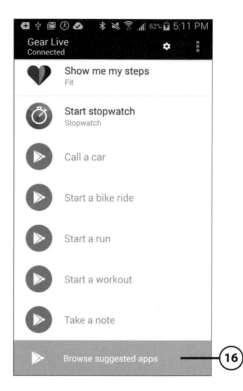

Choose a Watch Face

Your watch comes with some preinstalled watch faces, and you can use the Android Wear app to choose which one you want to use. You can also browse the Google Play Store for more. Some are free; some you must purchase.

1. From the main Android Wear app screen, tap one of the three most recent watch faces to set your watch to use it.

2. Tap More to see all watch faces you have installed.

3. Select a watch face to use.

4. Scroll down to the bottom of the screen and tap Get More Watch Faces to find more watch faces in the Google Play Store.

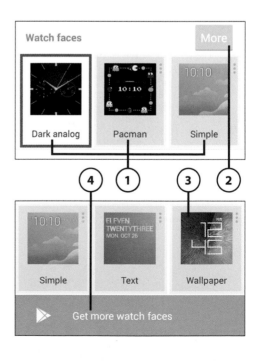

5. Tap to install a watch face.

6. Once your new watch face has been installed, it automatically downloads to your watch and is visible in the Android Wear app. Tap the watch face to make your watch start using it.

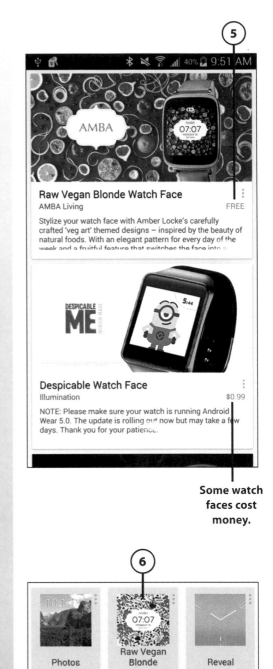

Some watch faces cost money.

7. Some watch faces have configuration options. If the watch face has settings that you can change that affect the way it works, the Settings icon displays over the watch face. Tap it to adjust the watch face's settings.

8. Tap to return to the main Android Wear app screen.

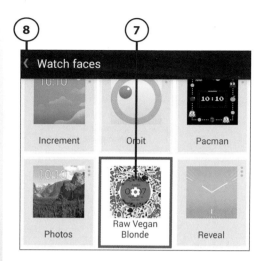

Adjust the Android Wear App's Settings

The Android Wear app does allow for some configuration, but also ways to view your watch's battery life and available memory.

1. From the main Android Wear app screen, tap the gear icon to see the settings.

2. Tap to choose apps that you no longer want to receive notifications for on your watch. By default, every notification from every app is sent to your watch. Use this setting to select which ones you really care about.

3. Check the box to set your watch to keep a low-resolution monochrome version of the screen on at all times, even when it goes to sleep.

4. Check the box to set your watch to wake up when it detects you tilting your wrist.

5. Tap to see how your watch's battery is performing and how much power each app is taking. Using this screen can help you identify apps that are draining the battery.

6. Tap to see your watch's memory usage, and how much memory each app is using.

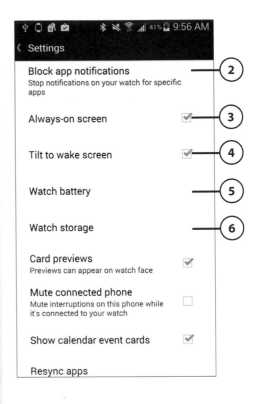

Watch Battery Usage

Viewing your watch's battery performance can help to determine how much longer your watch will last on its current charge based on current usage. You can also see which apps and watch faces are using the most battery time. Watch faces with a lot of animation can use a lot of battery charge. If you see a watch face or watch app that is using a lot of battery charge, you may choose to uninstall the app or stop using the watch face to help your watch last longer on a single charge.

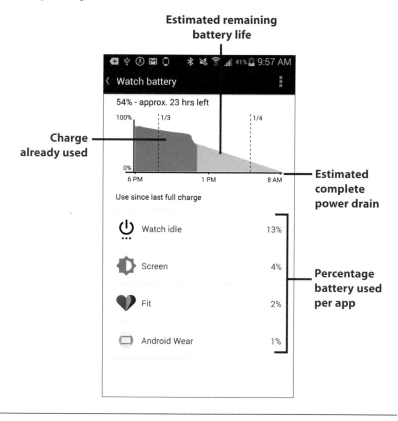

Watch Memory Usage

Viewing your watch's battery memory usage can help you see if your watch is running out of space, and if it is, which apps and watch faces are using the most memory.

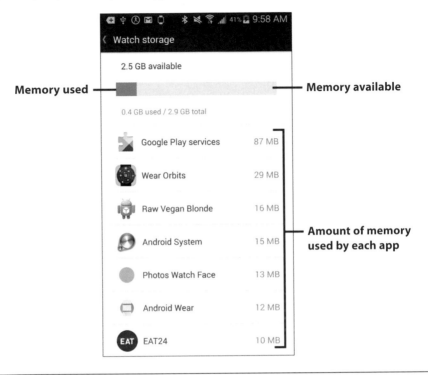

7. Check the box to allow a preview of an alert to be displayed on the bottom of the watch screen. If you uncheck this box, there will be no alert previews; however, you can still swipe up to view alerts.

8. Check the box to mute any alerts, notifications, or any other interruptions on your Note 4 while it is connected to the watch. Having this enabled helps cut down having alerts vibrate your Note 4 and your watch at the same time.

9. Check the box to show calendar events on your watch in the form of a card.

10. Tap to resynchronize apps between your Note 4 and your watch. You don't normally need to do this, but if you suspect that an app you recently installed on your Note 4 has not installed a mini-app on your watch, you can tap here.

11. Tap to return to the previous screen.

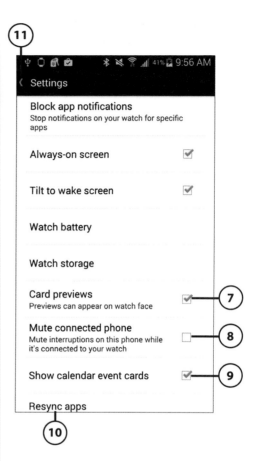

Install Apps on the Android Wear Watch

Some apps installed on your Note 4 will automatically install a watch app on your watch that helps you interact with the app from your watch. There are also dedicated watch apps that can be installed from the Google Play Store.

1. In the Android Wear app, scroll down to the bottom of the screen and tap Browse Suggested Apps.

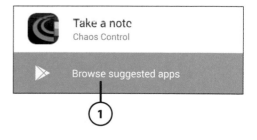

2. Scroll down to see all of the categories of watch apps. The categories are Watch Faces, New Year, Tools, Social, Productivity, Communication, Health & Fitness, Entertainment, Travel & Local, and Games.

3. Tap More to see more apps in a specific category.

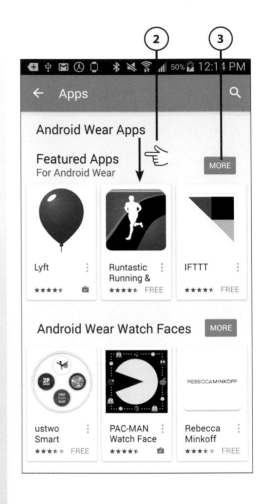

4. Tap an app you want to download. Some apps cost money. This example uses Reversi for Wear.

5. Tap Install.

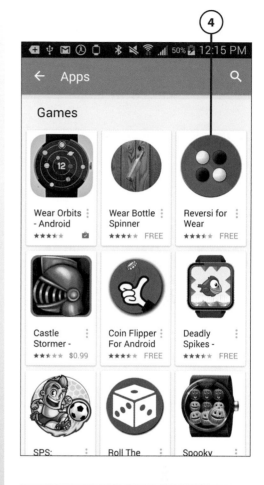

6. Tap Accept to accept any device or information permission the app needs to run. In this example, the app does not need any permissions.

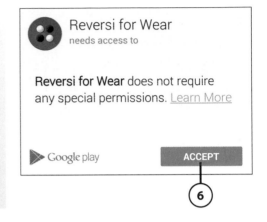

Using Your Android Wear Watch

Now that we have covered how to set up your watch via the Android Wear app, and you've installed some watch faces and apps, let's take a look at using the watch itself.

Watch Features

Your Android Wear watch actually runs on the Android operating system. As of the writing of this book, the version of Android running on Android Wear watches is Android 5.01 (Lollipop). Your watch either has a round or square face, includes an accelerometer to detect movement, a capacitive touchscreen so you can perform gestures such as tapping and swiping, and a microphone to listen for voice commands. Your watch probably also has a sensor to monitor your heart rate and a pedometer to measure your activity. Your watch relies on your Note 4 for the majority of its functions, including voice commands, so you must always have your Note 4 close by to use your watch. Although most Android Wear watches include a physical button, some do not.

Navigate Your Watch

Your watch responds to taps and swipes that allow you to navigate the interface, run apps, and see and respond to onscreen information.

1. While your watch is not being used, the screen becomes low resolution, monochrome, and dimmed to save energy.

2. Lift your arm to view your watch, and the screen will turn to full color.

3. Swipe notifications up to read them, and in some cases take actions on them. If you have more than one notification, swipe up repeatedly to read all of them.

4. Tap the preview of the notification to show more of it, and scroll down to read all of it.

5. Swipe the notification to the left to see any actions that you can take on the notification. This includes an option to block the app so that you don't see notifications from it again.

6. Swipe the notification to the right to dismiss it. To dismiss most apps while using them on your watch, swipe to the right.

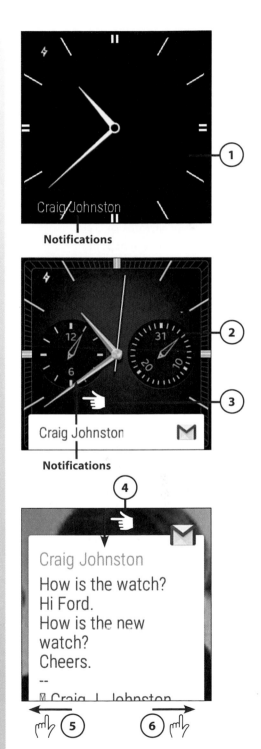

7. After you dismiss a notification, if you decide that you didn't want to, you can quickly swipe up from the bottom of the screen, and you will see a dismiss timer. Tap the timer to undo the dismiss before it runs out.

8. Swipe down from the top of the screen to see options and settings.

9. Tap to toggle mute on or off. When muted, your watch stops vibrating when alerts appear.

10. Swipe left to see more options.

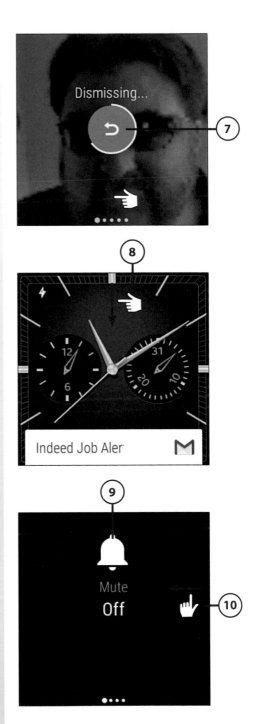

11. Tap to put your watch in Theater mode. When in Theater mode, the screen remains blank, you receive no notifications, and the action of lifting your arm to look at your watch will be deactivated. Press the watch button to exit Theater mode.

Alternative Method of Activating Theater Mode

If you double-press your watch's button, you will set it to Theater mode. Double-pressing the button makes the watch exit Theater mode.

12. Swipe left to see more options.

13. Tap to set your watch to Sunlight mode for five seconds. Sunlight mode sets the screen brightness to the maximum for five seconds to help with bright sunlight.

Alternative Method of Activating Sunlight Mode

If you triple-press your watch's button, Sunlight mode will be engaged for five seconds.

14. Swipe left to see more options.

15. Tap to change your watch's settings. See the next section for a description of all settings.

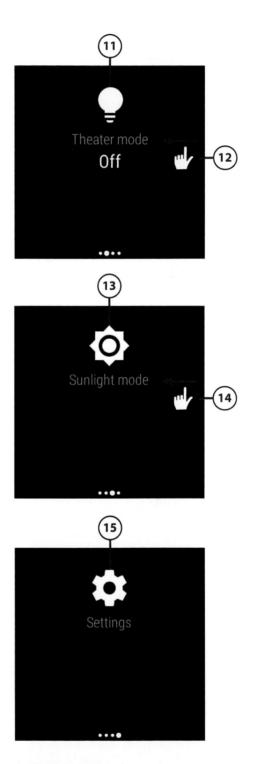

Adjust Your Watch's Settings

Use this section to adjust your watch's settings. To enter your watch's settings, you can either swipe down from the top of the screen and swipe left until you see the Settings icon, or tap your watch screen and scroll down to Settings.

1. Tap to manually adjust the brightness of your watch's screen.

2. Tap to pair your watch with Bluetooth devices such as Bluetooth speakers.

3. Scroll down for more settings.

4. Tap to toggle Always-on Screen on or off. When this is off, your watch screen no longer switches to the low-resolution mode when it goes to sleep; instead, it turns off completely.

5. Tap to toggle Airplane mode on or off. When in Airplane mode, your watch is not able to communicate using Bluetooth to your Note 4.

6. Tap to power off your watch.

7. Scroll down for more settings.

8. Tap to restart your watch. All your information remains untouched; your watch just restarts.

9. Tap to reset your watch. This puts the watch back to the way it came out of the box, and all your saved information will be lost.

10. Tap to change your watch face.

11. Scroll down for more settings.

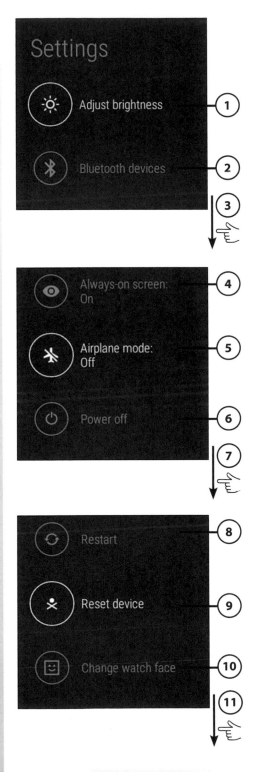

Choosing a New Watch Face

To change your watch face, swipe left and right to see all your installed watch faces and then tap the one you want to use.

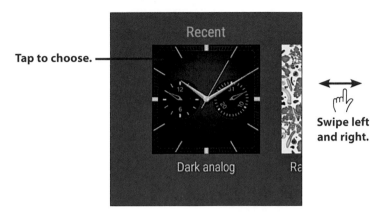

Tap to choose.

Swipe left and right.

12. Tap to change the size of the font used on your watch.

13. Tap to see information about your watch, as well as whether there is an update for it.

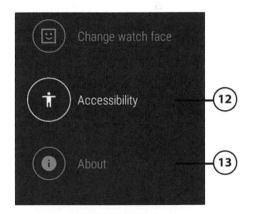

Use Your Watch and Run Watch Apps

Your watch was designed to be used with your voice. However, you can also manually select functions and apps by tapping and swiping on the screen.

1. Wake up your watch by lifting your arm. Alternatively, you can tap your watch's screen to wake it up.

2. After your watch wakes up and the screen turns to full color, say "OK Google." Alternatively, you can tap the watch screen.

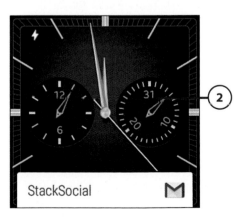

3. Your watch is now listening for a command. Say a command to perform an action or start an app. Use the next section to learn how to use each command and launch watch apps.

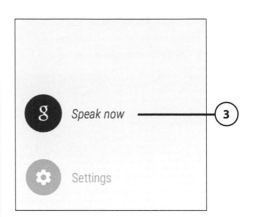

Use Watch Functions and Watch Apps

Your watch is designed for voice commands. However, if you don't speak, your watch stops listening and allows you to select functions and run apps using the touchscreen. It is your choice how you want to perform the following functions—either by speaking or by touching.

1. Say "Settings," or tap to see the Settings screen.

2. Say "Start Reversi" to start the Reversi app installed earlier in this chapter, or tap the Reversi icon to start it. Remember that Reversi is a watch app, so you must say "Start." You can also start watch apps by saying "Run" (for example, "Run Reversi").

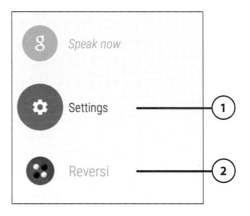

3. Say "Start Stopwatch," or tap to start the Stopwatch watch app.

4. Say "Take a note," or tap and speak the text of the note, to take a note. For example, you can say "Take a note to drink more water" and a new note will be created with the text "Drink more water." If you have previously installed an app that handles notes, the note will be saved to that app. Otherwise, your note will be emailed to your Gmail account.

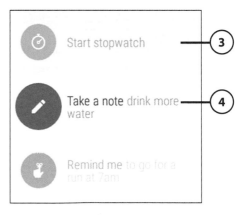

5. Say "Remind me," or tap and speak the reminder to add. For example, you can say "Remind me to go for a run at 7 a.m." and a new reminder will be created labeled "Go for a run" set for 7:00 a.m. the next day. You can also set recurring reminders. For example, you can say "Remind me to make coffee at 8 a.m. every weekday."

6. Say "Start a run," or tap to launch the app you installed to handle your runs. Start running and use the watch app you installed to monitor your run.

7. Say "Show me my steps," or tap to show how many steps you have walked. Your watch uses its built-in pedometer to keep track of your steps.

8. Say "Show me my heart rate," or tap to activate your watch's heart rate monitor. Follow the instructions to allow your watch to take your heart rate.

9. Say "Send text," or tap and speak the name of the recipient and the text message to send a text message to someone. For example, you can say "Send a text to Jim, see you later" and a new text message will be created to Jim with the text "See you later." If the contact has more than one phone number, you need to state which phone number to use, for example "Send a text to Jim mobile."

Contact Recognition

You must enable contact recognition for the "send a text" and "send an email" functions to work. To do this, on your Note 4, tap Settings, Accounts, Google, Accounts & Privacy, and check the box next to Contact Recognition.

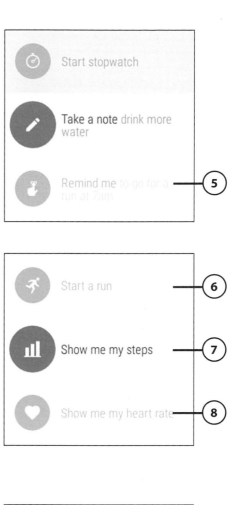

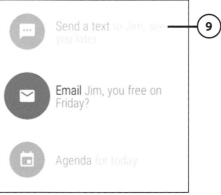

10. Say "Email," or tap and speak the name of the recipient and message. For example, you can say "Email Jim, you free on Friday"? and a new email will be created to Jim with the body of the message set to "You free on Friday?" If you have more than one person with the same name, and you are not specific, you are prompted to say the person's full name. If the person has more than one email address, you will be prompted to say the one to use (for example, Home or Work).

11. Say "Agenda" or tap to see your agenda for today.

12. Say "Navigate," or tap and speak the desired destination to start turn-by-turn directions to your desired destination. You can say things like "to a pizza place nearby" or "home" or "work," or you can speak an address. Turn-by-turn directions start on your Note 4, with a mini version of them being displayed on your watch.

13. Say "Set a timer," or tap and speak the time the timer must use. For example, you can say "Set a timer for 45 minutes." The timer starts on your watch.

14. Say "Start stopwatch," or tap to start the stopwatch app on your watch.

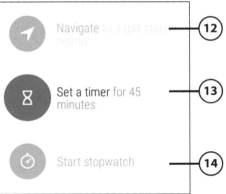

15. Say "Set an alarm," or tap and speak when the alarm must be set for. For example, you can say "Set an alarm for 6 this evening." The alarm will be created. Before the alarm is finished being created, you can tap Edit to edit the alarm and even make it recurring by selecting certain days of the week when it must trigger.

16. Say "Show alarms," or tap to show the alarms that have been set on your watch. You can edit or remove individual alarms by using the touch screen.

17. Say "Call a car," or tap to launch the car pickup service you installed on your Note 4 that supports Android Wear, such as Lyft.

18. Say "Play music," or tap to start playing an "I'm feeling lucky" mix on your Note 4. You can also say "Play Depeche Mode" to start playing all songs by Depeche Mode on your Note 4. See the "Play Music from Your Watch" sidebar at the end of this chapter for more information.

19. Say "Settings," or tap to see your watch's settings.

20. Say "Start," or tap and say the name of a watch app you have installed. For example, if you installed an app called Eat24, you would say "Start Eat 24."

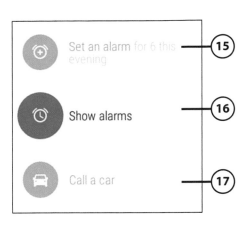

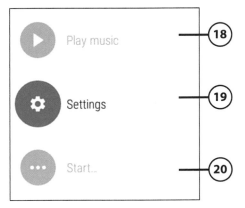

Reply to an Email Using Your Voice

When you receive a new email notification on your watch, you can reply to the email using your voice. To do this, swipe up the email notification. Swipe the notification to the left twice and tap Reply. Speak your reply. When you stop speaking, your watch sends the reply using the message you dictated.

Tap to reply.   **Speak your reply.**

>>>Go Further
MORE ABOUT NOTIFICATIONS

If there is more than one notification from an app (this is common for email notifications), you see a plus (+) symbol and a number indicating how many more notifications there are from this app. Tap the number, and all the notifications will be shown. Tap the one you want to interact with.

Digg

This Week's Best Videos: A Ruthless Dart-Throwing Man, North Carolina's

+3 more ——— **Tap to see all notifications from the app.**

Some notifications you see come from apps that do not provide any way to interact with them. Your only choice is to have your watch tell your Note 4 to open the corresponding app. You can then continue interacting with the app on your Note 4. To do this, swipe the notification to the left and tap Open on Phone.

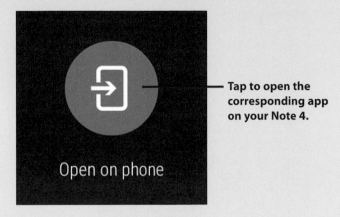

Tap to open the corresponding app on your Note 4.

>>>Go Further

PLAY MUSIC FROM YOUR WATCH

It's easy to command your watch to play music that is stored on your Note 4; however, you can also store music on your watch. To do this, open the Google Play Music app, open Settings, and check the box next to Download to Android Wear to download a copy of any music that you choose to your Android Wear watch. To switch to playing music from your Note 4 to your watch, after you say "OK Google, Play music," tap the blue X and tap Android Wear. This then allows you to play only music that is stored on your watch. To hear the music, you need to have a Bluetooth speaker paired with your watch. To switch back to playing music on your Note 4, say "OK Google, Play music," tap the blue X, and tap Phone.

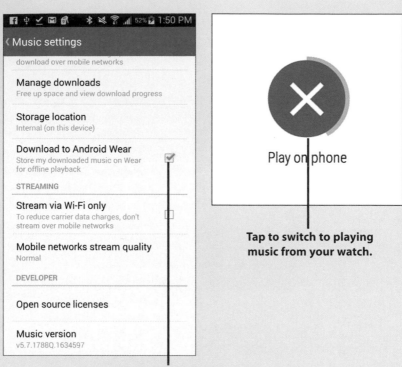

Check to load music to your watch.

Tap to switch to playing music from your watch.

When you choose to play music from your watch, swipe up and down to scroll through the albums. When you find an album you want to play, swipe left to choose to shuffle the songs on the album. Swipe left again to see the songs on the album. Scroll through the songs and tap one to start playing it. If you try to play music from your phone before you have paired a Bluetooth device capable of receiving the audio, you are prompted to complete the pairing process.

Swipe up to scroll through your albums.

Tap a song to play it.

Violator

World In My Eyes
Depeche Mode

Personal Jesus
Depeche Mode

Swipe up to scroll through the songs.

Shuffle

Tap to shuffle.

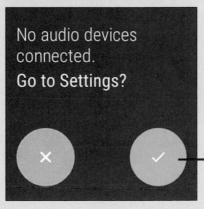

No audio devices connected.
Go to Settings?

Tap to connect a Bluetooth speaker.

See your battery usage trends.

In this chapter, you discover how to maintain your Galaxy Note 4 and solve problems. Topics include the following:

→ Updating Android
→ Optimizing battery life
→ Identifying battery-hungry apps
→ Caring for your Galaxy Note 4

13

Maintaining Your Galaxy Note 4 and Solving Problems

Every so often, Google releases new versions of Android that include bug fixes and new features. In this chapter, you find out how to upgrade your Galaxy Note 4 to a new version of Android and how to tackle common problem-solving issues and general maintenance of your Galaxy Note 4.

Updating Android

New releases of Android are always exciting because they add new features, fix bugs, and tweak the user interface. Here is how to update your Galaxy Note 4.

Updating Information

Updates to Android are not on a set schedule. The update messages appear as you turn on your Galaxy Note 4, and they remain in the Notification bar until you install the update. If you tap Install Later, your Note 4 reminds you at short intervals—30 minutes, 1 hour, or 3 hours—that there's an update. When to install the update is up to you. You might prefer to wait to see if each new update contains any bugs that need to be worked out rather than applying each update immediately.

1. Pull down the Notification bar to open the Notification shade.

Manually Checking for Updates

If you think there should be an update for your Galaxy Note 4 but have not yet received the onscreen notification, you can check manually by tapping Settings, System, About Device, and Software Updates in Tab view. (In List view, tap Settings, About Device, and Software Updates.) On the Software Updates screen, tap Update Now to check for an update.

2. Tap Software Update to display the Software Updates screen.

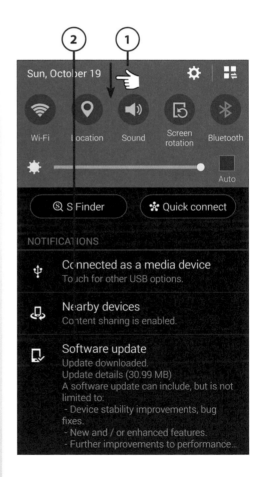

3. Tap Update Now. The Software Update screen appears, showing the details of the update the Galaxy Note 4 has downloaded.

4. Tap Install.

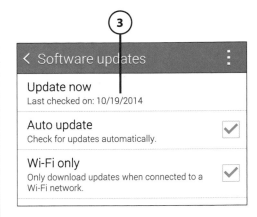

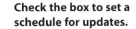

Check the box to set a schedule for updates.

Arranging Scheduled Software Updates

For simplicity, you can set your Galaxy Note 4 to install software updates on a schedule. To do so, check the Scheduled Software Updates box on the Software Update screen.

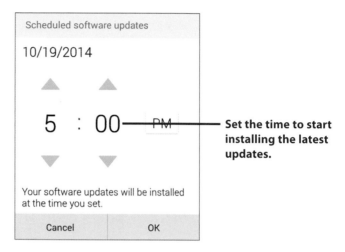

Set the time to start installing the latest updates.

On the Scheduled Software Updates screen, use the spin dials to set the time you want your Galaxy Note 4 to start installing the latest updates. If there are multiple updates, the Galaxy Note 4 downloads and installs them in sequence, so it might take some time to finish the updates. You can then tap the OK button, and your Galaxy Note 4 will run the updates at the time you specified.

5. Tap OK in the next Software Update dialog, which tells you that the device will be rebooted. Your Galaxy Note 4 restarts, installs the update, and then displays the Lock screen.

6. Unlock the Galaxy Note 4 as usual. For example, swipe the screen and then type your passcode. A Software Update screen displays, confirming that the device has been updated successfully.

7. Tap OK to close the screen. You can then resume using your Galaxy Note 4 normally.

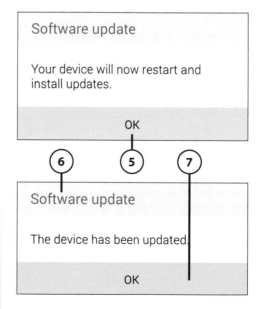

Optimizing the Battery

The battery in your Galaxy Note 4 is a lithium-ion battery that provides good battery life as long as you take care of it. You can change the way you use your Galaxy Note 4 to prolong the battery life so that the battery lasts long enough for you to use the phone all day.

Carrying a Spare Battery

One of the great things about the Galaxy Note 4 is how easily you can remove the back and change the battery. Given this feature, you might prefer to buy and carry a spare battery instead of scrimping on display brightness and phone usage. When your current battery runs out, you can power off the Note 4, pop in the spare battery, and restart it in less than a minute.

You can also buy higher-capacity batteries to get longer battery life. Some of these batteries fit inside the battery compartment and offer modestly higher battery capacity. Others are larger and include a custom back, or custom case, for the Galaxy Note 4.

Take Care of the Battery

There are specific steps you follow to take care of the battery in your Galaxy Note 4 and make it last longer.

Follow these steps to care for your Galaxy Note 4's battery:

1. Try to avoid discharging the battery completely. Fully discharging the battery too frequently harms the battery. Instead, try to keep it at least partially charged at all times (except as described in the next step).

2. To avoid a false battery level indication on your Galaxy Note 4, let the battery fully discharge about every 30 charges. Lithium-ion batteries do not have "memory" like older battery technologies, but fully discharging the battery once in a while helps keep the battery meter working correctly.

3. Avoid letting your Galaxy Note 4 get overheated because this can damage the battery and make it lose charge quickly. Do not leave your Note 4 in a hot car or out in the sun anywhere, including on the beach.

4. Consider having multiple chargers. For example, you could have one at home, one at work, and one in your car. This enables you to always keep your phone charged.

Monitor Battery Use

Android enables you to see exactly what apps and system processes are using the battery on your Galaxy Note 4. Armed with this information, you can alter your usage patterns to extend the Galaxy Note 4's run time on the battery.

1. On the Apps screen, tap Settings.

2. Tap the System tab. If the tab isn't visible, swipe left to find it.

3. Tap Power Saving to display the Power Saving screen.

4. Tap the Refresh icon to manually refresh the display.

5. Tap an app or Android service to see more details about it, including how much time it has been active, how much processor (CPU) time it has used, and—if the app has used data—how much data it has sent and received.

6. Tap the battery charge and usage diagram to display the History Details screen, which contains more details on the power consumption.

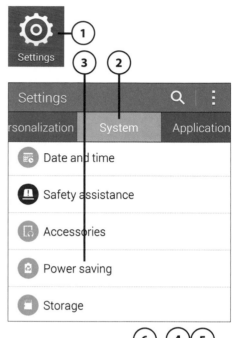

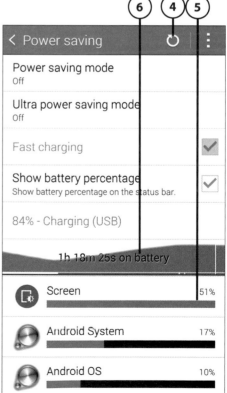

7. Look at the Mobile Network Signal readout to see when the mobile network signal was being used during the battery graph's time span.

8. Look at the Location On readout to determine when the GPS radio was being used during the battery graph's time span.

9. Look at the Wi-Fi readout to see when the Wi-Fi radio was being used during the battery graph's time span.

10. Look at the Awake readout to learn when your Galaxy Note 4 was awake during the battery graph's time span.

11. Look at the Screen On readout to check when your Galaxy Note 4's screen was on during the battery graph's time span.

12. Look at the Charging readout to find out when your Galaxy Note 4 was charging (if at all) during the battery graph's time span.

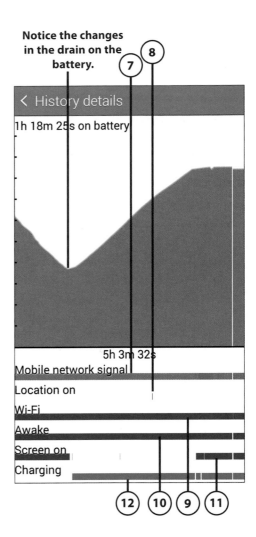

Notice the changes in the drain on the battery.

< History details

1h 18m 25s on battery

5h 3m 32s

Mobile network signal

Location on

Wi-Fi

Awake

Screen on

Charging

How Can Seeing Battery Drain Help?

If you look at the way your battery has been draining, you can see when the battery was draining the fastest, and you should be able to remember what apps you were using at that time or what you were doing on your Galaxy Note 4. Based on that, you can change your usage habits—for example, you can plan to charge your Galaxy Note 4 after a session of phone calls. You can uninstall any apps that appear to be power hogs, or you can simply avoid using them when running on the battery.

Choose Power-Saving Options

Your Galaxy Note 4 includes a feature called Power Saving Mode that enables you to reduce the amount of power it consumes. After choosing which of three power-saving options to use, you can turn Power Saving on and off by using its switch on the Settings screen.

For times when the battery is dangerously low, the Galaxy Note 4 also includes a feature called Ultra Power Saving Mode that reduces power usage to a minimum by changing the Home screen to grayscale and limiting the number of apps you can use.

Use Power Saving Mode

1. Tap Settings on the Apps screen.

2. Tap the System tab.

3. Tap the Power Saving button to display the Power Saving screen.

4. Tap the Power Saving Mode button to display the Power Saving Mode screen.

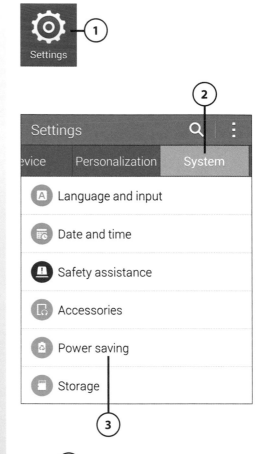

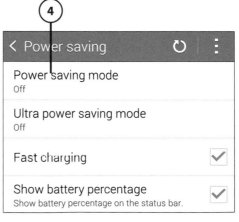

5. Move the Power Saving Mode switch to On to make the settings available.

6. Tap the unchecked Restrict Background Data box if you want to prevent apps in the background from transferring data across the cellular connection. The Restrict Background Data dialog opens.

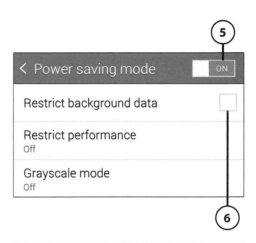

Why Restrict Background Data?

When you're actively using an app on your Galaxy Note 4 via the cellular connection, it's usually obvious when it's transferring data.

Apps can also transfer data in the background. For example, your email apps typically continue to download new messages when they're in the background, or the Settings app may download updates that have become available.

Background data transfer is usually helpful, but it can add up to a considerable power drain on your device's battery. So when you need to eke out battery life, it is a good idea to restrict background data transfer.

7. Tap the OK button to close the dialog. The Restrict Background Data check box is now checked.

8. Tap Restrict Performance to display the Restrict Performance screen.

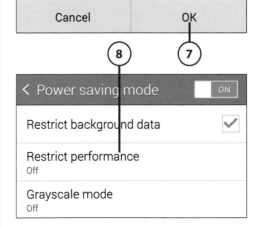

9. Move the Restrict Performance switch to On to make the settings available.

10. Check the CPU Performance box to enable throttling back the processor when the Galaxy Note 4 is running on battery power.

11. Check the Screen Output box to enable reducing the screen's brightness on the battery.

12. Check the Turn Off Touch Key Light box to prevent your Galaxy Note 4 from lighting up the Recent Apps button and the Back button when you tap them.

13. Check the Turn Off GPS box to turn off the GPS feature and disable all location services.

14. Tap Restrict Performance or the Back button to return to the Power Saving Mode screen.

15. If you want to use grayscale mode, tap Grayscale Mode. The Grayscale Mode screen appears.

16. Move the Grayscale Mode switch to On. The screen changes from color to grayscale.

17. Tap Grayscale Mode or the Back button to return to the Power Saving Mode screen if you want to choose further settings. Otherwise, press the Home button to display the Home screen, or tap the Recent Apps button to display the Recent Apps screen so that you can switch to another app you've been using.

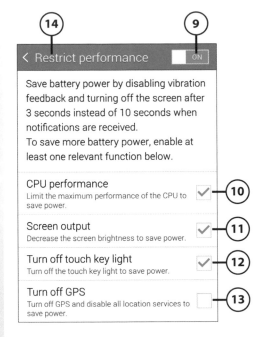

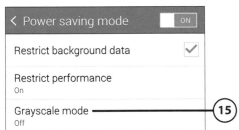

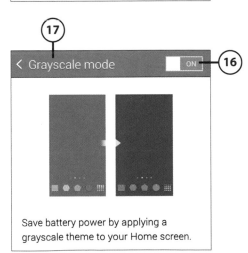

Turning Power Saving Mode On and Off Quickly

When you need to squeeze the most run time out of your Galaxy Note 4's battery, you'll probably want to turn Power Saving Mode on and off at a moment's notice. To do so, pull down with two fingers from the top of the screen to display the Quick Settings panel, and then tap the Power Saving icon.

Tap the U. Power Saving icon to turn Ultra Power Saving Mode on or off.

Tap the Power Saving icon to turn Power Saving Mode on or off.

Power Saving Mode uses the settings you have configured on the Power Saving Mode screen—for example, restricting performance but not turning on grayscale mode. If you want to change the settings, open the Quick Settings panel and tap and hold the Power Saving icon to jump straight to the Power Saving Mode screen.

Use Ultra Power Saving Mode

Using the regular Power Saving Mode can net you much more run time on the battery, but when you're in serious danger of running out of power, you can switch to Ultra Power Saving Mode instead. Ultra Power Saving Mode changes the screen to grayscale, restricts you to essential apps, turns off Wi-Fi and Bluetooth, and allows cellular data only when the screen is on. So it's really no fun at all. It's more of a get-you-home measure (or a get-you-to-a-power-source measure—the Galaxy Note 4's equivalent of a spare tire).

You can turn on Ultra Power Saving Mode in the Settings app, but because the mode has no configurable settings, it's easier to use the Quick Settings panel. Follow these steps:

1. Pull down with two fingers from the top of the screen to open the Quick Settings panel.

2. Tap the U. Power Saving icon. The Ultra Power Saving Mode screen opens.

Accepting the Terms and Conditions for Ultra Power Saving Mode

The first time you turn on Ultra Power Saving Mode, your Galaxy Note 4 displays a Terms and Conditions screen emphasizing that the run time that Ultra Power Saving Mode displays may not be strictly accurate because it depends on your device's network configuration, what you're doing with the device, and a handful of other variables, including the operating temperature (yes, really). You must check the box agreeing to the terms and conditions before you can tap the OK button to start using Ultra Power Saving Mode.

3. Look at the Battery Percentage readout and the Estimated Max. Standby Time readout to see how long Ultra Power Saving Mode may give you.

4. Tap Turn On to turn on Ultra Power Saving Mode. The screen changes to grayscale, and the Home screen appears.

Bare-Bones Home Screen

At first, the Home screen displays the icons for only three apps: Phone, Messages, and Internet. You can customize the apps (see the next task) on the Home screen by adding other apps from the meager selection that Ultra Power Saving mode offers; after that, you can remove any apps you've added, but you cannot change the default three apps.

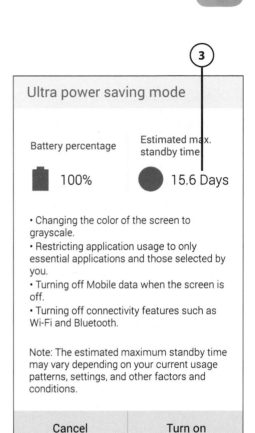

③

Ultra power saving mode

Battery percentage	Estimated max. standby time
100%	15.6 Days

• Changing the color of the screen to grayscale.
• Restricting application usage to only essential applications and those selected by you.
• Turning off Mobile data when the screen is off.
• Turning off connectivity features such as Wi-Fi and Bluetooth.

Note: The estimated maximum standby time may vary depending on your current usage patterns, settings, and other factors and conditions.

Cancel   Turn on

④

Customize the Home Screen in Ultra Power Saving Mode

1. Tap one of the Add (+) buttons to display the Add Application screen. Tap the button for the position in which you want to add the app.

2. Tap the app you want to add. The app appears on the Home screen. You can then repeat the steps to add other apps, up to the maximum of six.

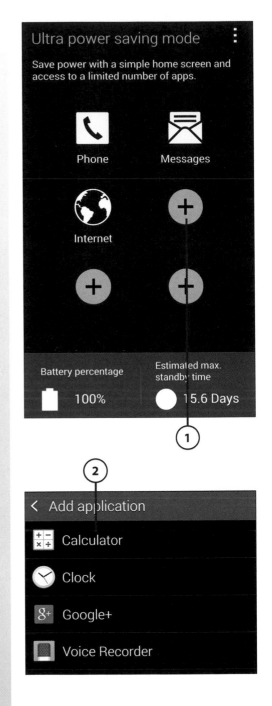

3. Remove one of the apps you've added by tapping the Menu button.

4. Tap Remove. A screen appears for customizing the Home screen.

5. Tap Delete (–) for the app you want to remove.

6. Tap OK to stop customizing the Home screen.

Choosing Settings in Ultra Power Saving Mode

Ultra Power Saving Mode enables you to configure a limited range of settings. To do so, tap the Menu button on the Home screen and tap Settings to display the Settings screen. You can then tap the appropriate button—Wi-Fi, Bluetooth, Airplane Mode, Mobile Networks, Location, Sound, or Brightness—and configure settings as usual.

Turn Off Ultra Power Saving Mode

1. Tap the Menu button on the Home screen.

2. Tap Turn Off Ultra Power Saving Mode. An Ultra Power Saving Mode screen opens.

3. Tap the Turn Off button.

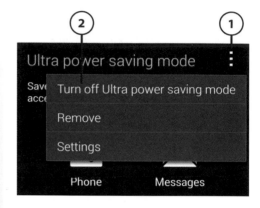

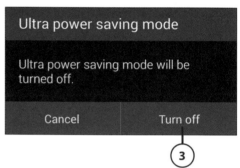

Managing Apps and Memory

Your Galaxy Note 4 can run many apps at the same time. With Android, you don't normally close apps between uses or after using them; instead, you leave them running in the background, which enables you to switch quickly to a running app when you need to use it again. However, when you want to close apps, you can easily close either individual apps or all the apps you're running.

The Galaxy Note 4's three tools for managing apps and memory overlap with each other and are somewhat confusing. Here are the essentials:

- **Recent Apps list**—You can close one or more apps quickly from the Recent Apps list when you no longer want those apps open.

- **Active Applications screen**—If you suspect that an app is slowing down your Galaxy Note 4, you can view the Active Applications screen to identify the culprit and close it from there.

- **Active App screen**—If an app or service seems to be causing your Galaxy Note 4 problems, you can use the Active App screen to forcibly close the app or service.

Close One or More Apps from the Recent Apps List

The quick way to close one or more apps is by using the Recent Apps list. Follow these steps:

1. From whichever screen you're currently on, tap the Recents button to display the Recent Apps screen.

2. Swipe each app you want to close off the list to the left or right.

3. If you want to close all open apps, tap Close All.

Close One or More Apps from the Active Applications Screen

In addition to using the Recent Apps list to close apps, you can close apps from the Active Applications screen in the Settings app. The advantage of this method is that you can see how much RAM your Galaxy Note 4 has free and how much RAM and CPU time each of the active apps is taking up, so you can identify resource hogs and close them to free up RAM and CPU time. Here, too, you can close either a single app or all the active apps.

1. From whichever screen you're currently on, tap the Recents button to display the Recent Apps screen.

2. Tap Active Applications to display the Active Applications screen.

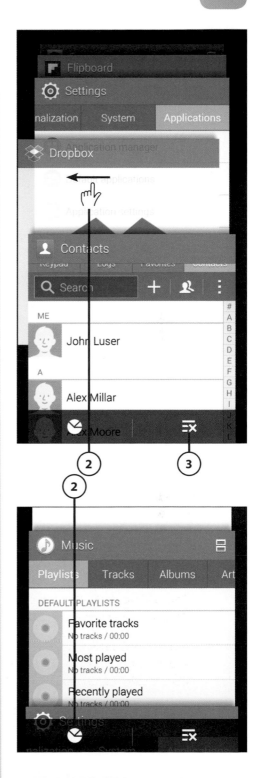

3. Look at the RAM Status readout to see how much RAM is in use and how much is free.

4. In the Active Applications list, look for any app that is using a lot of RAM or CPU time, as Chrome is in the example shown here. The End button for any app that appears to be having problems appears in red, whereas the End button for any app that is running okay appears in black.

5. Tap the End button for an app to close that app. The End dialog box opens.

6. Tap OK to close the app. You can then either close other apps as needed or resume what you were doing by pressing the Home button or tapping the Recents button.

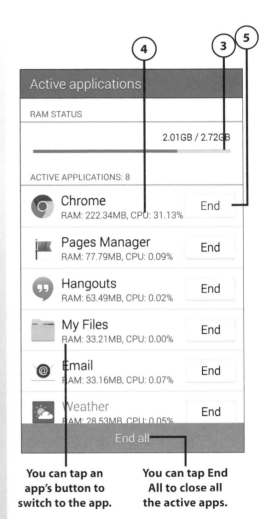

You can tap an app's button to switch to the app.

You can tap End All to close all the active apps.

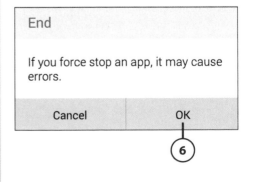

Force an App or a Service to Close

If closing apps in the ways just described doesn't solve the problems your Galaxy Note 4 is exhibiting, you may need to force an app or a service to close. This is an action you should take only to resolve problems, not as a regular move.

To force an app or service to close, follow these steps:

1. On the Apps screen, tap Settings to open the Settings app.

2. Tap the Applications tab.

3. Tap Application Manager to display the Application Manager screen.

4. Swipe left one or more times as needed to display the Running tab. This tab lists the apps that are currently running.

5. Look at the graph to see how much memory is being used by running apps and cached processes, and how much is free.

6. Tap an app to display the Active App screen, which contains more information about the app.

Tap to see processes that Android is caching.

7. Tap Stop if you believe the app is misbehaving.

8. Tap Report to report an app to Google. You might want to do this if it is misbehaving, using up too many resources, or you suspect it of stealing data. Some apps disable the Report button to prevent reporting.

9. Look at the Processes readout to see the processes that this app is using.

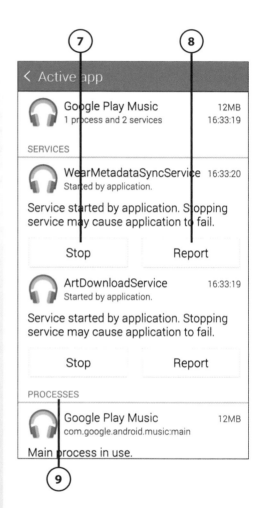

When Should You Manually Stop a Service or an App?

After you have been using your Galaxy Note 4 for a while, you'll become familiar with how long it takes to do certain tasks, such as typing, navigating menus, and so on. If you notice your phone becoming slow or not behaving the way you think it should, the culprit could be a new app you recently installed or a system service that has encountered a problem. Because Android doesn't normally quit an app or a service, the app or service continues running in the background, which might cause your Galaxy Note 4 to slow down. When this happens, it is useful to manually stop the app or service. If stopping one or more apps or services doesn't help, try restarting your Galaxy Note 4.

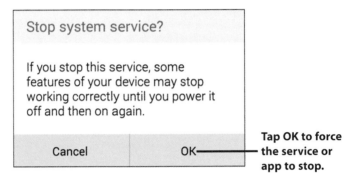

Stop system service?

If you stop this service, some features of your device may stop working correctly until you power it off and then on again.

Cancel   OK

Tap OK to force the service or app to stop.

Reining in Your Data Usage

If you are worried that you might exceed your data plan in a month, you can set a usage limit on your Galaxy Note 4. You can even prevent apps from using data while they are running in the background rather than in the foreground.

1. On the Apps screen, tap Settings to open the Settings app.

Settings

2. Tap Connections to display the Connections screen.

3. Tap Data Usage to display the Data Usage screen.

4. Make sure Mobile Data is checked to enable data transfer over your Galaxy Note 4's cellular connection.

5. Tap Set Mobile Data Limit to enable or disable mobile data limits. On the Limit Data Usage screen that opens, read the warning (that your service provider may account for usage differently than your Galaxy Note 4 does), and then tap OK. When the mobile data limit is enabled, your Galaxy Note 4 automatically cuts off all mobile data usage when the limit you set in step 7 is reached.

6. Tap the Data Usage Cycle pop-up menu to set the monthly billing cycle your cellular carrier uses for your Galaxy Note 4's account.

7. Tap the red handle and drag the red line up or down to select the mobile data limit you want to impose. This might or might not match your cellular data plan limit.

8. Tap the orange handle and drag the orange line up and down to set a data usage warning threshold. When you reach or pass this threshold, you see a warning in the Notification bar.

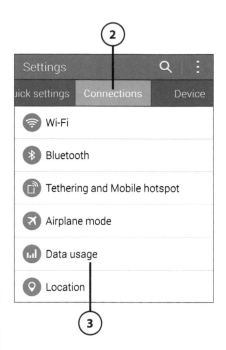

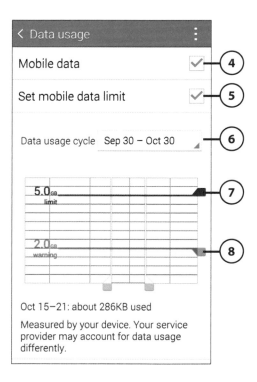

9. Scroll down if necessary, and tap an app to see more details about its data usage and to control how it uses data in the background.

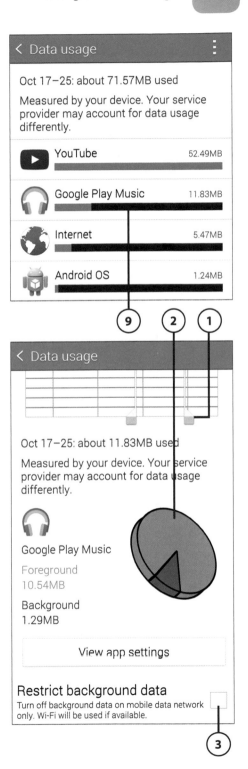

< Data usage

Oct 17–25: about 71.57MB used

Measured by your device. Your service provider may account for data usage differently.

▶ YouTube	52.49MB
🎧 Google Play Music	11.83MB
🌐 Internet	5.47MB
🤖 Android OS	1.24MB

⑨ ② ①

Set Background Data Limits

When you tap an app to see its data usage, you can also limit its usage when it is in the background. An app is in the background when you have launched the app but you are not currently using it. An app in the background still takes up memory and might still be transferring data.

1. Look at the Data Usage chart to see the data usage for this app specifically.

2. Look at the pie chart to see the breakdown of data usage in the foreground and background.

3. Tap the Restrict Background Data check box to restrict the app from using data while it is in the background.

< Data usage

Oct 17–25: about 11.83MB used

Measured by your device. Your service provider may account for data usage differently.

🎧

Google Play Music

Foreground
10.54MB

Background
1.29MB

View app settings

Restrict background data
Turn off background data on mobile data network only. Wi-Fi will be used if available.

③

Caring for the Galaxy Note 4's Exterior

Because you need to touch your Galaxy Note 4's screen to use it, it picks up oils and other residue from your hands. You also might get dirt on other parts of the phone. Here is how to clean your Galaxy Note 4 and how to avoid damaging its multipurpose jack:

- Wipe the screen with a microfiber cloth. You can purchase these in most electronic stores, or you can use the one that came with your sunglasses.

- To clean dirt off other parts of your phone, wipe it with a damp cloth. Never use soap or chemicals on your Galaxy Note 4 because they can damage it.

- When inserting the connector on the USB cable, try not to force it in the wrong way. If you damage the pins inside your Galaxy Note 4, you will need to take the battery out and use an external charger to charge it.

Protecting Your Galaxy Note 4's Exterior

Another way to care for your Galaxy Note 4's exterior is to protect it with a case. Many different types of cases are available from both brick-and-mortar stores and online stores. To protect the screen, you can apply a screen protector. When choosing a screen protector, make sure it is thin enough for the S Pen to work effectively.

Getting Help with Your Galaxy Note 4

There are many resources on the Internet where you can get help with your Galaxy Note 4.

1. Visit Samsung's official Galaxy Note 4 and Galaxy Gear site at www.samsung.com/global/microsite/galaxynote4/.

2. Visit Google's official Android website at www.android.com.

3. Check out Android blogs such as these:

   - Android Central at www.androidcentral.com/

   - Android Guys at www.androidguys.com/

   - Androinica at http://androinica.com/

Index

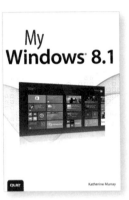

REGISTER THIS PRODUCT
SAVE 35%*
ON YOUR NEXT PURCHASE!

☐ How to Register Your Product

- Go to quepublishing.com/register
- Sign in or create an account
- Enter the 10- or 13-digit ISBN that appears on the back cover of your product

🔓 Benefits of Registering

- Ability to download product updates
- Access to bonus chapters and workshop files
- A 35% coupon to be used on your next purchase – valid for 30 days
  - To obtain your coupon, click on "Manage Codes" in the right column of your Account page
- Receive special offers on new editions and related Que products

Please note that the benefits for registering may vary by product. Benefits will be listed on your Account page under Registered Products.

We value and respect your privacy. Your email address will not be sold to any third party company.

* 35% discount code presented after product registration is valid on most print books, eBooks, and full-course videos sold on QuePublishing.com. Discount may not be combined with any other offer and is not redeemable for cash. Discount code expires after 30 days from the time of product registration. Offer subject to change.

quepublishing.com